Stuat James Conlon

...1.4108

THE
LAST
CIGARETTE

THE
LAST
CIGARETTE

Simon Gray

Granta Books
London

Granta Publications, 12 Addison Avenue, London W11 4QR

First published in Great Britain by Granta Books 2008

A CIP catalogue record for this book
is available from the British Library.

1 3 5 7 9 10 8 6 4 2

ISBN 978 1 84708 038 7

Typeset by M Rules
Printed and bound in Great Britain by
William Clowes Ltd, Beccles, Suffolk

For my beloved Victoria

PART ONE

A RESOLUTE MAN

2005

I'm still in Suffolk, where it's a typical August afternoon, cold and damp, with England losing a test match in Birmingham, and things can't go on like this. I say that, but how can they change? Well, I can make them change by stating categorically –
> That intend to give up smoking.

I've left out the 'I'. Do it again, with the 'I' in it.
> I intend to give up smoking.

There. I've put it down. It's legible, in firm, blue ballpoint. There's no getting away from it because it's plonk in the middle of the page, and to tear it out would be cheating.

This diary is going to be about my attempt to give up smoking. It is also going to be my main help in giving up smoking. By the time I've finished it I will be a free man, able to leave the house without my two packets of cigarettes, and my two lighters, able to sit down and read without compulsively checking that I've got these four articles in place on the desk in front of me or on the little table beside me. I shall never again have to grope for a cigarette while watching television, fly into a panic when I can't put my hand straight on the package – is that an unintended double entendre, 'put my hand straight on the package'? I have an idea that 'package' has a salacious meaning, or am I thinking of 'parcel'?

Nor worry that I might fall asleep with a cigarette burning on the brink of the ashtray, or while hanging from my lips.

There will be no cigarette burns – at least of my making – on my trousers and my shirt fronts.

The cuffs of my cardigans will no longer be singed. No, that's not right. I am devoted to my two cardigans, which are identical in every respect, including the location and the extent of the singes, so to put it accurately, there will be no further singes on my two cardigans. In the unlikely event that I ever have a new cardigan, and that I wear it, it will never be singed at the cuffs. At least not by me.

Socially

I will no longer need to check whether smoking is permitted at any unfamiliar restaurant at which I want to book a table.

And when smoking is banned in all restaurants, cafés, pubs and bars, as it surely will be, I shall no longer contemplate having to spend my last years in my two clubs solely because smoking will be permitted on their premises. If it is permitted. It's entirely possible that, as in Scotland, smoking will be banned even in private clubs. It makes my blood boil even to think of it. Banning smoking in private clubs! In all restaurants, bars and cafés, come to think of it! What a nonsense! What an impertinence! What an infraction of the fundamental liberties of an Englishman, let alone his human rights!

Hold on, though. Hold on to this. You are going to give up smoking voluntarily. The bans are irrelevant. It is your choice.

I read in one of the papers the other day that they're going to ban smoking in California prisons, including in the cells on death row. As all things Californian, except its weather, eventually spread around the world, there's more than a good chance that smoking will also be banned in prisons near home, the ones in which, if I am sent to prison, I'm likely to be housed. I once spent almost a month in Los Angeles, but apart from a misunderstanding with an attractive Jewish lesbian stand-up comic whose breasts seemed, from a drunken male heterosexual point of view, more Jewish than lesbian, I don't believe I did anything in California for which I could still be extradited, although you never know, with new sex laws being introduced every day, no doubt all of them to be retroactive, I might conceivably end up in a prison there, perhaps even on death row. On the other hand, as I'm trying to give up smoking, that could be the sort of extreme solution I'm looking for. Turn myself over to the electric chair and that would be the end of it – though given the American system, I could end up on death row with years and years of no-smoking appeals all the way up to the Supreme Court ahead of me, and then be put down without a last cigarette. Surely this would approach the 'cruel and unusual' treatment that their constitution forbids? How can anyone decide what is 'cruel and unusual' for someone else? Only I know how unusual it is for me not to have a cigarette, how cruel it is for me to be deprived of one. The judges in the various American courts who would decide against me, as they doubtless would, what sort of men and women would they be? If they were told that if they allowed me a last cigarette their lives would be blessed with peace and joy, as would their children's, and their children's children's, even unto etc. would they say, 'Hey, it does seem a little tough to send the old English guy to the chair without letting him have one last cigarette'? Or would they remain true to – what? What would they be true to? Is it just or decent or humane, no, it is unusual and cruel! It is American! Is any of this helping me to give up smoking? How am I going to do it?

Perhaps the solution is to throw away all my packets and my

lighters – Yes, I might do that. Tomorrow we go back to London. Perhaps it would be more sensible to start stopping then. I'm not sure that I can do it entirely by willpower – there are various aids – patches, lozenges, gum.

But I've tried nicotine gum – about twenty years ago, when you needed a prescription, which made it more appealing by making it seem almost illicit. In no time, it seemed to me, I'd swapped clouds of nicotine in the lungs for pools of it in the stomach. Just as I'd never been without something between my lips, I was now never without something between my jaws – I kept this up for six months, six months of worse than the usual indigestion, a drain-like smell around my mouth, the grinding of teeth upon teeth, and I might still be doing it, or more likely be dead from it, if I hadn't undertaken to direct one of my plays in New York, and had to deal with a very difficult actor, an eye-rolling, shoulder-shrugging, gesticulatory young ham of an actor. One night, in the interval of a preview, I found myself at the bar nearest the theatre, trembling with rage at a new on-stage walk he'd developed, as if he had two wooden legs or had soiled himself. I ordered a double whisky, then plodded to the cigarette machine, put in the right number of quarters, pulled out a packet of Marlboros and a book of matches – it wasn't until I was on my third or fourth cigarette that I realized I was smoking again, and knew that from then on there was no going forward – well, until now, of course – but my point is that gum, lozenges, patches won't do the trick, it really does have to be by a sustained act of will, by resolution.

Give myself a date. If the purpose of this diary is to accompany me on my journey as I struggle not to have a cigarette, day after day, hour by hour, minute on minute, struggle to go without a cigarette – then why, as I write this, have I just put out a cigarette, why am I now lighting another one? I should put it out. Why not put it out? NOW. Start stopping smoking NOW.

IS TOTO, TOO, A CHILD OF HER TIME?

I was sitting in the kitchen reading about the snug little world of Moscow's elite in the early 1930s, all the prominent families living near each other in their apartments in the Kremlin, with neighbouring dachas by the sea, all the droppings-in, the children playing together, the drunken evenings, the gossiping, flirtations, adulteries, all the men chummy and drinking together while vying for the boss's ear and promotion. And then this tight and sociable group, almost an extended family, began to poison itself. Lifelong friends, husbands and wives, brothers and sisters betrayed each other, all at the behest of the avuncular psychopath who connected them each to each –

It made for miserable reading, but I kept at it, miserably, until Toto, who'd been sitting under the table by my feet, suddenly growled, reared up, ran through the dog flap into the garden, and began to make a screeching noise. When I went out she was standing over what I took to be one of the mounds of earth that the moles throw up – they are all over the lawn, like little prehistoric citadels. She was butting at it with her head, then lifting her head and screeching, then butting, and I realized it wasn't a mound of earth it was a pheasant, about half her own size, and more than half dead, but shuddering. I couldn't think of any way of getting her away from it, short of kicking her.

I went out again just now. The corpse, at least I hope it's now a corpse, was sodden and still. Toto was crouched over it, also sodden, her haunches quivering, licking at it. She sensed me watching her, crouched lower, and snarled. So here I am, back in my study, writing about it. And there is Victoria, in her study, writing about something else, probably.

It's stopped raining, the sun is out, and I'm back from the kitchen, into which I tried to lure Toto with leathery-looking strips which come in a cellophane bag and are called Doggie Treats, something like that. The first few times I held them out she ran towards me, then wheeled around and whipped back to the pheasant. This happened four or five times, though each time she got less far from the pheasant, until finally she didn't come at all – she adjusted her position so that she couldn't see me, and resumed her snarling, licking and butting. So I'm back in my study. It's raining again.

Toto has at last left the premises. Victoria effected this by putting the lead on George at the garden gate, then holding up Toto's lead and summoning her in a soft, coaxing voice. I waited for a while after they'd gone, then scooped up the wretched mess and heaved it into the organic field at the end of our garden, right out into the stubble. This field has received many corpses over the years, mice, moles, voles, birds, all victims of our two cats, Tom and Errol. I don't know whether the pheasant was in the first instance a victim of Toto's, it might have dropped into the garden from the sky, from a stroke or a heart attack. We can assume, surely, that animals in the wild sometimes die from natural causes, perhaps even from their vices. The phone is ringing – Victoria on her mobile to ask whether I'd disposed of the remains. I said I had. She said, well the walk's impossible, Toto's lying down and refusing to move. I said that I'd go and meet her, which I'm just about to do, after I've tied my shoelaces and lit a cigarette, which I've just put out after a very few puffs.

*

It was a gorgeous walk, with the sun setting, the fields and woods so green and fresh, George trotting along obediently, Toto skipping in front of me, pulling a bit but quite content to be doing what we do every evening in the country. Now and then she ran to a fence and looked for a horse. She likes to lick their faces and they seem to enjoy it, cantering over to her and lowering their muzzles so her tongue can reach them, but this evening they were too far off, standing together in little clusters, their coats shiny in the light. When we got back to the garden Toto ran immediately to where the pheasant had been, sniffed around forlornly, eventually gave up, came into the kitchen. In a minute I suppose I shall pick up the book about Stalin, reluctantly but with purpose – many of the things described in it happened in my time, after all, and I am a child of my time, as are we all, or so they say.

I, SOLIPSIST

It's still cold and wet in Suffolk and we've just won by two runs the test match that I said yesterday we were losing. This proves that I am a pessimist; also that I'm bad at predicting the outcome of sporting events; also, and most importantly, why I am right to go on watching cricket. The best thing about international sporting events is that the team I passionately hope will win is called England, not Britain, or the UK, but England. My team. From my country. Well, they're not all from my country. Our best batsman is from South Africa, our wicketkeeper grew up and learnt his trade in Australia, and is called Jones, one of our fast bowlers is also called Jones, but wherever they come from, or learnt the game, they all represent England, and therefore me.

I wasn't always so insular, so solipsistic. In fact, in my early years I was a citizen of the universe. I wore a cape that carried me from pole to pole, where evil resides. As I grew into my maturity I became a Continentalist, though not a European. What's the distinction between a Continentalist and a European? Well, I suppose a Continentalist likes to be in Paris, or Rome or Madrid, or dabbing himself in the Mediterranean, he likes to sit at a pavement café with a bottle of wine on the table, a book in his hand, a cigarette between his lips, and have at his command not so much a command of the language as an appearance of fluency in the demotic, an ability to slur vowels and consonants into a seamless flow, accompanied by a flurry of gestures with hands, shoulders and eyebrows, so that his speech both sounds and looks like the native tongue, though incomprehensible to any native.

The other trick was to pass oneself off in Italy as a Frenchman, in France as a Spaniard, and in Spain as an Italian etc. One only wanted to be taken for an Englishman when there was a danger that one would be taken instead for Dutch, Scandinavian or, above all, German. The Continentalist has of course passed into history, if he's remembered it's only with tender embarrassment by people of my age and background. Besides nowadays we have our own seedy version of the Continent here at home. Many people on the streets or in shops speak English as I once spoke Italian and French, and there are cafés and restaurants on the pavement, though it has to be said that they're mostly uncomfortable and unhygienic because our pavements are narrow – your moules marinières, however wholesome when brought out of the kitchen, are swiftly layered and peppered by grime and whatever else comes out in the fumes of passing exhaust pipes – not necessarily passing, either. The other day a rubbish truck was parked belching and farting alongside the Renaissance café for the whole half-hour that I was drinking my coffee, and the men, who seemed to be stuffing rubbish into the back and shovelling it out again before scooping it back in, were hawking, spitting, banging up against the table, bellowing in tongues – what in other words you'd expect from London when it goes Continental, alien and disgusting but also, in an unanalysable way, Anglo-Saxon, and endurable –

The Europeanization of England begins with the enfolding of this little country into a larger organization called the UK, which isn't so much a geographical place as a dead thought in a bureaucratic head. Nobody with a decent sense of self would say, 'I live in the UK', unless you were a desperado dealing with a customs or immigration official in, say, Libya. Where do you live? London, England. And where were you born? Hayling Island, England. And that's it, really it stops there, in the particular. You can't be a European without becoming yourself simply an idea, and not your own idea at that.

There is rumoured to be a law pending, or perhaps it is already secretly passed, that will make it a criminal offence – treason, I suppose – to slander or to libel the European Union. I suppose that by making it into a potential victim of a crime – the victim of a crime of utterance; the next step the victim of a crime of thought – they hope to convince us that it actually and specifically exists, as a person exists, and that we can feel its pain when unkind and disbelieving things are said and thought about it.

When I ponder such matters, I consider it astonishing that I have decided to attempt to give up smoking.

THE FACE IN THE OMELETTE

Let me resist lighting a cigarette by thinking about Mao, Stalin and Hitler. The other day, on a radio phone-in, I heard the old argument repeated – Hitler was the most wicked because he murdered millions in the name of fascism and racial superiority. Mao and Stalin were less wicked because they murdered millions in the name of communism, a noble if possibly imbecilic ideal. Therefore people who supported fascism and Hitler are much more wicked than people who supported communism – in fact, people who supported the USSR, those of them in this country who are still alive, are to be considered rather endearing, to be cherished and even honoured. Their hearts were in the right place when they argued, with decent regret, that you can't make an omelette without breaking eggs – which actually is only a pleasantly domestic way of saying that Lenin and Stalin couldn't make a communist state without breaking heads, legs, lives, families, spirits – without maiming, torturing, starving, killing – all the things that Hitler did but in one respect more terrifyingly because more arbitrarily. If you were Aryan and an indifferent servant of Hitler's state you were safe, and knew what to do to remain safe, at least until the war came. If you were a good servant in Mao's or Stalin's state you were in danger every minute of your life, and if it decided to extinguish you because, say, of a joke you were rumoured to have told, or to have laughed at, you went to your end knowing that your legacy to your parents and your children, your friends, colleagues, even your neighbours, was likely to be torture or death, or a labour camp, certainly ostracism and penury – their crime, of course, being you, knowing you and perhaps loving you.

So what was Osip Mandelstam thinking when he recited the famous but unpublished, indeed vanished, poem that evening in Moscow? Supposing you were there, pleased to be numbered among his friends and colleagues, your excitement as he takes the paper out of his pocket, unfolds it, begins to declaim it – you relish his mischievous smile, the sparkle of his eye, the familiar, expressive voice, old Osip with a new poem! And then you hear the words 'Stalin', 'murderer' – but for a second or two you don't grasp their meaning, and you hope that you're not going to, but when you look away from Osip's face in all its merriness and mischief you see in the other faces what they're probably now seeing in yours, and you know that you all know what you've just heard – a suicide note, a collective suicide note because all your names are on it, you signed it with your ears – so if you value your life, and the lives of your loved ones, you'd better hurry to the authorities, describe the poem, provide a list of everybody in the room, and hope that you are the first to inform, because if you aren't it will seem that you've only informed because you're afraid that you've already been informed on. But whether you're first or last it is unlikely that you will survive, in fact not even the officials to whom you've informed will survive, the time will come when they will be swept away with all the muck and eggshells from 'those days', that's how the historical process works, after all, these days become 'those days', the subjective becomes the objective, the executors the executed, more and more and more eggs get broken, the omelette gets bigger and bigger and bigger, it has a face with a moustache and a pipe, and Joe's your uncle! Yes, dear old Uncle Joe, the human omelette.

AN EGG FOR THE OMELETTE

Really it doesn't matter whether a state becomes an omelette for reasons that sound virtuous, if imbecilic, or for reasons that sound nasty, the sounds are irrelevant, the intentions are identical – to control all its members through terror. The state of terror is the state itself. And the state itself is the man himself. Hitler, Mao, Stalin were the state and the terror, and in the end you can only decide morally between them in quantitative terms – Which of them killed most? The one who had most to kill. And after him, Stalin. Or the other way around. And after them, Hitler. Once the debate takes this form, it isn't worth having, even on a radio phone-in. They were foul states, created by foul people by foul means for a foul purpose, they spoke different languages, used a different vocabulary, but the experience of living in them would have been pretty well identical – unless, as I said, you were an Aryan in Hitler's Germany, but that's scarcely a moral distinction.

It's now three in the afternoon, my lights are on, the rain is drizzling down, and I'm cold. I'm cold in mid-August, but I'm not smoking – he's not smoking! – so supposing you while away the rest of this non-smoking August day by deciding which, among your literary contemporaries, would have survived if they'd lived in, say, Moscow through the 20s and 30s. I would like to say none of them, but I suspect there would be several. Of the playwrights – let's think: well, let's begin with yourself. Would you have gone under? I don't think I'd have lasted long, but not because I'd have been full of defiance, I know that I'm a coward in almost every respect, that is, morally, emotionally and physically. I can't bear to be hurt, and I can't bear to hurt people, but the two are intertwined, aren't they, the fear of hurting people seems to have within it an element of virtue, or at least sensitivity to others, but it hasn't, in my case – it's not really that I can't bear hurting people, it's that I can't bear the consequences – no, let's be scrupulous and precise – I can't bear the consequences for myself of hurting people. I think if my actions had only bad consequences for others, and not for me, and I didn't have actually to witness their suffering, I wouldn't at all mind committing bad actions. How true is this? I don't know. What is true is that I would want to survive. I'd try to keep my poems and my jokes to myself, but I have a loose and wayward tongue which might shorten my life under a malign regime, just as it's shortened a few evenings under a comparatively benign one – and what is also true is, look, without your noticing he's lit up and, yes, smoking, he's smoking again. Perhaps the sensible thing is to put off giving up until we get to Spetses.

SHARKS V. RATS

We go to Athens tomorrow morning and we should be on Spetses by the early evening, in time for a swim. I've sent instructions to the mayor, to ban smoking everywhere on the island, including in private houses. That should settle my hash, this long disease my hash.

I wonder, though, what sort of accommodation we'll find ourselves in when we get to Spetses. We've put ourselves, orphan-style, in the hands of an old friend who lives there, an intelligent and practical woman in whom we have an absolute trust. She has found a house that she describes in terms that doom us to disappointment. No place could conceivably match our desires and needs as, according to her email, this one does. It would have been better if she'd found us somewhere Greek and hopeless, so that we could draw on our limitless resources of stoicism and declare it 'Not as bad as all that! Good heavens, we'll make do! Besides we're out most of the day! And much of the night! And it's only for three weeks!' – that sort of house.

The house we used to stay in, that we had come to love, changed its aspect and its atmosphere as I either reached the end of my drinking years or began the days of my abstention, depending on which way around you look at it. It was my habit to sit on the stone steps leading down from the house to the heavily scented garden late at night, reading under a dim lamp – this was my habit for five summers running, but in the last of these summers, when I was either at the end of my drunk period or at the very beginning of my sober period, I began to hallucinate enormous rats coming and going up and down the stairs past me, vanishing into the darkness in the corner of the wall at the top or into the bushes at the bottom. They should have been pink, of course, to qualify as the alcoholic's perfect rats, but they were the usual grubby grey, long pale tail, prominent teeth – common or garden rats, much more terrifying as hallucinations than surreal rats. I couldn't give up reading outside at night because, as I say, it was my habit, and I'm very bad at giving up habits, so I bent over my book and tried to concentrate on not being aware of the comings and goings of the rats, though I could hear them and sense them, and if I looked, see them, coming and going.

And then one night there was a massive sort of presence at the door, a lurking, unmoving, antediluvian rat, and I bent deeper into my book.

'Christ!' he said. It was Piers's voice. 'Christ! Look! There's a rat.' Now it's true that Piers was as drunk as I was during my drunk period, and as prone to hallucinations as I was during both my drunk and my early sober periods, so one way and another we might both now and then have hallucinated rats, but not at precisely the same time surely? Which meant that there were real rats coming out of the house, rats to be faced up to, that couldn't be dodged by concentrating on a book.

Piers, as a matter of interest, wasn't terrified of rats, real or hallucinated. He was terrified of not getting another drink, but nothing much else frightened him – oh, apart from the sea, but that was with just cause, he'd nearly drowned years before, off Bondi

Beach, and since then had virtually given up swimming, going in perhaps two or three times during his weeks in Spetses, and they weren't really swims, they were grim-jawed, fist-clenched wades out to just below his chest, a dozen turbulent strokes back towards the beach, then to his feet and a lunging, splashing, panic-stricken run to dry land and a drink.

Also, of course, he had spent years in Hong Kong, with its actual and rumoured shark attacks, about which he nevertheless affected, when we went out to visit him, to be blasé.

I have a horror of sharks that is quite different from my horror of rats. Rats come out of the unknown, yet seem to be in some foul way secreted in oneself. Sharks, on the other hand, come upon you, drag you down, bite you to death. Any man swimming in shark-infested seas who is not afraid of sharks is, in that one respect at least, an imbecile – I don't really expect to be eaten to death by a rat that comes across me, though it could happen of course, especially if he has a pack with him (rats are always male, in my grasp of them). I would expect to be eaten to death by a shark that wouldn't have just come across me, he would have sought me out, perhaps not specifically me, but one of my kind which might well turn out to be me. Almost the first thing I asked Piers when Victoria and I arrived in Hong Kong was, 'What's the shark situation?' 'Look,' he said, in a calm, mature voice, thus turning himself from younger into older brother, 'I know what you feel about sharks, Simon, and yes, there are sharks in these waters, naturally there are sharks, of all kinds, but the last shark attack was fifteen years ago, Simon.'

The next was a week away. We heard about it on the news, from the radio of the car we'd hired, a magnificently upholstered, air-conditioned affair. A man had been 'taken' at Clear Water Beach that morning, his leg had been ripped off, he'd died on his way to hospital. This was the first of four fatal attacks, and the most startling in that the victim, a hairdresser, had been witness to the fifteen-years-ago attack Piers had mentioned, when a woman standing at waist-height had been 'taken'. The hairdresser, who went to Clear Water every morning for a swim and had been standing near her, virtually beside her, was so horrified by the experience – he would never forget, he said in an interview in the papers, the sight of her standing there, her hands on her hips, and then, on an instant, her being upturned, her bewildered screams as she was dragged out to sea, the kerfuffle of her dismemberment, her torso bobbing to the surface – these weren't his exact words, but the gist of his account as Piers remembered it from fifteen years back.

Piers also remembered that the hairdresser had sworn that he would never swim in the sea again, certainly never ever in Clear Water Bay, and for fifteen years he had stuck to it, this simple and most sensible of promises to himself. But the years went by, no attacks, he began to be tempted, the weather so sultry, the wonderfully clear water of Clear Water Bay so close, just a short drive – so he went one morning, and stood in the water not even waist-high, knee-high, and the shark came and took him. It was thought to be the same shark. So what does this tell us about sharks, fate, will, broken promises made to themselves by Hong Kong hairdressers?

Well, about sharks, or this one anyway, it might mean that it had been gone a long time, snacking off faraway shores until eventually his travels had brought him back. Was there some palpable memory of a place he'd come across where a good meal was to be had? And unlike the rest of us, who return for that fondly remembered meal in that now-vanished little restaurant, his restaurant was still there – as indeed was the meal himself, standing waiting, legs spread, hands on hips, exactly as he remembered him. Is it possible that the shark had sized him up on his previous visit, and tucked him away in the recesses of his extraordinarily complicated yet simple brain. Or perhaps he didn't wait for fifteen years, he came back frequently and impatiently, desperate to find his meal in place, prepared and on the table, so to speak, *la specialité de la maison.*

But the hairdresser, what was tucked away in the recesses of his far more complicated brain? In the forefront it was simple enough: 'Do not swim again in the sea. Do not swim again in the sea. Particularly do not swim again in Clear Water Bay.' The physical shock of what he'd seen must have lingered in his body, would linger there for the rest of his life, surely, so why, why on earth? After all, this wasn't an idle promise, of the sort he made and broke every day of his professional life – 'Madam, let me cut this little bit, lop off this, shorten that, and you will look twenty years younger, that's a promise, madam!' His promise to himself about the shark wasn't really even a self-injunction along the lines of 'Never again allow a play of yours to be done at Milton Keynes!' It was a statement of fact. Nothing could be more certain than that he would never again go to Clear Water Bay, let alone stand in the water. But he went. He stood. Did his will insist that he follow the diktat of reason: 'Nothing has happened for fifteen years, it's probably long dead, the odds on your being taken must be one in trillions, you're being a silly-billy, a cowardy-custard.' And all the while something in him demanded a date with destiny: 'Go and be taken, go and be taken, you know it's you. Think of the splash you'll make. People will remember and wonder. The very man who witnessed! Who swore he'd never! Yes, the very he, the very same he! Go. Go and be taken!' Or perhaps he sleepwalked, programmed from birth. Or accepted into his unconsciousness a direct command from the shark's appetite. 'Be back here in fifteen years. Fifteen years. On the dot.'

What is incontrovertible is that sharks have their ways. They know things that we don't. Perhaps they know things about us that we don't. There's the story of the two sailors who survived a capsized ship far out in deep water. They swam for hours and hours and hours, until exhausted, all hope gone. 'Look!' one of them suddenly cried, standing up, 'I can stand up!' but the land turned under him, opened its mouth. I don't know what happened to the other sailor but he must have survived. How else would we know the story?

I don't know any equivalent stories about rats, but then rats don't move to the profound, impersonal laws that sharks move to, if indeed sharks move to profound, impersonal laws. The sharks featured above may merely have been lucky – 'Could you believe it, my dear! In the exact same spot! Like he was waiting for me!' and 'Stood right on me, all I had to do was roll over and open wide!' – but I don't think so, I think destiny comes into it somewhere, even if it's the victim's destiny, the shark only the instrument.

The rat's way of being seems much more haphazard, secret and dark. He doesn't 'take' his food in public off a sunny liquid snack bar in front of lots of people, he snuffles through holes and crouches in corners, waiting his chance on a dead body or a dying one, otherwise it's crumbs and larder raids, although I seem to remember a film called *Herbert* or *Hubert*, which told the story of a super-intelligent rat that made himself, Hitler-like, the leader of an enormous pack with which he planned to take over the world, but then something happened to thwart him, I don't know what as I didn't see it, nothing could get me to see a film about rats –
But the thing about the hallucinatory rat that passed me as it went down the stairs that turned out to be a real rat that passed me as it went down the stairs, and was confirmed as such by my brother Piers, is that from then on I moved about the house in a suppressed state of terror, even in broad and sunny daylight, and even in the

enchanting and sweetly scented garden – sometimes a little too sweetly scented for my taste, especially at night, it made you long for a blast of wintry Suffolk air – but until the rat it was a safe place, is my point, and after the rat its thick perfumes suggested putrefaction, and I stepped carefully through it, eyes darting into shady crannies during the day, all over the place at night –

I phoned up the owner, a most kind and intelligent woman who had made us a present of this house every August for five years running, phoned her up and said, 'There are rats in your house.' Not as baldly as that, I hope, I hope I asked her about her health and so forth, but I got to the point very smartly, my eyes no doubt hopping around the floor. There was a pause as she waited for me to go on, and when I didn't she said, 'There are rats all over the island, in every house, why should mine be exempt?' 'Of course,' I said. 'Of course. Just thought you'd like to know – and was wondering if there's anything I can do about them. Anything you'd like me to do about them.' 'Oh, ignore them,' she said. 'That's what I do. It's probably why I never see them.' 'Hard to ignore if they keep brushing against you.' 'Well, if they upset you, you have my permission to do anything you can think of to get rid of them.' I thought immediately of setting the house on fire, then thought beyond that to the eventual solution, which was to take rooms the following year in a house with a majestic terrace overlooking the sea that I persuaded myself was too high up, too light and airy and breeze-swept, to attract the attention of rats. The landlady was a middle-aged Greek/German woman, kind, thoughtful, practical and sometimes playful, called Alex. From her house a steep path, with steps, leads to the beach, an arduous climb down and up. This year Alex is not letting out her rooms, but she has found us the house that we go to tomorrow, the house that she is sure we'll love, and sounds so perfect for our needs that we must prepare for disappointment. Come to think of it, Alex said that this most perfect of houses is only a few yards on from her own, so there will be the steep path, the steps, the arduous climb down and up – I hope that's our disappointment taken care of.

MY TRAVELLING COMPANIONS

I think that the loud woman across the aisle from me on my left is probably very pleasant, everything she says is certainly pleasant enough, to do with adjusting her watch to Athens time, helping her husband, whose face I can't see but whose hands were quite prominent during the watch-adjusting business – odd hands, foreshortened, without fingernails, in fact I think their tips are missing, but he uses them with authority, stubbing a knucklish stump into her lap, where the watch is again because she's started the whole business again, having set it two hours behind instead of two hours ahead, and is now having, starting from there, as he points out in a slow, emphatic, German-accented voice, to put it four hours ahead – all this would be all right except that she shouts, really shouts, as if he were deaf and in a different room, a distant room – no, in a different aeroplane almost, furthermore she repeats everything he says in this shout, as if she were deaf, too, deaf to her own voice as well as to his. She's a sensible-looking woman of about fifty, I suppose, long feet in flat shoes planted on the floor, a floral skirt of the kind that women of what I take to be her disposition have worn all my life, I remember them from when I was knee-high to such ladies. Though they are evidently women, they look as if they're cross-dressing. Not like men cross-dressing as women, but women cross-dressing as women, de-sexing themselves. Her voice is like that, too, not a man's voice but a woman's voice, loud and de-sexed – ah, she's got some magazines from the stewardess or whatever they're called these days, hostesses, anyway quite evidently not chosen for their looks or their appealing little ways – the particular one who is serving us dumped a pile of magazines in the woman's lap, the woman spread her floral skirt to receive them, plucked out a gourmet magazine, then shovelled the remainder into her husband's lap – 'Jolly good, have these, *Newsweek*, you like *Newsweek*, it's American.' So he's got three *Newsweek*s, same issue, to read from. He's now got his foreshortened fingers around a magnifying glass, is studying an article in *Newsweek* through the magnifying glass as if it were a specimen in a lab. I still haven't seen his face, only his fingers, and the sleeve of a grey suit – and heard his voice, of course, like something from a 1940s espionage film with Conrad Veidt in it.

There was one Conrad Veidt made with Valerie Hobson – a beautiful woman – so stylish and playful – she's tied to a chair for a good ten minutes, a very good ten minutes, black stockings (pre-tights after all), high heels, arms raised, *Contraband*, that's it, the name of the film, *Contraband*, now the thing about Conrad Veidt, whose name nobody remembers when they're talking about *Casablanca*, is that he was the highest-paid actor in the film, which also featured Marcel Dalio, the Jewish count in *La Règle du Jeu*. In *Casablanca* Dalio plays the part of the croupier, a very small part, though he does get to say, '*Faites vos jeux, mesdames, messieurs, faites vos jeux*', and wears tails, I think, though perhaps only a dinner jacket. There was something poignant, unbearable really, in coming across Dalio in a bit part, his great years, the pre-war years of French cinema, behind him. I suppose he got out before the Germans came, he wouldn't have lasted long as he was so patently both Jewish and homosexual, a small, portly man, he had the saddest eyes, a natural aristocrat, but one always feared for his feelings – he was also one of the escaping prisoners in *La Grande Illusion*, I think, at least I see him in my memory in conversation with Erich von Stroheim, who has his cigarette in a long holder, a monocle in place, or is it an eye-patch, a lost eye and a lost arm too – he and Dalio, the Prussian nobleman and the French aristocrat, at one in spirit, divided by war, preserving the civilities. Can you imagine a film like *La Grande Illusion* being made these days? – but oh, don't start, don't start on your 'these days those days', and I don't really remember *La Grande Illusion* clearly, I'm only going on like this because we're on the verge of taking off, we've been on the verge for half an hour, revving up, jolting forward, fading down again, the cabin full of fumes and suppressed ill-temper, along with the usual dose of fear, not all from me – false starts on aeroplanes are worse than false starts in sex really, because on an aeroplane you're anticipating relief from the anxiety of being on the ground just before you go up in the air where you don't want to be, while in sex you're anticipating relief and pleasure, pleasure through relief – I'm not sure the analogy can be pursued any further, I shouldn't have embarked on it, it doesn't hold – we're now rocking down the runway, the barking woman in the floral dress has seized one of her elderly Germanic husband's deformed hands – he reminds me of Isaiah Berlin, I realize, though his voice doesn't, I could never understand a word Sir I.B. said, I know it was in English because he talked to me as if he assumed it was in my language, and also friends assured me he spoke in English, it was obvious, therefore, that I lacked some part of the brain that could decipher his accent, we're in the air.

Now we're flying. We're in business class, BA, horribly cramped, the man in front of me has just put his seat back so that it's pressing into my knees, and I can see, with very little adjustment to my position, the fine, thick grey hair across the top of his scalp, with a whorl right in the centre – an astonishingly healthy scalp, marvellously lustrous hair, nothing moving about in it or flaking off from it, it would be a pleasure to damage it in some way, to make up for my being able to see it so clearly because the selfish sod has his seat back. The young woman beside me keeps blowing her nose into a scrap of tissue, the non-cross-dresser on the other side of the aisle has a cough like a horse, an explosive whinny, I can now see her elderly husband, his deformed hands are part of a deformed package, his face, which might once have been an Isaiah Berlin-like face, is peeled and scabbed, his eyes are naked, no eyelashes or lids, must be the victim of a fire or bombing, his lips are loose, pendulous, but they could be undamaged, loose and pendulous by nature.

The only good thing about the flight is that no food is served on it. Owing to an altercation the catering staff are on strike – Gourmet-Gate I believe the managing company is called, and it seems that BA is incapable of providing food except through the services of Gourmet-Gate – but where, in these cramped, claustrophobic conditions, could you put a tray of food without getting most of it over yourself? I daren't ask Victoria how much we paid for this flight, how much extra to go business. Economy can't conceivably be more cramped and uncomfortable without breaching all kinds of human rights laws. I'm going to have a look, if I can get up.

Well, yes, economy is worse. The rows on either side of the aisle have three seats, the rows here in business have three seats on one side, my side, and two seats on the other side. Victoria is in a two-seater, on the aisle, further down the plane. So what it comes to is that people sitting in the three-seat blocks in business, like me, have exactly the same deal, in terms of space, as people sitting in economy, while the people seated in the two-seat blocks in business

would seem to have a better deal. I tested this by trying out
Victoria's seat. It had the same leg-space as mine, i.e. almost none,
but she has a much more charming companion – mine is now
blowing her nose on little shreds of Kleenex about twice a minute,
long, thick, wet blows, then she screws up the Kleenex and places
it in a paper cup, already bulging, in the rack on the back of the seat
in front of her. There is an already full paper cup beside the one she
has now nearly filled. She is frankly a very disgusting person to find
yourself sitting next to on a flight. The third person on our row, on
the window seat, I can't see properly. He's a middle-aged man, I
think, and I imagine he's inclining himself as close to the window
as he can, to escape the nose-blowing girl who separates us.
Victoria's only companion, on the other hand, is a wiry old
Australian woman with a twin in San Francisco and she would, I
think, be a fizzing conversationalist if she weren't crumpled and
drained from exhaustion and hunger. She's flown BA and therefore
foodless from Sydney to Heathrow, had to transfer to the Athens
flight so hurriedly that she didn't have time to pick up anything to
eat between planes, and here she is now, not having eaten for a day
or so, not even in possession of one of the clumsy blue cardboard
boxes that those of us who arrived, fully breakfasted, were issued
with in the business-class lounge. These boxes contain smatterings
of this and that, a little roll of ham that looks like a boiled thumb,
a smudge of cheese, two lumps of bread, a chocolatey lump of
dough, and a plastic container of small shreds of fruit – altogether
like scraps left over from a reception, really, and repulsive to look at.
I offered my box, and virtually all its contents – I'd taken a bite out
of the chocolate dough – to the Australian lady, who refused it for
reasons I didn't want to enquire into, perhaps I look unhygienic,
and she suspected that my fingers had poked and delved into each
item, or perhaps she was too proud to accept charity, or perhaps,

driven by fatigue and hunger, she is in a delusional state and thinks that by not eating any food not provided by BA she is punishing BA for not providing any food. But wait a minute! This box of soiled tapas was provided by BA, so perhaps her plan is to be so enfeebled by malnutrition that she will have to be carried off the plane, put into an ambulance and driven to a hospital, from there to initiate successful lawsuits, the proceeds of which I hope she'll share with her Frisco twin – anyway, she managed a short but sprightly conversation with Victoria, Victoria told me, in which she said that Australian boys are having immense sexual successs when they visit England by telling the girls that they are writers, although they aren't and don't want to be. I am surprised and proud to learn that our girls still care enough about literature to go to bed with its practitioners.

The girl beside me is starting on her third paper cup. I don't think I can go on doing this without describing her in detail, and I'm anxious these days not to write from hatred, so I'll take out a book. All the books for serious reading are packed into a capacious leather bag that's been checked in, but in my floppy briefcase there is a last-minute chuck-in for the plane, I'm not sure what it is, but think it's an old Penguin, yes, I remember choosing it exactly because it's an old Penguin, yes, an orange Penguin.

The Light and the Dark – how can a novel with a title like that conceivably be any good? It's almost a parody, *The Light and the Dark*, by C. P. Snow, Charles Percival Snow. Percival? You're just guessing, why not Philip? Or Patrick? Why not Clive, come to that? Clive Patrick (or Paddy) Snow's *The Light and the Dark, The Wet and the Dry, The Hot and the Cold, The Pie and the Sky* – are you sure that retitling the novel and fiddling about with the author's name is more interesting than actually reading?

– actually, actually, her last one took about thirty seconds, longer than you would have thought possible to blow a nose, and where does it come from that she keeps having to blow it out? Open, turn the pages, read – She's taken a fourth paper cup out of her carrier bag – perhaps she's collecting it for a scientific experiment, or on doctor's orders, we'll see what she does with the cups when the plane lands, if she repacks them it's germ warfare – against whom? The Greeks? But bringing germs to Greece would be like bringing coals to Newcastle, every sandwich is like Russian roulette. Surely she's just being thoughtful, what can she do with her germ-laden tissues but put them in a receptacle, and it's not her fault that we're squeezed so closely together – the tip of her nose is very red, her eyes watery, she has an annoying habit of thrashing over the pages of the newspaper (*The Times*) with maximum noise and fuss – she has long, elegant legs – if there were some way of getting her upright, hands bound behind her back, would she suddenly become a bold, proud, defiant beauty? Or would the consequences of her not being able to get at her tissues make her even more disgusting? Better leave her as she is, making her way through her fourth paper mug – give myself over to Carlos Pepe Snow.

More like fog, really, but an odd sort of fog, everything described so clearly, and yet everything important obscured, obscured by clarity, in fact – he describes his world without seeing it, almost as if he thinks adjectives are in themselves full of detail and content – a girl is 'passionate, generous, capable and free' – and that's it, it's no good you wanting this passion, generosity, freedom and capability in action because there's no girl to act. I've read fifty pages so far, in that old, small Penguin print, and I still have no idea what the story is about, or who the characters are, apart from their names and their positions in life, or rather their positions in a Cambridge college in the mid-30s of the last century. I know, in a vague sort of way, what it purports to be about – a brilliant young linguist who is subject to bouts of depression, bouts of manic behaviour, so a manic-depressive therefore, and old Snow describes and analyses these bouts with responsible lucidity, grave, deliberate, well informed, hollow, lifeless – so that the hero, Roy Calvert by name – dashing sort of name – really becomes very irritating. He's a character without a pulse. The narrator, who of course has a name like two surnames, let me check – yes, yes, of course, Lewis Eliot – Lewis Eliot, doesn't have much of a pulse either. He's a ponderous and bulky man, one feels, but as a character weighs nothing. I suppose he's a front for old C.P. himself. One of his tricks is to bring himself to our attention by having himself complimented. A character will say, usually apropos of nothing, something like 'There is no doubt, Lewis, that you are one of the most intelligent/compassionate/understanding of men' or 'You, above all men, Eliot, know what suffering is' – but the tone of the novel is that of a man who really doesn't know what suffering is, though he certainly ought to, as he has a mad wife that so far – as far as I've read – he keeps buried in London, I suppose she might turn up, but I'm not too worried about meeting her because however mad she is she won't be mad where it matters, in my imagination – a moment ago the pilot said we would be landing and the plane has just done two big downwards hops, stomach-jumping hops – here is a sentence: 'Once I saw them in a party, when she thought herself unobserved: she looked at him with a glance that was heavy, brooding, possessive, consumed with the need to be sure of him.' All his adjectives come in threes and fours as if he has to fill a quota, it's like reading P. G. Wodehouse without the jokes.

We're coming in now, coming into Athens, hoppity-hop, I don't know whether we have an old plane or an ungifted pilot, but this is not the way you want to land in a place where you haven't been for five years – oh, how I could do with a cigarette, thank God I'm not giving them up until we're settled into Spetses.

GREEK WELCOMES

Here we are, in our magnificent little house, a few yards further
along the path I was describing back in London. I'm sitting on its
narrow terrace, it's 11 p.m., and when I look up from writing this
I can see the moving dots of the sea-taxis taking people at high
speed from one part of the island to the other, from one bar or café
to another. In daytime they remind me of little dogs, they scamper
across the water, their bows like little snouts, but at night they
become mysterious and urgent dots of light, travelling through dark
space because you can't separate the sea from the sky – there's a great
field of dark punctuated in its lower half by the skimming dots, in
its top by the stars.

So we're in Greece again, Spetses again, home after five years
away. As soon as we were out of Athens airport, walking towards the
car our friend Alex had arranged for us, we could feel the difference
in the air, the dry lightness of it, and the feet correspondingly light
as we zipped along after our driver, a jolly well-dressed man called
Soros, whose only discernible flaw at this stage was that he'd been
waiting at the wrong exit – there was an interminable business, with
mobile phones, Victoria phoning Alex in Spetses to say her man
wasn't there, Alex phoning her man to find out where he was, then
phoning us and saying her man was at the bureau de change
carrying a placard with the name SIMON on it, then when we went
to the bureau de change Victoria phoning Alex to say that there
were lots of drivers holding up placards with names on them, none
of them SIMON, so Alex phoned the driver again and I spotted a man
holding up a placard that had no name on it because it was the
wrong way around because he was hurrying away from us, so I ran
around to the front of him, saw SIMON on the placard, led him back
to Victoria and our bags and then we were out of the airport,

sucking in the air and thinking we'd made it, actually made it to Greece, and we smiled triumphantly at each other, smiled forgivingly at the driver, this jolly, eager, roly-poly man whose name was Soros and who was smartly dressed, a picture of respectability, unlike the furry, slovenly, dark-aspected (I mean in temperament, not race) drivers on the rank that we passed on the way to our car. We could see that Soros was a very careful and steady driver, even in the hundred yards or so he drove us before we were stopped by the police –

A young man in a slick brown and green uniform stepped out on to the street and waved us down, then came to the window and ordered Soros to get out. A police car drove up behind us, and another, older policeman got out, dressed exactly like his partner but unlike him in that he looked ill-tempered and authoritarian. The younger one, who was merely passive and low-voiced, could speak English, quite reasonable English, as transpired when he began to speak quite reasonable English about our situation, which was complicated and possibly dire – we were being driven illegally, our driver, Soros, was a bandit, he had infringed the law by the mere fact of having us in the back of his taxi, he and his taxi would shortly be taken away, the one to be placed in custody, the other to be impounded. He said all this, or what amounted to all this, in his pleasantly broken English through the window in the back of the taxi where we sat stiffly, as if under arrest ourselves. I got out, having noticed that there were no ashtrays in Soros's taxi, and that it was probably a non-smoker therefore, and lit a cigarette, grateful really – in these oppressive days you have to snatch your opportunities as they present themselves, which means that most bad situations can be transformed into good ones if, while they're going on, you can take your cigarettes and lighter out of your pocket and enjoy a good smoke under pressure – a better smoke for its being under pressure.

In fact, here's an interesting thing – if I had been able to smoke in Soros's taxi, I would have been much more worried by the sudden intervention of the police, I would have sat in the taxi smoking, but not noticing that I was smoking, and concentrating on our situation. As I couldn't smoke in the taxi, I was mainly thinking about wanting a cigarette, and then delighted when I saw I could have one by getting out of the taxi – without the police I wouldn't have been able to get out of the taxi. For this small but intense pleasure I had to thank a) the Athens police and b) the anti-smoking laws.

So there I was smoking on the pavement – no, it wasn't a pavement, it was the edge of the wide road that leads out of Athens airport – presumably nobody walks, or is allowed to walk, out of an international airport. Victoria got out to join me. The superior, or anyway older, policeman was listening with a grim, unkind face to the explanations of Soros, who kept laughing in disbelief. The young speaker of reasonable if broken English, who was clearly beginning to suspect that he was taking part in a mistake, began to question us as to how we had come by the services of Soros. We explained slowly, calmly, a touch loudly, however, to penetrate the foreign layer of his understanding, that Soros was a perfectly legitimate taxi driver who hadn't been cowboying for tourists outside the official ranks, but had been commissioned by our friend in Spetses. He asked if he could speak to our friend in Spetses. Alex was no longer answering her phone, she was on the answering machine – Victoria held her mobile to the young policeman's ear and he listened to Alex's rather gruffly important voice announcing that she wasn't there, and then he went to his superior, to convey whatever information he had to convey. The superior and Soros were now standing facing each other in silence. I lit another cigarette and put an arm protectively around Victoria's shoulder, a proud gesture, also defiant and noble, except that there was nothing she needed protection from except my smoke. Soros and the two policemen fell into quiet discourse, the whole tenor of the engagement seemed to have changed, they shook hands, the two policemen went to their car, Soros got into the taxi, gestured us in with a boisterous, angry laugh, and off we went, I hanging on to my cigarette, on the grounds that a legitimately lit cigarette can stay lit until it comes to its natural end. I used the open window as my ashtray and half hoped I missed the open window of a parallel car when I finally flicked it away. Victoria can sometimes speak Greek, and even sometimes understand it, so she bent forward and she and Soros had a cheek-to-cheek about what had happened. The senior policeman had been implacable, was going to impound, fine etc., because he refused to believe that Soros wasn't a bandit and a cowboy, a stealer of other men's fares, until Soros decided to tell him that his brother-in-law was a policeman, and that was that, we were on our way. I asked Victoria to ask him whether his brother-in-law was really a policeman. Yes, he was, of course he was, Soros said, and gave his rank, where he was stationed, so forth. Although he continued to smile and laugh a little, he was evidently hurt and a little indignant that his integrity had been questioned – Soros was an honourable man, and expected to be treated as such, was what his demeanour conveyed. He also drove very well, through the foul and dusty suburbs of Athens to the port of Piraeus.

It took about an hour, and when we got there it was foul too, as foul as I remembered it from five years ago, and all the years before that, the afternoon sun beating down, no bars or cafés, and the only shade from a long strip of tarpaulin some distance from the quay, so that when your boat comes in you have to walk fifty yards or so through the naked heat, with all your luggage, and dragging children and great-grandparents and whatever other burdens you have, how is it, how is it, that one of the most famous ports in the world, that receives so many of the country's eager guests and dispatches them to all its lovely islands, can be allowed to be so unwelcoming, so positively and aggressively hostile? It's as if it's set out to show that an ancient seaport can be as nasty as a modern airport, and the fact is, to come to the very heart of the matter, we had four exceptionally heavy bags, two of which could be rolled along on their attached wheels, but two of which had no wheels attached and had to be carried. Victoria spoke to Soros, asking if he could help, he said he would be glad to stay – it would be half an hour before the boat to Spetses came in – and get our bags on board. He accompanied Victoria to the ticket office and helped her to collect the tickets, while I stood by the taxi, guarding our bags and admiring the shapely young men in smart white sailor suits and peaked caps that were strutting about – two of them were quite close, and getting closer, they were both handsome, no, sharply and darkly pretty, and in those crisp outfits and rakishly angled caps reminded me of a film – now what film can it have been that they reminded me of? Who were the actors? Two sharp and darkly pretty men, crisp white uniforms, caps – oh yes, Tom Cruise and Demi Moore in *A Few Good Men*. Demi Moore is a woman, of course, but throughout the film she seemed to be the same sex as Tom Cruise, so really you could equally well think of them as a pair of crisp, dark, pretty women or a pair of men, crisp, dark and pretty. Of the two of them I think Tom was the more fanciable, had more sex appeal whether you took him for man or woman, while poor little Demi was really his sidekick of either sex – what kind of name is Demi anyway? It's a size, surely, half of semi, as in demi-tasse, but what would a demi-attached house be like, or a semi-mondaine, on the other hand, or a semi-Moore, would that be twice as much Moore as Demi, who though small and tightly built would never move you to call her petite? But could you call Tom Cruise petite, by any chance, if you came across him in something frilly, suspenders glimpsed – he has very showy teeth, slightly rat-like but too white and unused for a rat, and he doesn't actually bare them, he flashes them, 'mine eyes dazzle' teeth. But back to the film itself. Although Tom and Demi rattle their way through it, crisp, dark and equivalently gendered, it belongs to Jack Nicholson as a psychotic admiral (no, not perhaps an admiral, but high in the chain of command), rather like Humphrey Bogart in *The Caine Mutiny* but up a notch or two, or down a notch or two, depending on whether you're talking of the power or the subtlety of the performances. Bogart was hateful but poignant, Nicholson merely, but swaggeringly, hateful. We saw Nicholson in Spetses one year, sitting in the wagon of a motorized tricycle, the wagon really rather flimsy, made of canvas and wood, just about wide enough, long enough and strong enough to hold three suitcases, or two Al Pacinos or one Jack Nicholson. It had tiny wheels, so that Jack was also very close to the ground, and looked rather as if he were being hauled around in his container like a trophy in one of those big old movies about the ancient Romans. You expected, say, Charlton Heston or Susan Hayward to be his captor and driver, but it was only your usual Spetsiot, seedy and out of sorts. I suppose they were going off to a yacht, or to the island owned by the Niarchos family – anyway, Jack didn't look as if he enjoyed being in transit in Spetses, in the wagon of a motorized tricycle, he lacked his crazed, mischievous grin, in fact he looked downright sullen, possibly hung-over.

In the film, made when Jack was in his prime, he is a spruce and gleaming monster of the liberal imagination, who believes in discipline, order, punishment, cleanliness, wholesomeness, death, and here were his creatures in front of me, Tom and Demi, one of them was holding in his hand a flapping booklet of pink forms that reminded me, for some reason, of the kind of booklet carried by London traffic wardens. Well, of course these weren't London traffic wardens, these were Greek maritime traffic wardens, Piraeus was their beat, and they were writing out a ticket for Soros, who was standing, incredulous, incredulous once more, on the step of the ticket office, staring at them, Victoria beside him. He came over, expostulating. They shrugged. Tom wrote while Demi took off his sunglasses and put them on again, they were completely impassive. One of them had an eye-catching golden buckle on his belt. Soros phoned Alex in Spetses. This time she was in and, being of a forthright and frequently furious disposition, demanded to speak to Tom and Demi. She stayed on the line as Soros held the phone out, they waved it away, Tom going on with her writing, Demi taking his glasses off, etc., I with one arm hung over Victoria's shoulder as I smoked my cigarette, until the ticket was completed, a fine for seventy euros, then they gestured Soros towards the car park, a few hundred yards further into the heat. We got in and he drove us there, we got out the bags, and between us dragged them all the way to the quay. The Dolphin arrived, in unexpected colours, reds and greens. The last time we'd been in a Dolphin, and during all the years we travelled between Piraeus and Spetses and back again, they were yellow and always reminded me of a torpedo, because they looked as if they could travel under water, indeed had been built to do so in spite of the lofty skis on which they rode, but this new Dolphin, probably redecorated for the Olympics, had VODAPHONE written on it in large black letters, just as the cricket pitches for the recent test matches have VODAPHONE written on them, at least on the screen – it seems actually to be written on the pitch, as if the bowler is going to run through the letters, but it's a digital trick, I suppose, because it can't actually be carved and painted into the grass, surely? Anyway, here's my point, not much of a point really –

the name of the thing that gets into one's life by ringing in one's pocket, or more irritatingly in other people's pockets, bags or purses, and then shears itself across one of my favourite television pictures, the pitch of a test match, is now smeared on the side of the familiar and beloved – no, that's crap, Dolphins aren't beloved, not by me anyway, they're uncomfortable, usually very crowded, and you can't see the passing islands when you're seated, because the windowed hole – the porthole, I suppose it technically is – is too small. In fact it's rather like being on the London tube if it went just under the sea rather than under the ground. Still, a Dolphin is a familiar, if unloved creature, and I hate to find it transformed and abused in this way by Vodaphone, just as I hate to see the sacred turf of our cricket grounds turned into a Vodaphone advertising hoarding.

Also familiar and unloved is the business of getting on a Dolphin. All the tickets are numbered, your seat is your seat, whether you get on first or last, so why is there always a desperate scramble to be first up the gangplank, people shoving each other, stepping on each other's feet, swinging their enormous knapsacks or bum-packs or whatever they're called from side to side in the hope of buffeting the people behind them or to either side of them. My own instinct, being an elderly and in some quarters highly regarded playwright, is to get in among them and barge and shunt and kick my way to the seat that is reserved for me and which I could therefore get to in peace if I only waited, as Victoria advises, for everybody else to be settled. Why do I do it? Perhaps it goes back to prep school days, when the amount of cake you got depended on your rough-housing skills, or to nursery school, when one had to jostle for a turn on the pottie. But I didn't go to nursery school. Well, back to Mummy's teat then. But who would have been my rival, Nigel, sixteen months older than me? Would he still have been on the breast? And did Mummy breast-feed anyway? I don't think so, I can't remember, although sometimes when I light a cigarette and suck in, I have a soothing, backwards-rolling feeling that I'm on the end of something life-sustaining, no, life-enhancing, almost as if it were unfiltered. Of course Mummy was a heavy smoker, so perhaps I was suckled on nicotine milk. And now a word from his sponsor. He smokes Silk Cut. He is now smoking a Silk Cut. He is not feeling bilious. He has not just coughed. He is by no means on the verge of throwing up. He is as happy as a babe on the teat, and why not, as he cannot distinguish between mother's milk and nicotine, as long as he sucks, sucks. You too can be suckled by Silk Cut. Five pounds a packet. Five pounds × three times a day = £15 × 7 = £105 per week × 52 = somewhere under £6,000 a year, wow! Is that all? All those headaches, phlegm-driven coughing fits and rancid stomachs for only £6,000. And just think of all the things you can't get for £6,000!

I threw myself into the hurly-burly, determined to be the first person to my reserved seat, but fell back almost immediately, having been caught in the stomach by a particularly knobbly bum-pack, or perhaps just a knobbly bum – anyway, I was winded and slipped out of the ruck, reached for Victoria's hand, and left it to Soros to do the man's work. He got the bags on board, got the only porter, a large, stocky man with a viciously curling moustache above a snarling mouth, to put the bags in the rack. Soros then, always smiling and sometimes laughing, cleared a way through the mob and settled us into our seats, and then settled beside me to sort out our account. He scribbled some sums on a piece of paper and handed it to me. The sum of sixty euros was underlined. Preposterous, clearly preposterous, he'd incurred a seventy-euro fine, been bullied and threatened by first the land police and then the maritime police, hauled four heavy pieces of baggage aboard when surrounded by a tumult of Greek and tourist desperados, on top of which he'd performed his basic professional task of driving us for an hour from the air- to the seaport, on top of which, through all the stress and injustice, he'd remained unfailingly good-humoured and courteous. I gave him forty-euros extra, 100 euros, not as much as he deserved but seemingly, from his expression and gestures and from the words Victoria understood, more than he expected. It strikes me now that there is a rich paradox in all this. Out of the worst possible, and completely characteristic, welcome from the Greeks had come the best possible, and also completely characteristic, welcome from a Greek.

THE WHOLE WORLD'S A HOSPITAL

I phone Harold every evening. We're each on a mobile. I think Harold has learnt how to use his since he became ill the first time around. His voice is stronger than it was when we last saw him in London a week or so ago, but then it was little more than a whisper, the husk of the barking, powerful voice it used to be. We have little to say to each other. Well, what is there to say, really? He's over there in London, in a hospital, quite possibly dying, and I'm here in Spetses, swimming, eating, reading, writing, and though I'm also dying, it's only in the *sub specie aeternitatis* kind of way, as people are, everywhere. I feel abundantly, even boisterously, healthy. I would write obscenely healthy because it would make me seem less callous, more aware of the contrast in our two states, but I know that whatever's on his mind he can't share with me properly, and it would be – yes, obscene, actually – to share with him what's on my mind, although in fact very little is on my mind except the thought of him, the image of him so ill. I can hardly tell him how I spend my days – 'Well, over here, Harold, all is well, the sun shines, the sea shimmers. We walk down the path that leads to the beach several times a day, plunge in, drift around for as long as we feel inclined, climb out, dry ourselves, drift along to one of the cafés on the front, read the English papers, drift back for another swim, then up the steep but dappled path to the little house perched above the bay, and loiter there, reading, writing, living.' Or I could complain about the insects – 'Bitten by mosquitoes, Harold, I'm taking vitamin B because Victoria says that mosquitoes hate vitamin B, also I have little pencils of repellent I dab over myself, Harold, and if they fail to repel I have little pencils of after-bite, so you see there are serious irritants and inconveniences to the otherwise blissful days, and to be quite truthful about the dappled path to and from the beach, it's actually very steep, very steep indeed, it may only take three minutes, I timed it, to go up, but it feels like three hours, I find myself dragging myself up the last steps, and going down isn't easy either, I stumble sometimes, and overbalance, and what's more the food in Spetses is mostly pretty foul, and what's more, and more and more –'

So what happens during our conversations at the moment is that I ask him how he is, he tells me how he is, clearly and concisely, but with an exhausted fatalism in his voice. He says a little about his eating, whether he's managed to get anything down and keep it there, and then his voice comes to a halt, then falters into news of the test match, which we discuss with fraudulent animation. Fraudulent for him because the effort of seeming to care is enormous, I think. And fraudulent for me because I already know the news, having picked it up from someone else a little earlier. Still, it gives us a subject, for which we're both grateful, keeping us in touch with all the conversations we've had over the years about cricket, test matches, so forth. Then we say to each other, 'Let's see how tomorrow goes, fingers crossed for tomorrow,' and we hang up, and I try not to keep the thought of him sitting upright, absolutely drained by the effort of our conversation with his mobile in his hand. Does he fiddle with it first, looking for the little red switch-off symbol, pressing it with a feeble and unpractised finger, then put it carefully by the bed? In what state of mind does he watch the cricket? I wonder where the television set is in relation to his bed? Does he have to look at it at an angle, or is it above the foot of the bed? I can't imagine the layout of his room. I've been in the hospital he's in quite a few times for this and that, but I have no sense of its rooms, or of its exterior even. I have an idea that its nurses are pleasant. I wonder if he loses his temper with them, whether he has the strength to lose his temper, and then the further strength to apologize. I hope that if he can do the first, he can also do the second – it's not safe, really, to be on bad terms with your nurses. Anyway, there he is, in a place I can't visualize even though I've been to it, and here am I, in a place he certainly can't visualize as he's never been to it, with the moon above and the sea below, and the cicadas clicking their knees.

Actually, Harold is very good at apologies, an outburst over the dinner table will be followed the next morning, or sometimes very late the same night, with a self-denunciation on the telephone, and the manly hope – and I mean manly, I don't know if this word is much used now, it may have passed out of the modern vocabulary, an archaism as unusual as the creature himself – forthright, unadorned, full of strong and delicate feeling, manly. His voice seems to have peeled off layers of bark, as in both tree and dog. In the ordinary currency of life it always has a bark to it, even when – as often, in rehearsals – he was being gentle with an actor in trouble, there would be the rough, brusque coating that went with the outthrust jaw and the glittering eyes. When he becomes angry the eyes go milky, the voice a brutal weapon that is virtually without content. What I mean by this is that he speaks violently, really violently. His voice is like a fist driving into you, but he uses almost no words, three or four at the most – 'shit', 'fuck', 'I' are the ones you hear – recognize anyway, the other words aren't words, they aren't even inexactly uttered expletives, they're dark and ugly sounds, incomprehensible because not intended to be comprehended except as dark and ugly sounds, and full of eloquence therefore. You may not have understood what he was saying but you knew what he meant. Thus he will preface his subsequent apology with 'I don't know exactly what I said last night, I went off the rails a bit, I drank too much and – well, I hope you'll forgive me.'

It's the drink, of course, but it isn't only the drink, of course. The primitive, I really wanted to write the primeval, savagery of Harold's rages comes from somewhere or something drink may have opened the way to, but isn't itself created by drink. It is a chaos of self. 'Seething with rage' is an often used phrase, but I've never felt its truth except with Harold, he 'seethes' as things in nature seethe or he 'erupts' as things in nature erupt – volcanoes, naturally – a volcanic temper, but if you could see into the depth of the volcano what would you see there? Certainly nothing to explain it, you would see only molten substance, and if you could peer into Harold's depths when he seethes and when he erupts, I don't think you'd find the explanation – friends invariably use phrases like 'I think what set Harold off –' and out will come some plausible motive, based on biography. I can't remember any of the explanations now, but they're always perfectly reasonable, with due acceptance of the irrational influence of drink – 'all that, you see, and then he was slightly drunk of course' – but hopelessly inadequate because they omit their own often physical responses to the rages, the assaults, in fact we're struck dumb by them, sit white-faced and in shock as expletive follows expletive. Women cry, mostly. I can't remember anyone standing up to him. Well, how could you? He's like a man having a fit, if he was having it in the appropriate context, a psychiatric ward, for instance, he would be restrained physically, a strait-jacket and then chemically. Then you think about the plays and you wonder if the genius of them is that they both contain and express the dark turbulence they come out of, in some ways they are more like people than works, you feel you might bump into them in a pub or in a dream, you see them living from moment to moment, impulse to impulse, but you don't quite understand how the moments and the impulses connect, which is why you're never sure, even if you've seen one many times, how it's going to end, or whether you're safe in your seat while it's happening, it might come down from the stage and beat you up.

On the other hand, there is his gentleness. What makes him seem so very gentle is the contrast with what we remember and dread. The eyes that go milky when he is in a fit are luminous with concern, the voice becomes soft but – more importantly – tentative, almost shy. Unlike most people he is actually more exposed, more simply and directly himself, when he is concerned and touched than when he is angry, beside himself. Harold tender and gentle is Harold in himself, gathered together and at your service, which has the specific effect of liberating you, so that you become intimate and uninhibited in your confidences and confessions, and in that respect he is oddly priest-like, and gives you a sense of being protected. If I try to distinguish this Harold, the perfect Harold, from my other close friends in similar circumstances, I would say that there is a sense of almost religious seriousness in the exchanges with him, and of absolute concentration – the subject is the subject, not to be

deviated from until it has been explored in all its possibilities for
help, whereas with my other friends there is always, however
desperate the subject, an element of rough and tumble, unrelated
complaints and confessions intervene, they offer examples from
their own experience that make you equal confidants, and
sometimes, by the end, you have forgotten which one of you has
come to talk about what problem. This is never so with Harold, if
he has something to discuss he will place it before you and you will
begin, quietly and gravely, to discuss it, you'll bring to it the sort of
attention he brings to you, there are no byways or turnings off, no
bursts of hilarity. These are rather moving experiences, the
dominating image, for me, always being Harold's eyes, wide and full
of soft feeling.

I've just phoned Harold. He sounded exhausted, but his voice
was again clear and stronger. He gave me the test score, which
isn't too good, the Australian openers still batting with 101 on
the board, I said that both sides had a habit of collapsing when
apparently set, and then reviving when all seemed lost, perhaps
we'll take lots of wickets tomorrow, he said, 'Yes, well, we'll see.'
And then said he was being taken to the hospital on Monday for
another look to make sure that the cancer hasn't come back. I
said, 'Oh.' I couldn't think what to say really. There was a pause,
just like the one that had followed our conversation about the
cricket. 'Well, we'll see,' he said, and we hung up. I don't think
I was of much use. His going into the hospital seems to me
distinctly ominous, how can they not know, after all these
months, during which he has seen specialist after specialist,
whether he's in remission or whether the cancer has come back?
And yet a mere few days ago we were celebrating the news that
they had identified his illness. It was a dental problem, all they

had to do was to fatten him up and give him the appropriate drugs.

In remission. It's such a hopeful word, but when you think what it means, you realize that we're all, always, in remission, even the healthiest of us. In fact from the day we're born. Does that make it a less hopeful word? I keep remembering how, when Alan was, according to the doctors, a day or so away from death, and there was nothing more to be done but to wait for the end, they'd make the process as painless, as peaceful as possible – at least that is what they said to Alan's son Ben. They nevertheless subjected him to a last dose of chemotherapy, the chemo being some chemical not available in England, that had had to be shipped over especially from Switzerland. Ben couldn't understand why they insisted on doing this, it was completely useless and upset the equilibrium of Alan's last days, and upset Ben, who had to encourage his father through needless discomfort and to pretend that it might be a dramatic step towards recovery. Alan was really past taking in what they were doing, all he registered was the physical unpleasantness, and as I say, it made no sense at all to Ben, no sense until he saw the bill, which arrived with cruel punctuality on his father's death and included a vast charge for the last dose of chemotherapy.

How can one trust doctors? They seem to know more and more about their own specialities, less and less about their patients. If they are ear, nose and throat people, then they know the ear, nose and throat of you, but not what these are attached to, you're not present as a living and ailing organism, you're there in the bits and pieces he knows about, and he's unlikely? unwilling? unable? to speculate about alternative explanations for your illness, there's nothing wrong with your ear, nose and throat, so you'd better go to someone who specializes in something else and if you're lucky you might eventually hit on a man who happens to specialize in whatever is killing you.

I'm not ready to give up smoking yet. Insufficiently settled. I tried yesterday, managed until dinner, but then sitting in the café, a coffee in front of me, the sea lapping softly a few yards away, and such a moon! It was the moon that did it, the moon's fault.

THIS ISLAND NOW

The beach we swim from is a couple of minutes away from here, down some steps between grand houses at the top, fairly humble new ones at the bottom. When you've gone down the steps you turn right into another little alley with a wall on one side, behind the wall is a dry river bed, and small apartments on the other side. Each apartment has a poky terrace on which a man or a woman is sitting, serenely reading a paper or smoking a cigarette. They're all and always very polite, and utter a greeting (at least I hope it's that) in Greek, and I doff my straw hat, in the manner of an English gentleman of the old school. It's pleasant going down these two alleys, as there are great trees and dappled shade in the first alley, and the sides of the apartment and the wall create shade in the second. When you emerge, though, you are on a shadeless main street along which motorbikes and the motorized tricycles roar and whine, emitting exhaust fumes that you have to close your mouth and screw your eyes against. The tourist brochure about Spetses tells you that no cars are allowed on the island, which is almost true – there are three officially sanctioned taxis and some delivery trucks – it also says that you can travel about the island in a horse-drawn carriage, which is completely true, you can indeed travel that way if you can afford it, and it's undeniably lovely, late at night, when most of the other traffic has stopped, to come clip-clopping home in a rocking, swaying carriage. The horses are remarkably strong and gifted. They know the intricacies of the island roads so well that the drivers scarcely have to use the reins, just saying a few words now and then to indicate left or right. They do complicated manoeuvres, U-turns and so forth, with economy and skill.

What the tourist brochure doesn't tell you, though, is that the no-cars, horse-drawn-carriages stuff is strictly for the tourist brochure, and leaves out of account the fact that any other form of motorized transport is allowed – tricycles, Vespas, and motorbikes from the frailest to the most powerful, some of them so large that with a burly man on them, his elbows and knees sticking out, they virtually fill the narrower roads. All the drivers go very fast, and very noisily, and if you come in July and August, as Victoria and I used to do, the island is a bedlam, and dangerous. On our first year we saw so many people, from children to ancients, in plaster casts – ankles, thighs, whole legs up to the hip, wrists, whole arms up to the armpit – we thought that there must have been a seismic catastrophe. In fact, they were only the season's regular harvest, either the drivers themselves or their victims.

So you cross this road in your swimming trunks and your loosely buttoned short-sleeved shirt, with your espadrilles under rather than on your feet, your towel over your arm, taking great care to look both ways, and when you arrive on the opposite pavement, you take three steps down through a gap in a low wall and you are on the beach, a long slab of concrete with cracks and holes in it, and uncomfortable sun-beds on it, and on the sun-beds a selection of bodies, all heavily oiled and unnaturally gleaming, and for the most part it's a pretty disgusting sight which would be rendered more disgusting if you added your own body to it, but you don't, you shed your shirt, drop it on the wall along with your towel and hat, and totter to one of the ladders down which you climb in a burdened – burdened? Burdened by what? Worry? Responsibility? Years? Wrinkles and fat? Well, all those, but just let's just say that you climb down the ladder in an ungainly fashion and lower yourself into – and this is the point – the soft Aegean Sea. Once you're in it you can lie there for hours, or do as the Greeks do and form impromptu little parties – you see them in groups of four, five, six, seven, their heads form a loose and bobbing circle as they gossip, laugh, quarrel, their voices rising to shrieks, dropping to conspiratorial whispers. It's really very charming to watch them at it from the shore, in fact watching them at it is about the only charming aspect of being on the shore, where the sun beats right through the umbrella which you can hire, along with a beach-bed, for a quite outrageous price – I hate it, and even Victoria, who loves the sun, finds it uncomfortable, but the Greeks sit and sprawl in it, many of them without hats, and they seem not only comfortable, but happy and grateful – I don't understand it, why don't they feel ill and angry, as I do after two minutes, what is it in their pigmentation or their souls that makes it possible for them – and many of them don't even swim. There's a certain type of middle-aged woman, hair dyed yellow or reddish, with freckled, almost ginger breasts on full display – she struts up and down this strip of cement, promenading, so to speak, with her mobile to her ear, her voice piercing, she never swims, but occasionally lowers herself down the ladder to a rung where the water is knee-high, she stays like that, still on her mobile, for a couple of minutes, then climbs back up, shakes her legs irritably as if something slimy has got on to them, then goes to her bed, lies down, still on her mobile – something about her reminds me of bacon.

You can't spend much time on the cement beach, even if the

Greeks can. Or rather you shouldn't. Get into the marvellous welcoming water as quickly as you can, stay in it until you feel yourself going cold even in the warmth, and the skin on your hands begins to pucker and whiten, then get out, jostle your way to your clothes and towel, dry yourself, go away. You don't, of course. You stay for a cigarette or two, to watch the people on the beach, observe them with the detachment of a writer on the make, is how you like to see it, but in no time you're loathing them, and the ones chatterboxing in the sea, with their bobbing heads and their rasping laughter, seem suddenly to be a coven.

And then there's bound to be a blonde, there is one now and I'm looking at her as I write this – leggy, with a little strip of material between her legs and nothing over her breasts. The stocky, bullet-headed brute lying indifferently at her side, sucking from a can of beer, is almost certainly English, and possibly she is too. They seem to have no physical interest in each other even when they rub oil into each other, the man, so unappealing, is as narcissistic as his appealing girlfriend – if she is his girlfriend, she might be his sister, or his probation officer, he might be on one of those therapeutic outings that the British prison or social services offer, on some bizarre but carefully worked-out system, as an alternative to a prison sentence – The general policy, as we all know, is to bung as many people as possible into prison – all political parties seem to agree that the British public likes to have the most overcrowded, educationally depriving prison system in Europe, but every so often, and equally incomprehensibly, they like to single out a sociopath with a particularly obnoxious criminal history, and send him on an experimental holiday, so why not include in his package a leggy, bare-breasted prison officer with a voice you could grate cheese on, she's now on her mobile, talking to Lav – a nickname, I assume, short for Lavinia, or a joke name for a man whose behaviour it sums up, or who knows? Who cares? I seem to care as I rest briefly on a white plastic bed, the sun pouring through my straw hat like a molten headache, my cigarette jammed into my mouth, as I scrawl down that suddenly I loathe her pert breasts, her long legs, her pretty, unsensual face, her voice above all, and Lav above all that, to whom her voice could reach without benefit of mobile. She's talking about Tone's hangover, Tone being, I suppose, the inert lump basting himself at her side, an absolute catch, and already half prepared, for an enterprising cannibal who could take him off in the back of a motorized tricycle and deliver him to one of those old-fashioned butchers who specializes in human flesh, there's always one in an out-of-the-way quarter, you'll find him if you look.

I say it was the heat beating down on the cement strip without affecting anyone but me that made me hateful, so the sun, the sun's to blame, but the fact is that now that I'm back on my terrace, with the fan whirring above my head, the cool sea gleaming in the darkness, when all appears to be right with the world as far as the eye can reach, I am still hateful, by which I mean full of hate, and it's nothing to do with the memories of the beach, because between being down on the beach at midday and being here at midnight on the terrace there should be other memories – let them find me, the memories of some other day, let them be good and unchoke me from this hatred that comes on me like a sickness more and more.

THE MAN IN THE WHITE PLASTIC CHAIR

We still haven't been to Zogheria, though it's only a short water-taxi ride, fifteen minutes if the sea is rough, from the harbour. On still days the water is so clear that you can see to the bottom when you are out of your depth, and you can stay out of your depth without thinking about it, lazily, dreamily stirring a few yards on your back or rolling on to your side, and if you look out to sea there will be the outline of the mainland, and if you look to shore there will be the beach sloping up to the taverna, set in pine trees, the pine trees cover the slopes around the beach, and at evening the light –

The last time we went, five years ago, I sat at a table in the taverna. It was evening, about six I should think. I watched Victoria sitting on the sun-bed by the edge of the sea, she was bent over a small pad, doing a watercolour, and the light – It really felt like the last time, the light so soft and closing down gently, the end of the day, the end of the season, love in September, the end of a great deal in our lives –

In the first year we came the family that ran the taverna consisted of a father (Taki), a mother (Elena) and two sons (Yannis and Bright-eyes) and a Labrador puppy, bouncing and playful, called Kim. There was also a very pretty, dark young woman who was Yannis's fiancée, and the next year she was his wife and pregnant, the year after the mother of a baby girl – we dropped in on these lives for eight consecutive years, saw the baby become a little girl, saw the young wife pregnant again, then Bright-eyes absent, doing his national service – and there was the grandfather, a retired fisherman who sat in a small wicker armchair, his hands on his knees, not talking much, and an uncle with a trim grey moustache and furrowed grey hair who was still an active fisherman with a small blue boat – now the odd thing, the odd thing about either these people or my memory of them, is that, in spite of the dramatically changing circumstances, the pregnancy, the baby, the absence of Bright-eyes, nothing seemed to change, it was as if a tableau sprang to familiar life every time we re-entered it, and one memory could serve for all memories – for example, on one of our earliest visits there was the most perfect young woman, Scandinavian, surely, lying alone on the beach as the afternoon sun became twilight, she wore bikini bottoms only, her bra spread along the handle of her basket by her head – short blonde hair, long, long legs, her face turned, impassive and lovely, the inevitable sunglasses, she really was a delight and a mortification to the aged eye I kept trained on her from my table in the taverna, I hoped she would get to her feet and I could take in the full-breasted length of her, but she showed no sign of moving, and I could hear the distant hum of the taxi, Michaelis or Martina, growing louder behind the promontory – then lo! the puppy Kim tumbled down the terrace of the taverna on to the beach and bounded up to the girl, who reached out a leisurely hand to stroke him – he darted away, skipped back, plucked up her bra, scampered around her, and lo! there she was, up and frantically about, an arm across her breasts as she tried to catch Kim, who was one moment at her feet – so over she bent – the next jumping away from her – so she darted and pirouetted this way and that, reaching for him with both arms at last, in an abandoned and despairing fashion, and her breasts, elegant and shapely, like two upside-down puddings – I don't think puddings is quite right, doesn't give the sense of contour and grace, though it does catch the mingling of desires – the nicest thing about it, though, was that in spite of the indignity, the necessary immodesty of her movements, she was convulsed with laughter, she clearly adored Kim for the puppy he was, even when she was caught in the hurly-burly of a tug-of-war. She'd managed to snatch back one of the straps and was trying to jerk it free with both hands, and Kim, settled back on his haunches, was determined to keep hold. I don't know how it worked out, the memory stops there, on that image. I wonder if she ever remembers it, wherever she is now, perhaps married, with children, and with a dog or two, I bet.

So that was Kim, in subsequent years a proper-sized dog, and then a lame one, and then he was gone, he died quite young, at six, possibly seven, anyway between one summer when he was there and the next, when there was a puppy instead, another Labrador.

And so, having been in Spetses a week, we've still hadn't done the thing we always used to do the day after we arrived, go down to the new harbour to find Michaelis or his daughter Martina to take us in their water-taxi to what is probably our favourite spot in the whole world. Each evening we say, 'Tomorrow we'll go to Zogheria. Or perhaps Wednesday, we'll go on Wednesday.' I suppose we're afraid that something might have changed for ever, a death most likely, the uncle or the grandfather – after five years they won't remember how things were the last time we saw them – if, say, the grandfather died two years ago it won't be on their minds when they see us, so that when we look around, look towards his small wicker chair, say, and they follow the look, and realize that we don't know, they'll shake their heads sorrowfully, etc., so forth – that's the sort of thing we're afraid of, or worse because it might be one of the children, God help us all – I am beginning to doubt that we will go at all to Zogheria this year.

We used to have five Spetses friends, Athenians who spent the whole of the summer on the island and who were more than holiday friends. We kept in touch one way or another throughout the rest of the year. Now three of them are dead, they died during the winter months, of course, one of them no longer comes to the island, and only Nata is left. She's become more and more a year-round friend, coming to stay with us in London, or in a nearby hotel. We have in our sitting room in Holland Park a bull she cast in metal. It stands on the table by my armchair. It's about a foot long and six inches high, its head is lowered to a butting position, and its shoulders are gathered together, all compact, muscular force, its front legs bent, its back legs lunging forward, so in shape, if you follow its line down from the top of its head to the tip of its tail, it's a model of noble and powerful aggression, but on its bent face there is the most curiously shy and timid expression, a sweetness, and its testicles are small and delicately shaped bells that tinkle slightly if you shift its body about – not easily done, as it's very heavy, I can only just lift it, and if I do I need to put it down again immediately. When Nata arrived from Athens she was carrying it under her arm. She'd carried it under her arm on to and off the plane, and while at the airport waiting for a taxi. It's true that this was some years ago, seven I should think, when she was – if I deduct seven from eighty-three, which she now is – so when she was seventy-six. Yesterday she joined us on the beach, she had a cheroot hanging out of the side of her mouth and hanging from her hand her elegant little basket, decorated with flowers and leaves – well, there she is, Nata – on the one hand, the cheroot, her eyes squinting through the smoke, a tough, almost manly image – on the other hand the charming and feminine basket – she is very like, in that way, in the contradictions of her nature and her appearance, the bull that I love so much. She's quick to denunciation and shows of anger, banging her fist on the table or shaking it in the air, the cause of these outbursts never personal, but general, generous, political – the state of the world, the moral and mental health of President Bush, the ancient and future quarrels with the Turks, the iniquities of the Northern Barbarians. Once she denounced us – Victoria and me – it was only the second or third time we'd met her, we were having dinner with her and a number of her friends – she was talking passionately in Greek at one end of the table, we were talking calmly in English at the other end, and suddenly Nata was on her feet, her dress flowing around her like a toga, she pointed a finger at us, and said, in a tumultuous voice, 'Yes, it is the fault of you – your fault – you Northern Barbarians!' I can't remember now what was our fault, but it was historical, and went back a long way, something en route, no doubt, to the Elgin Marbles. And then, of course, being Nata, she laughed, though adding, 'But still, it is true. I am sorry to have to say it, but it is true.' Her English is upper-class *circa* 1930s, as she was brought up, as were so many Greeks of her generation and class, by an English nanny. She makes grammatical mistakes and her vocabulary is sometimes faulty, but the accent is impeccable even though she invests it with so much un-English feeling, not only passionate feeling but tender and concerned. In repose she has the face of an owl, and she walks like an owl, too – her feet paddle along, her body swaying from side to side – but when she's swimming, the water flattens her hair so that it is sleek against her scalp and neck, and she has the head of a seal. This morning she came down to the concrete beach and sat beside us smoking a cheroot and talking about her work, her family, her plans for her grandchildren's careers – she admits to being, no, boasts of being an oppressively ambitious grandmother, and she entangled her conversation about her grandson, a brilliant mathematician now teaching in London, at Imperial College, with a consideration of the problems she's having with a statue she's working on of Poseidon, King of the Fishes. Poseidon will be carrying in one hand his three-pronged fishing spear, and in his other hand a fish he has just caught – it is going to be larger than human-sized and is designed to be placed in the sea by the Spetses lighthouse. I asked her if this King of the Fishes planned to eat the caught fish, and she said, 'Yes, of course.' I started to debate this with her – I mean, what kind of king would eat his own subjects? A king was a god, she said, who could do what he liked with his subjects, and I suppose that makes sense, in that every god that man has created seems in some way or another to consume his children, who are also his parents – this idea is running out of meaning, I can't pursue it here, prefer rather to dwell on Nata, in her leather espadrilles and her voluminous dress flowing to the metal ladder that people like me

clamber down, rung by rung, and that Nata dives over, her arms
stretched out, unbending, the sides of the hands and the sides of the
feet pressed together in a straight and true dive, classical, but with her
dress billowing around her as she hits the water. She remains under it
for quite a while, and then surges up and settles into a steady crawl,
her cheroot drifting in her wake. She likes to fill her mouth with the
sea and then, lying on her back, jet it out in an enormous arc. It's
much more difficult than it looks, neither Victoria nor I can manage
half the distance that she manages, then she swims out quite a long
way and there remains, her seal's head turning this way and that as she
engages other swimmers in conversation –

'The fact is that I am diseased,' he said on the phone this evening.
'I am a diseased man.' He said it huskily and in wonder, as if to be
diseased against one's will is an almost ungraspable concept.
Everything I said to him seemed to be completely inadequate.
Perhaps the time has passed in myself when I can be of much good
to anyone in need of support of a moral kind. The truth is that the
moment I begin to consider it, I can't think of any reason, moral or
otherwise, why Harold shouldn't be dying, everybody else is, after all,
though not many of my acquaintance are as consciously close to
death, but unconsciously – I mean by that unawares – who knows?
Perhaps I myself, or Victoria or my children. This thought I cannot
pursue, on no account can I pursue this thought, which nevertheless
remains the case – 'remains the case', there's a Harold phrase for you.

This evening, on a sudden impulse, we went to the harbour, in
search of Michaelis. We found him sitting at a table outside the bar,
where all the sea-taxi drivers sit. He is a short man with splay feet
and only one good eye, and you can't be sure that his one good eye
is actually any good, at least as far as seeing goes, but it's good to

look at, as it sparkles with life, friendliness, ironic malice. He damaged the other eye in a motor accident here on Spetses, went to England to have it treated privately – this was about thirty years ago – and came back without it, having spent a year of his life and all his savings trying to save it. It had been extracted for reasons that I don't understand, and replaced with a dull, false one that remains fixed and staring, while the other glints and swivels expressively – but he can't see even with the good eye at night, he becomes a blind man when the sun goes down, as Victoria and I discovered one summer, when he took us across the gulf to the mainland. We set out just as twilight was becoming darkness, Michaelis standing upright at the wheel, his face blank with apprehension that became more than that as we approached the shore, a bulky black mass pierced here and there with little dots of light – his wife, a handsome woman – a hairdresser by profession who once cut my hair so brutally – no, she didn't cut it brutally, she cut it easily and pleasantly, patting my head as she closed in on the skull – it was the final effect that was brutal, I looked like an elderly version of the beer-swigging lout on the beach this morning – anyway, this practical and pleasant-looking woman was seated in the small cabin of the boat, the whole boat being not that much larger or more capacious than a London cab, knitting. She'd come along for the ride, she'd said, for the pleasure of a jaunt across the strait, the night air – she really did communicate this in gestures and half-phrases that Victoria and I could understand. As we approached the lump of blackness in the darkness that was the shore, I noticed that Michaelis was standing sentinel-like sideways on to it, that his face was frozen and that the glitter in the eye was the glitter of panic. His wife came out of the cabin quite casually, stood beside him, chatting in low, wifely fashion and smiling warmly at us, as we sat there on the low wooden seats in the prow, Victoria on one side, I on the other, Michaelis and now his wife between, he physically and she morally at the wheel – so the wife guided through the calm, impenetrable dark the clearly completely night-blind Michaelis, who steered, slowed, reversed, lurched forward, according to her directions – but though she spoke calmly and gently, smiled warmly, a picture of wifely companionability, she had a gesture – plucking at tufts of her hair over her ears – which became like a neurotic tic at what were key moments, in fact one knew they were key because of the tic – but why am I going into all this? We didn't hit anything, we didn't sink, nobody fell into the water, nothing really happened at all. We got to the jetty belonging to the man who'd asked us to dinner, he was waiting with a torch to guide us in, we disembarked, we walked along the path to his home, had dinner – actually I remember nothing at all about the dinner apart from the dread of the return journey, which was exactly like the journey there, in reverse. Getting away from shore was the nightmare but once we were out at sea, and safe, the wife went back to her knitting.

And there he was this evening, Michaelis, at the sea-taxi drivers' bar, facing us as we approached but not really recognizing us until he caught us out of the corner of his functioning eye. He adjusted his head so he could get a view of us, then he exclaimed, encircled us with his arms, kissed me on both cheeks, took Victoria's hand with formal gallantry, and held it but didn't kiss her, was in fact shy, I think. Martina came gliding along the side of the harbour in her taxi, saw us, moored the taxi and was up the quay steps and on us like an enormous and friendly dog. Now we were with them there was no turning back. We established we'd be there tomorrow at 1 p.m., and that one or the other, Martina or Michaelis, would take us to Zogheria.

Midnight. I am sitting on the terrace in a white plastic chair, the sort of white plastic chair you see in bars and cafés across the world,

and staring at this yellow pad with a kind of angry listlessness – I
long to want to pull it towards me and write about the lovely
afternoon we had in Zogheria, but instead I find myself writing a
sentence about the white plastic chair that I'm sitting in and – and
in short –
in short
and in short
I am afraid.

2 a.m. We go home tomorrow. Home. London in autumn, and the
light fading earlier and earlier, day by day – and I'm sitting here on
the terrace for the last time this year – and who knows, perhaps for
the last time ever. It's balmy, with the gentlest of breezes, the lights
of the sea-taxis zipping through the darkness below, and I feel that
I should be able to draw on a rich vein of melancholy, write an
elegy, valedictory, Greece, Greece, oh my Greece, when shall I—?
But really all I want to do is sit here in the white plastic chair on
the terrace, as blankly as possible, smoking. Smoking. Yes, well,
perhaps when we get back to London – remove all the ashtrays.
That might be a start.

4 a.m. It's beginning to get misty and there are only two lights down
there on the water, they're doing zigzags, rather sinuous zigzags, one
behind the other – the one in front has stopped, the other has
caught up, they're moving again, so close that they make just one
light in all that dark sea.

Dawn soon, so no longer home tomorrow, home today.
    Home today.
    God help me.

OLD MAN DROWNING, BUMPITY BUMP

We're on the tarmac at Athens airport. Waiting to take off. There's a slight delay, owing to something or other – a late passenger, a pregnant stewardess, a terrorist trying to get an upgrade – I didn't really take it in, it is enough that the pilot had the usual soothing voice, that Victoria a few rows behind me is looking quite relaxed from a mild overdose of Temazipan. Why are we going backwards for take-off? Pay no attention. Concentrate instead on this and that. Think of a word

racist

Is a reasonable definition of a racist someone who thinks anyone of a different race inferior, simply by virtue of being of a different race? Or is that simply another definition of stupidity? What about attributing someone's bad behaviour to their racial origin – as in 'Well, of course, he would say/do that, wouldn't he, given that he's Aryan/Jewish/Welsh/Asian?' But what if you attribute their good behaviour to their racial origin? 'Naturally he did the honourable thing, how could he not, he's Arab/Scots/African/Oriental' – which should be, logically, as insulting as its reverse – the notion that, for racial reasons, a man can no more help his virtues than his vices, he is his race, etc. – 'What do you expect from a Czech/a Pole/an Englishman, except cowardice/courage?' Let's make it personal, if someone said to me, after I'd rescued an old man from drowning –

– which, actually, I did once,

on a beach in Liguria, an old Italian – heaved him on to the shore after his legs buckled under him in about three feet of water, there was no danger to myself actually, as I was standing almost next to him, I only had to scoop him up by his armpits and hold him steady as he tottered back to land, but there was danger to him because he had fallen face down, so my virtue, if it was a virtue, was in my alertness, I'd had on my eye on him because he'd looked out of his depth in water just above his knees. His wife said to me, 'Oh, thank you, thank you, you are an Englishman, are you not, so naturally you are brave and strong, noble and true' – would it have been reasonable of me to take offence, and to reply curtly that my bravery, strength, nobility and truthfulness had been acquired by hard work, constant self-scrutiny and self-discipline, as I had decided at a very early age, in my sole self and independently of parental influence, social background, and above all my racial inheritance, that my task in life was to look out for the good of other people, take minute-by-minute note of who might require help of any kind – myself I did it, madam, I, I, I, not some Englishman, but I, Simon Gray, rescued your husband from the broiling sea – or would I have swelled up with pride at having my race identified as brave, strong, noble and true? I think I would, yes, I would like to be thought a credit to my tribe. As I say, this is reduced to the personal – if I were a *Guardian* reader I might well have replied, 'Madam, I acted not as an Englishman, but as a member of the human race, from impulses that know no frontiers' –

But supposing I'd been observed swimming away from the old man drowning, and he'd drowned, and his wife had said to me, 'Oh, you cowardly Englishman, you are all alike' – would I have felt more ashamed? Personally, yes, for having brought discredit to my tribe, though I suppose I could have said, as a *Telegraph*-reading person, 'Madam, I behaved as any sensible, risk-assessing, self-interested member of the human race would have behaved – I realized that there was a good chance that if I went to his aid he would have taken me down with him, I have a wife, children, grandchildren, two dogs, two cats to consider, I had no reason to suppose on the evidence available that your husband contributes more to the general good than I do, in fact, now that I see him properly, laid out on the towels and turning blue, I suspect that both justice and nature have been properly served etc. in that he is evidently very old (thus nature's claim) and (justice's claim) corrupt, if not corrupt, venal – after all, he's a Greek, isn't he? Furthermore show me a Greek, madam, or a Jap, come to that, or an Afro-Caribbean that you can swear would have behaved differently – I can certainly show you quite a few Englishmen, several of them friends of mine, who would have behaved exactly as I behaved, equally I can show you quite a few Englishmen, even better friends of mine, who would have given an assist to your husband in the form of a downwards shove, before duck-paddling rapidly away, not out of malice, but out of an apprehension that your husband's desperate last thrashings and gropings might pose a danger to their own continued existence.' So in my imagination, the squabble between me and the freshly minted widow rages on over the purpling corpse of her husband, carrying me further and further from my discussion of the meaning of the word 'racist'.

Have we established anything at all? Apart from my inability to think sequentially or coherently.

Well, this at least.

Anyone who calls anyone a racist in an argument has lost the argument. Unless, of course, the person he's calling a racist is a racist.

I've just woken up. Must therefore have fallen asleep. What was I writing?
we're touching down,

bumpity-bump
bumpity bumpity bumpity
bump
bump

ANDREW AND LILIANNE

It takes an act of will, now that we're back in London, to put on my shoes, my scarf and coat, and get down the stairs on to the pavement, where often I do a lumbering pirouette and within a few minutes find myself back where I started, taking off my coat and shoes – or I make it up Holland Park Avenue as far as the Renaissance, drink down two coffees at a table on the pavement, and then labour home, take off my coat. This is no life for a sentient man, or at least sentient enough to know that this is no life for him. The question arises, therefore: what can I do? To what end should I eke out my remaining days? Furthermore, a question that excited me in my adolescence, when I first came across it in *The Myth of Sisyphus*: why bother to eke out my remaining days, why not just kill myself, and so put an end to the eking? Now how do you answer that question, which Camus, if I remember correctly, says is the first question we should put to ourselves – actually I don't think that's quite how he formulates it, I think he begins by saying that the question 'Why do men kill themselves?' should be replaced by the question 'Why do men not kill themselves?' and of course he puts it in French, and I read it, at the age of sixteen, in English, and haven't looked at it since, so really I'm not guessing, exactly, because it's very clear in my memory, but hoping, let's think of it that way, hoping that my very clear memory of the opening sentences of *The Myth of Sisyphus* is correct. It certainly makes perfect sense to me now, is in fact the question I might have put to myself without reference to Camus if the memory of Camus hadn't intruded – what I'm doing here is stalling, because in fact I don't want to answer the question 'Why don't I commit suicide?' After all, the best I can hope for is another day like this, of which the best that can be said is that I don't believe I've caused anyone any harm, or done any damage in the world. As far as I know. I may have done incidental harm and damage quite unawares.

I might, for example, have reminded somebody of somebody they had loved and lost, and stirred long and hitherto successfully repressed feelings which then engulfed them. Well, suppose a woman, suppose she was driving by in a car, had glanced out of the window and my face, my body posture, the dreary drum of my feet heading up Holland Park Avenue had brought to her mind a husband or a dog, yes, more likely a dog, that she buried a year ago, the dog that had been a mere pup when she had – had what? Her first child? Got married? Got arrested? Got her driving licence? Does one remember dogs as pups anyway? I don't think so. I think one remembers them, carries them about in one's heart, as full-grown dogs, with their characters firmly established. Besides, if it was the sight of me plodding up Holland Park Avenue that reminded her of her dog, it would scarcely be of a puppy, would it, that I reminded her? It would be of an elderly dog, the equivalent of a seventy-year-old man, which would be a 420-year-old dog if you multiply by six to translate dog years to human years – which can't be right, is clearly nonsensical in fact, a 420-year-old dog would be a dead dog, surely, even in dog years, so have I got the multiplication factor wrong? But let's get back to the point I started from, which was whether I might have done unintended harm today by reminding a woman driving past me on Holland Park Avenue of a beloved husband or dog, now dead. There. That puts it all very clearly. She saw me, into her head surged a memory of her dead husband going about a particularly

beloved piece of business, what? My imagination fails me, I can't
make up a beloved piece of husbandly business, I seem to picture
him coming out of the lavatory, shuffling out, doing up his belt – not
much hope that she'll remember that as a beloved bit of business, but
possibly its very characteristicness will have something lovable about
it, perhaps just its regularity – 'Every morning, on the stroke of eight,
I'd see him coming out of the lavatory. He had a way of fumbling
with his belt, such a way of fumbling with his belt! It was so him!'
She may, of course, remember it, particularly the regularity, with
revulsion, in which case he would be likely to be in all his aspects
unbeloved by her – surely there are other bits of business you can
give him that don't have lavatorial associations and that she might
remember with, well, a degree of affection at least –

'He is remembered with a degree of affection' might be a decent
enough epitaph, come to that, it's certainly more precise and
therefore more convincing, than 'Beloved', which is what I put on
my brother Piers's tombstone. Now, when I sit on the bench
opposite his grave and look at the word, it no longer seems simple
and eloquent, but brutal and pretentious. I used to distract myself
from it by getting up and walking around for a while, and then
pausing in front of one of the graves eight down from Piers, on the
right, as you face him. Actually I've described it somewhere else –
    The headstone is rather jaunty, yellowy-grey in colour, with a
photograph of a young man embedded in a little glass dome at the
top. He is bare-headed, dark hair cut short, round, handsome face
with slightly child-like features, unformed anyway, as if he hasn't
grown into them yet. He is dressed in shiny black leather, mounted
on a powerful motorbike, a helmet under one arm, the other resting
on the handlebars. Underneath this is inscribed 'In Loving Memory
Of Andrew Crabb' and underneath that 'A Dear Son, Brother And

Friend' and underneath that 'Born 12th February 1963 Died 10th April 1996' and underneath that is written in curling, flourishy letters the following poem:

> He rode through life
> Fast and Free
> His candle burning bright
> And through the smoke that we still pass
> He left us with his light

Once, when I worked out from his dates that he was just two days short of thirty-three years and two months old when he smashed himself up on his motorbike, I suddenly became interested in this question of ages, how long the dead in Piers's vicinity had spent in the world. I suppose I must have checked on about fifteen gravestones, and found two, both men, on which the arithmetic worked out at forty-nine – the age Piers was when he died. Altogether three out of sixteen, if one included Piers – must be unusual, surely, a freak clustering – 'clustering', isn't that the right word, the word they use when compiling statistics of this sort?

Now a new grave has come between Andrew Crabb and Piers, of a woman who, like Andrew Crabb, died in her thirties, and on the tombstone which marks it there is a poem in italic letters:

> Do not stand at my grave and weep
> I am not here. I do not sleep
> I am a thousand winds that blow
> I am the softly falling snow

and above it, etched into the stone, is the figure of a woman who could be an angel or could be a nurse, it's so vaguely, rather than delicately, executed. I suppose the statement of the poem could be described as pantheistic, sentimental-pantheistic, anyway it's certainly not Christian and it's self-evidently untrue, you might even say that it's a lie, just as the nurse/angel etching is a lie, she wasn't like that in life and she isn't that in death. I wish I could remember her name, her Christian name was Lilianne, I'm sure of that, but why I mention her, or rather her tombstone, is that it always gives me comfort, because it speaks well of the feelings of the people – parents I think – who buried her, and makes me feel less well about the people who buried my brother Piers and if I exonerate my brother Nigel, who was in shock and not well, I am left with me, as the family member I feel less well about, the unexonerated. I always slide some of the feeling on Lilianne's tombstone on to Piers's, although he would never have thought of himself as softly falling snow, or as a thousand winds that blow, furthermore he might well have wanted me to stand at his grave and weep, but to what avail as he is to be found, if he is to be found anywhere, At The Still Point Of The Turning World, which is where I plonked him, according to the line I had inscribed on the bench. Furthermore I attributed the line, as if to give it added value, to T. S. Eliot. 'Piers Gray, At The Still Point Of The Turning World. T. S. Eliot.' Lilianne's lines, unattributed, seem simply to have drifted down and settled on her tombstone – when I say them aloud I don't say them directly to Piers, of course, as that would be a sort of thieving. I say them almost directly towards Lilianne but keep Piers in the corners of my eyes.

CAN WRITING FICTION REPLACE SMOKING?

But what was I doing up at the graveyard? What chain of thought, if it can be called thought – ?

Oh yes, my wondering whether I did unintended harm today by being mistaken by a passing woman driver for a beloved husband or dog. Well, how would that develop? I'm shambling up the street, heavy-limbed and flu-ridden, she glances in my direction just as she approaches the traffic lights, her heart leaps or her mind drifts, either way coordination disintegrates, the car bounds through the red light or stalls at a green one, then either runs over a pedestrian or is run into by the car behind, she either faces criminal charges or is seriously injured – in one way or the other her life is ruined. Or is it? Who knows how she would emerge from either catastrophe, seeming catastrophe? Take seeming catastrophe one: she runs over a child. She – Adele, let's call her, after her French grandmother – Adele has had a heavy lunch with Miriam, an old friend from schooldays. The school was St Muphet's, a boarding school in Shropshire which has long since been converted first into a hotel and more recently into a halfway house for sex offenders who are being returned to the community. It was that sort of school, the seeds of its future already in it. It was also the sort of school that girls like Adele and Miriam found themselves being sent to by parents who wouldn't contemplate state education and couldn't afford the best or even the better private schools.

Adele's father was a doctor with a long history of migraines, insomnia and adultery, her mother was consequently, or so a rationalist would argue, a bit of a dipsomaniac, who grew fat and developed a heart condition, and was subject to asthma attacks, some of them wilful – cats brought them on, but whenever she saw one she picked it up and buried her face in its fur. She had a small but genuine gift for painting, and did surreal landscapes from her sofa, which one of her husband's rich patients would sometimes buy when Adele's school fees were in the offing, but were otherwise stacked in various rooms around their house in Barnet, in those days a cheap and inconvenient London

suburb. Adele was still living there at the time of the accident on
Holland Park Avenue, which happened when? I must look back – Oh,
today, this morning, when I went up to the Renaissance – so she's still
living in it as I write this, along with one of her daughters, Wendy, who
is a single parent and an unsuccessful freelance photographer – her one
exhibition, in a small studio in Whitechapel, consisting of shots of her
two children, three-year-old Seraphina and seven-year-old Jacques
(different fathers) playing on the beach, in the bath, in the garden, all
in the nude, was closed by the police and almost led to Seraphina and
Jacques being taken into care by Social Services. This crisis brought out
the sleeping tigress in Adele. She adored her grandchildren with a
passion she'd felt for no one and nothing else in her life. She hired
lawyers and wrote letters to her MP and went from door to door
collecting signatures for a petition and got interviewed on afternoon
television and finally managed to gain custody, which Wendy resents
far more than she would have resented losing them to the state – other
than when she was photographing them she found them 'a fucking
nuisance' were her actual words to Klaus, the seventy-five-year-old
father of Seraphina, a Swiss violinist whose concert career came to an
end when he lost the use of his left hand in a beer-house brawl in
Stuttgart in '83 with some English football fans from West Ham.
Where is Wendy now, then? Is she with Seraphina's father, Klaus, the
one-handed violinist? No, she's gone to join Jacques's father in
Morocco, a faith-healing drug dealer, or a drug-dealing faith healer,
depending which way round you look at him, and gay – his name is
Willard and he comes from Texas. This is surely all the background I
need on Adele. The key points I should try to keep in mind are that she
is in her early sixties, she's the world's best grandmother, a well-
intentioned but spurned mother, a conscientious if little-loved daughter,
a dutiful if undervalued friend, and this is what she looks like –

ADELE RAPED IN PRISON! IS THIS JUSTICE?

Adele has curly grey hair, a round, gentle, thoughtless sort of face with a snub nose and large grey eyes that don't see much or well – her spectacles have an odd effect, they make her eyes seem small and crafty, which won't help her cause at her upcoming trial, although the real problem is going to be the amount of alcohol I've had her consume – two vodka turganovs before the meal, a bottle of red wine and a bottle of white wine during it, more than she'd drunk altogether in the previous six months, and certainly enough to see her sent to prison – and how can she not be, given that she badly maimed a mother, her child and their dog – a dog? Yes, yes, the child was carrying the dog when the mother scooped her up and bam! Adele got the lot of them. I can't bring myself to decide who lives and who dies. The sentimental side of me is inclining towards the dog as the sole survivor, but is it wise to introduce another dog? The whole business only arose, the accident and so forth, because Adele mistook you for a dog, surely this other dog just gets in the way, so kill off the dog, no, not kill off, eliminate it from the child's arms, also take the child out of the mother's arms and put her in a pram – so Adele smashed into a pram. Christ! – let's leave that for a moment, toy briefly with the idea of making Adele herself her only victim, paralyse her from the waist down or up or both – no, no, just leave it that she hurt her knee slightly, the point is the drunken driving and jail time, that's what we want to get to, that's where all this is tending, redemption, a Tolstoyan redemption in jail, a bit like *Resurrection* but without all the mystical stuff, or a Dostoyevskian redemption, like *Crime and Punishment* but again without all the mystical stuff, just a straightforward, no-holds-barred Anglo-Saxon account of a middle-class, middle-aged soul discovering herself through rough Anglo-Saxon justice and sexual humiliation, in jail she was the particular favourite of brawny inmates with child-like dispositions, but eventually her innate dignity, her gentle manners, her generous and unreproachful acceptance of the needs and desires of the socially deprived and less fortunate whose sexual appetites –

All this coming about because she a) drank too much at a lunch with her old friend Miriam and then b) glimpsed through her car window an elderly man (me) who reminded her of a beloved dog. Now all that really remains for me to work out is the nature of her conversation with Miriam, and what it was about the man (me) she glimpsed that reminded her of the dog, and then what it was about the memory of the dog that caused her to lose control of her car – what sort of car, by the way? Oh what does it matter what sort of car, a car is a car – well, it is to you, because you can't drive and have therefore never owned a car, so it's hard for you to visualize Adele driving past you up Holland Park Avenue, glancing out of the window – no, actually it's not hard, I see her quite clearly, her round face purplish-tinted from all that alcohol, her spectacles slightly askew, her mouth half agape and her jaw slack, like something seen through the window of an aquarium, I see her in fact from what would have been my point of view if I'd turned my head as she drove past – but I didn't turn my head, I kept plodding listlessly on, thinking little angry thoughts about not wanting the coffee I was forcing myself towards, not wanting the cigarette I was about to smoke that would make me feel worse and thinking I really wanted to be back in my study, or, better still, back in bed –

What did Adele and her friend Miriam talk about? What did they drink about? I don't think I've said yet that Adele didn't really like her friend Miriam. In fact she thought of her as a responsibility she'd been saddled with at the ghastly little school whose name I've forgotten and can't be bothered to look back for – actually I think it was St Moppet's, an unlikely name for a school, it might have been Mupphet, St Mupphet – in the narrow, damp and underlit dormitory in their first term Adele had had the misfortune to be bedded next to Miriam, but 'next to' doesn't give the sense of the closeness, it was almost as if the ten girls in the dorm shared a vast mattress with gaps in it, Adele had only to reach out over the blankets, an instinctive and uncontrolled maternal gesture, and the sobbing child was in her arms, and there she remained. It was as if some strange adoption contract had been drawn up, in which Adele had had no say and the terms of which were absolute: it was Adele's task in life to look after Miriam, Miriam had assumed it when she had lain, snivelling, with her head against Adele's soft young bosoms, her long lean legs locked around Adele's short sturdy ones, and her thumb in her mouth – her own mouth, that is, though so complete had been the act of possession that it might easily have been Adele's, the image would have perfectly represented what Adele sometimes felt about the relationship.

At St Moppet's it was rumoured from time to time
but really nobody believed it.
I don't believe it, I can't even imagine it.
Just because I can't imagine it doesn't mean it didn't happen.
Well, possibly once. Just the once. In the library.

WHAT HAPPENED IN THE LIBRARY

On a fine spring afternoon. The 2.30 cooking class that had been cancelled because its teacher, Miss Sally Twark, had had to rush to the sanatorium with gastroenteritis, so Adele and Miriam went to the school library, a small room, not much bigger than, say, a room in the Hilton, that contained a free-standing bookcase, a low understuffed armchair and a wooden three-legged stool. There was also a wrinkled brown leather sofa – courtesy of a governor and parent, the distinguished psychiatrist R. de Witt Witt, who at the time being written about (1969) championed hallucinatory drugs, spontaneous violence, chaotic sex and was a crusading enemy of the family ('only psychically healthy when engaged in incest') – but at the time of writing this (Nov 2006) he is a vegetable resident of what would have been called, at the time being written about, an asylum for the criminally insane –

Look, what happened in the library?

I don't know. I'll have to come back to that tomorrow. The important thing is that I've been writing steadily through the story of Adele and what's-her-name without smoking a cigarette. It must be the longest sustained piece of writing in my whole lifetime written without a cigarette, and I suddenly notice how dry my lips are, and that my lungs and my blood are pleading – no, no cigarette! Back to the library. Find out what happened there. Bondage? Rape? Murder!?!?

Miriam is as we left her.

She is lying on the sofa, one leg dangling over the side, so that the heel of her squat brown shoe (regulation school issue) is on the floor. The hem of her pleated grey skirt has slipped under her buttocks. Her long and shapely legs are thus exposed up to her thighs – her left one, stretched to the floor, is straight and true, almost no sign of a kneecap, just a small inverted pouch, while the line of her sinewy calf is tautly curved. Her head is flung back over the end of the sofa, her fine blonde hair cascades to either side of her narrow head. Her small beaky nose and tight, almost lipless mouth seem both sharpened and softened by the light that falls through the latticed window – it may be her abandoned posture, or her almost translucent skin, or the general impression she gives of having been drowned in a lily pond and then dried out in a linen cupboard – hush, she's speaking:

'I wish I was Ted.'

Adele, doing her best to ignore the drip sliding down the runway from Miriam's nostrils, responds with her customary warm-hearted curiosity.

'Ted? Who's Ted, dear?'

'Dead, I said. I said dead. I wish I was dead.'

'Oh.' She tries to think of something new to say. 'I think you have a cold coming on.'

'That's why I wish I was dead, is it?'

'It's why I thought I heard you say Ted instead of dead. The "d" sounded like a "t" – Ted. Instead of dead.'

Adele is sitting on the stool, which has a shiny top off which her bottom skidded when she first sat on it. She has hitched up her pleated grey skirt so that her buttocks can have a purchase – actually there is only enough surface for one buttock to purchase, and she is aware of how unseemly she looks, as if lopsided on a lavatory, but feels, more sadly than bitterly, that this is appropriate for her relationship with Miriam –

'But why would you want to commit suicide?' Her eyes are on the base of Miriam's nostrils, where another drop, so shiny, like the morning dew, so shiny –

'I didn't say I want to commit suicide.'

'Oh. Why don't you?' She was surprised to feel a throb of pleasure. She smiled.

'Why don't I? What do you mean?'

'Well, you haven't got anything to live for, have you, from what you tell me, and from what I can see for myself. You say your parents never wanted you, your father says you're not his and your mother wishes you weren't hers, your father likes boys, that's why he went into the navy, and your mother drinks all night and sleeps all day –'

'I never said any of that.'

'Yes you did. You say it all the time. In your sleep. That's why you cry and I have to put my arms around you.'

'Daddy's an admiral, and Mummy's ill, she can't help it –'

'That's what you say when you're not asleep.'

Miriam wipes her sleeve across her nose, as if just waking up. 'You're trying to hurt me.' It's a whisper, child-like. 'Why are you trying to hurt me?'

'Because I'm just like everybody else who knows you. I can't bear you.' Without seeming to herself to move she has shifted her bottom from the stool and is grinding it into Miriam's face.

You can see them there, if you concentrate. Adele is suffocating Miriam to death with her bum, and she is grinning while she's doing it, no, actually she's more than grinning, she's making noises through her grin that might sound sexual, but come from deeper in her, and are in fact homicidal. She wonders vaguely why Miriam isn't trying to bite her – but ah! How can she bite, given that her mouth, whether opened or closed, is being crushed by mounds of flesh and wads of cloth, and that's why her legs aren't threshing, her fists have fallen away, why she has become still, quite still.

The sigh that Adele sighed as she rolled her bottom off Miriam was one of regret. She wished she'd done what she wanted to do, but it was too late to clamber back and finish the job, there were voices that at first she thought were outside the library, faint but clear from a distance, and then were inside the library, and then inside her head –

She slid her buttocks into their previous uneasy position on the stool, and sat watching Miriam's return to consciousness with a cool, unworried eye.

Miriam twitched and gobbled, the white began to return to her nose and cheeks, which had gone puce under pressure, and foam gathered at the corners of her mouth. Her legs and arms trembled and her bony chest sucked in and out, raspingly. She reminded Adele of an ungainly young bird, say a gosling, just rescued from the jaws of a cat, except, except for her lips – Adele felt a stirring of desire, and such was her state might well have – might well have – if Miriam hadn't – but Miriam did. She pulled herself up, and she looked at Adele with such a vague, puzzled look of terror –

'We must never do that again,' Adele said firmly. 'We don't know what came over us.'

'No' Miriam's voice was feeble but eager – 'I don't know what came over us.' She winced as she spoke, and touched her lips, which were swollen and bruised, like the plums of August, and had provided Adele with the thought – they looked, those lips, as if they'd been kissed and kissed, which in a way they had been.

'It was wrong of us,' Adele said huskily. 'I blame myself most.'

'No, no, it was my fault, I know it was.' Miriam was pleading, yes, but was she pleading for her life? Or pleading to be forgiven for being such a temptress? Or did she merely sound pleading, because she had her whiniest voice on? And did Adele care? She felt such a surge of freedom, such a surge of lust and power combined –

'Well, yes, it was your fault because you looked so pretty – but I shouldn't have done it, and I promise I won't, ever again.'

'Do you promise, honestly, honestly?'

'Only if you promise never again to look so sweet.'

'I shan't, ever again, I promise.'

'Then I shan't, ever again. So we're safe, aren't we?'

'Yes, safe!' But she squealed when Adele got off the stool and went to her and bent over her. She drew her knees up and she hunched her shoulders.

'But we must kiss a little kiss, to seal our promises. Mustn't we?' Adele put her finger under Miriam's chin, and turned the thin, sharp strip of a face towards her, and pursed her lips. Miriam squeezed her eyes shut, and tried to purse her lips –

If Adele had known what rape was, she'd have raped Miriam on the spot. She'd have thrown her on the floor, bound her hands behind her back with her own flaxen tresses, ripped off her blouse and bra – whoops, whoops, whoops! Forward. Forward to a cigarette.

Alas, alas, now two.

PART TWO

JERRY ORBACH AND LENNIE BRISCOE
ARE SORRY FOR YOUR LOSS

I've spent most of the day looking at the chaos on my study bookshelves and wondering what I can do about it. Just now I noticed, half hidden on a top shelf, Ian MacKillop's biography of F. R. Leavis. I took it down to put it somewhere more visible, somewhere more honourable, found myself dipping into it and then thinking not so much about Leavis as about Ian. We met when we were in our early twenties, in our second year at Cambridge, both taking the English tripos and both teaching in the same language school for foreigners in the vacations. At that age he was tall and thin, like a comically doleful but good-hearted cleric as conjured up by Boz and illustrated by Phiz, with spiky hair and the confused, sometimes desperate expression natural to an undergraduate with a wife and baby to support – and yet there was this oddly ecclesiastical aspect to him, partly a matter of his dark clothes and his pallor, but also the timbre of his voice and particularly in the carefulness with which he chose his words –

But there was never, at any time, anything ecclesiastical about his thinking, or the things he was willing to talk about. He seemed to have a completely uninhibited mind, I can't remember him being shocked by any subject or event. His curiosity was limitless, willing to go through endless byways for the pleasure of the journey.

Actually, the Leavis biography was a brave undertaking, given that Ian had been a pupil of both the Leavises. His critical impartiality was bound to offend their acolytes, his even-toned sympathy to irritate their enemies, but it succeeded in its main aim, which was to make us aware of what at his best Leavis represented, and what the personal cost had been in broken friendships, lost trust, isolation. The last stretch of the book, on Queenie Leavis's attempts to usurp her husband's reputation by laying claim to his work, make for pretty desolating reading, but Ian tells it scrupulously, unflinchingly, with a deliberated kindness all his own. I think he was a man of great tolerance and geniality but no softness – in his writing, with his friends, or in his living.

He knew so much about so many unexpected things – horror films, pulp fiction, westerns as well as thrillers, early Agatha Christie, every poet alive writing in the English language, dozens and dozens of poets that one, this one anyway, had never heard of, and he enjoyed reading them even when he didn't understand them – in fact not understanding them was part of his pleasure, it made him puzzle, worry and think, and he had a plan, not altogether a fantasy, to travel in a caravan around the British Isles and the States, park outside their homes, observe them in their habits, quiz them about their poetry.

He made a calm comedy out of the worst events in his life, out of even his last illness. I don't know anyone else who could make a dispassionate tone so droll – he was never ungenerous, except about himself in abrupt little asides, mutterings really. On our last meeting he remarked that there was something, I forget what, that he was really determined to do, really was obliged to do, then he chucked in, in a low voice, as an afterthought, 'Unless I'm dead, of course. And then I won't have to.'

When he came to stay he would bring a gift, anthologies of seventeenth- and eighteenth-century verse, or a little bundle of mid-twentieth-century detective stories – we have a charming wooden angel, hand-painted, from Guatemala on our mantelpiece. On his last visit he brought half a dozen eggs laid by his recently acquired hens. He'd carried them with him all day, while he'd gone about his London tasks – a visit to the British Library, meetings with colleagues and with publishers – before coming to us late in the evening. It made the eggs more delightfully and specially a gift, the thought that he'd had to keep them in mind all day, carry them carefully –

'I'm sorry for your loss' is what television detectives say when interviewing the victim's widow, widower or children, the phrase has become so inert that you no longer listen to it, if the actor changed it slightly, to 'Thank you for your loss' or 'We're happy for your loss' or 'Have a nice loss now', none of the characters, or the actors, or the audience would notice – but an actor who managed to give it unexpected poignancy was the late Jerry Orbach, who played the late Lennie Briscoe in *Law and Order*. In his last episodes one kept noticing his make-up, presumably he wore so much because without it he would have been visibly ill, visibly dying – when he said, 'I am sorry for your loss' his old, cynical roué's face, though powdered and covered in rouge, with eyeshadow, and even lipstick, seemed suddenly to get so much older, more cynical, and he would switch his eyes sideways as if he were sending a message to those in mourning on the other side of the screen, and how could there not have been quite a few of us, given the size of the audiences, though very few of us would subsequently be charged with murder – it's a fair bet that one out of every three of the characters to whom Lennie Briscoe says, 'I'm sorry for your loss' will end up in prison gabardine – the effect is really double, on the one hand the actor Jerry Orbach intimately consoling the grieving multitude with 'Hey, me too, I know what it's like, furthermore I'm on the way out myself' and on the other hand Detective Lennie Briscoe saying to a character, 'We'll continue this conversation down at the station, we're going to have to ask you for a DNA sample, and oh, hey, sorry for your loss.'

I wonder if Americans actually do say it to each other, and if they do whether they say it in an attempt to nullify the fact that gives rise to it. 'I am sorry' has the primary meaning of 'I feel sorrow', but still trails a slight suggestion of apology, perhaps for the inadequacy of the phrase, while 'loss', well, it means at its simplest that you don't have it any more – loss of money, loss of time, loss of patience and of temper, loss of a child – your son, your daughter, your mother, father, best friend, but what exactly is lost? This gesture, that expression, the early morning cuddle, the endearing laugh and endearing smile, her uniquely irritating laugh and his noisy way of gulping down his coffee, his way of not leaving the table when blowing his nose, 'Sorry for your loss.'

The trouble with the dead is not that they are lost, and therefore might be found, but that they are beyond finding and are not therefore lost, they are absent to this world, in all the places that they were accustomed to be present in, and that you were accustomed to their being present in, the space at your side, the opposite seat at your usual table, the other half of the bed, the neighbouring pillow – nothing can be more finally absent than a dead person, and yet the dead persist in being almost present in traces and glimpses, whisking around the corner of your memory to drive you mad, like the incompletely forgotten name of a film star from many years ago – there was one I was trying to remember the other evening, a man in the restaurant reminded me of him, a slim, middle-aged man eating by himself, not out in the open part of the restaurant but in a cramped bit by the bar – he reminds me, I said to Victoria, of that actor, in that film – I could see the actor's face quite clearly, though in the film it was usually half in shadow, a neat little moustache, opaque eyes, and he had a cleft in his chin, more dimple than cleft, shiny black hair pasted back, and there was the voice, drawling but toneless, I knew him so well in my teens, but who was he? In what film, *Zorro, Mask of Zorro?* No, no, Peter Lorre was in it, *Dimitrios, The Mask of Dimitrios*, and he was Z, Z certainly comes into it – in the film I'm trying to remember he generally lurked in alleys and hallways, or in a seedy hotel with large, bogus-looking rooms and cluttered corners you couldn't see into – I can't remember a particular scene, or a line of dialogue, or the plot, or even the climax, just Peter Lorre and Zachary Scott – Good Lord, there it is, Zachary Scott, what a name! And now I've got it written down I'll have it here to tell Victoria – Zachary Scott, I'll say, in *The Mask of Dimitrios*. He died not too long ago, there was something anomalous in the obituary, he went to Harvard to study Classics, or he played chess at international level, or fenced in the Olympics, something like one of those things but not actually any of those things. The next time the film turns up on television I must watch it to the end and at the end of it, when the credits roll and there is his name, I'll try to remember to feel sorry for the loss. Our loss. Our losses.

I've been sitting here for half an hour, still thinking or thinking yet again about the word 'loss' and wondering why I can't leave it alone, a bit of grit in my inner eye.

As my life has emptied of friends over these last years, I shouldn't find it strange that I frequently feel lonely –

LOVE BEFORE THE TIME OF THE ANSWERING MACHINE

I think I miss the voices most, on the telephone. What was friendship like before the invention of the telephone? We know of its intensity for Tennyson, say, or Pope, for Milton or Matthew Arnold, all of whom wrote about their friendships, about the deaths of their friends, and all their poems, so different in form and vocabulary, strike the same note of grief and yearning, they make the same attempts to catch and hold the lives that have gone, we know the nature of the friendships from the manner in which they are missed – but it's hard for us now to grasp the developing of friendship before the telephone, when it depended on physical presence and letters – and before that, before the invention of the railway and the penny post – you can convert an impulse into a disaster within seconds now, and from pretty well anywhere in the world – why, merely by taking my mobile out of my pocket while strolling down Holland Park Avenue I could ruin friendships with people in New York, Rome and London in five minutes. It would have taken weeks in 1907, months, many months, in 1807 –

But for decades now most friendships have developed partly through the voice, disembodied but full of character, though not exactly the same character as the embodied one – does this mean that in those days, before the telephone, the physical meetings of friends were more intense – we know, but are still surprised, that Victorian men publicly kissed, embraced, touched each other in a way that modern men don't, except, I suppose, for theatricals and homosexual men in love with each other, who presumably touch and fondle like heterosexual couples in love with each other – well, not entirely like, as they don't do it in public that I've seen, though come to think of it young heterosexual couples today don't fondle and caress, or even hold hands very much, in public, although some of them don't mind being seen fornicating on beaches in the Mediterranean or in Greece, in Spetses actually, during the high season they hump away, all the night long, all the short night long –

As for the changing nature of friendship – when once a friendship was sustained by correspondence interrupted by intense physical presence, it's now sustained by telephone and more and more by email – I suspect email is most often used by friends when a) they don't want to waste the time and b) they can't face the emotional complications of a conversation – or, embedded in this proposition, that they want to present their side of the case without contradiction or diversion. I've noticed that people don't really enjoy receiving chatty emails, it's something like getting tightly written postcards – such stuff is for letters, in envelopes, that you open when you're ready – I was going to say that there are letters you open at breakfast, others you keep until lunch, others you face up to after midnight, after a few drinks if you're lucky enough to be a drinker, or after a few cigarettes if you're unlucky enough to be a smoker – but where we live, in Holland Park, we don't get letters at breakfast, or by lunch, we get them, when we get them at all, in the early evening, or later, when our neighbours return from work and redistribute the post according to the addresses on the envelopes –

When I talk of letters I mean, of course, personal communications, written by hand or on a typewriter, or if on a computer with an accompanying apology – i.e. my handwriting has degenerated so much from under-use that nobody can read it, therefore I have to write this on the computer, therefore if you don't understand it, it will be because of a failure of clarity on my part or of intelligence on yours – although I admit that I've never actually written an apology of that order in one of my computer letters, but – but – but to get back to telephones, or rather the era of the telephone, before the invention of the mobile, right back to the old telephone, lying in its sturdy cradle, when it used to ring just as you opened the front door, went on ringing while you pounded up the stairs, went on ringing as you hurtled along the hall, flung open the sitting-room door, lunged across the room, ring-ring, ring-ring,

ring-ring it went, until you closed your hand around the receiver,
ring-ring, ring-ring until the instant before you lifted it off its cradle,
and you knew even as you lifted it that you were too late, you'd get
the low, impassive buzzing sound that was the dialling tone – then
you could do a number of things, depending on who you suspected
or hoped had made the call – I'm going back, note, past the
telephone answering machine, when there was nothing from the
telephone except the ring-ring when it rang, and zzzzz when you
lifted it a fraction of a second too late to your ear, so there was
absolutely no way of knowing whose call you'd missed – it could
have been a wrong number, why not? But you hoped not, you
hoped it was a real call, an important call, so you did one of two
things – you either sat by it, lifting it now and then to make sure it
was working, and zzzzz, it was, or you phoned up everybody you
knew who was 'on the phone' to ask if they had just called you –
that was the telephone fifty years ago, you were its prisoner if you
were in love, it gave you enormous freedom if you were out of love –
if the phone rang, nobody could prove you were actually there,
listening to it ring, waiting it out – however often and pleadingly
it called you, you could never be proved to have heard it – you
would think of the person at the other end giving up at last, or
going out for a walk, a half an hour walk, before allowing herself to
call again – and then another half an hour – but don't forget that
you never knew, when the phone rang, who was calling you – you
might have thought you were waiting her out, and then discovered
weeks later that it was in fact somebody who would have changed
your life if you'd answered – 'I did phone you a couple of times,
when I was passing through London, to see if you still wanted to
take me to bed, but you were always out, and so I assumed', 'I did
wonder if you'd be interested in the job, but I could never catch you
in and then somebody mentioned somebody not quite as well

qualified as you but –' But it was most probably the one you knew it was, that you didn't want it to be, sometimes it took a lot of icy-hearted cowardice not to answer the phone in those days –

Most of my time – eight years of time – at Cambridge I didn't have a telephone – the nearest one to my lodgings was a public telephone booth in the nearby park. Many hours of my life were spent in its vicinity, either making calls at an appointed time or waiting at an appointed time for it to ring. I would arrive half an hour early, and take possession of the booth, with the directory opened in front of me, the telephone to my ear, acting out an intense conversation – when the precise moment came for the arranged call, I would hang up with a little pantomime of exasperation, fumble open the directory as if I had to make an urgent call as the consequence of the last one – this for the benefit of the queue of four or five waiting with heads bowed, which in those days was the usual position for people waiting their turn – only in films did you see people pantomiming impatiently, beating on the little square windows etc. – in life they stood there, however desperate, in calm despondency, with their heads, as I've said, lowered, never meeting your eyes, or mine, especially mine as they glued themselves to the pages of the directory until the phone rang – or didn't ring. On one occasion it was, in a sense, the other way around – in all senses the other way around, actually, in that the booth was occupied by a man with parcels around his feet, and he was reporting into the phone very slowly from a notebook, a thick notebook, perhaps he was a journalist – and the reason I needed to be in the booth was that I needed to phone the girl I had been in love with, to tell her not to come for the weekend, actually it was essential that she didn't come, because – because – I can't remember what reason I was going to give, probably not the truth, that I'd fallen out of love with her. I'd put off making the call and suspected

I'd left it too late, certainly too late if this man went on and on – I was still standing outside the booth when I saw her in the distance, walking across Parker's Piece towards my rooms, with her overnight bag swinging from her hand, she'd caught an earlier train than usual so that we could have more than usual of the weekend together –

There had been so many times before then when I would be at the booth, inside it, at the precise moment of her call, and we'd discuss which train she'd take, and we'd talk about whether I'd meet her at the station or not, I adored seeing her get off the train, she was an exceptionally pretty girl, only just seventeen – I was twenty-five – and I would feel such a thrill of ownership – 'See that lovely young creature you can't help looking at and thinking about, she is going to be in my bed in about twenty minutes, yes, that pretty young girl with the breasts you can't find the nerve to look at, mine, me, belongs to me.' She, on the other hand, preferred to make her own way from the station, walking across Parker's Piece with her overnight bag swinging from her hand, thinking, she would tell me, of all the things she would be doing to me in twenty minutes or so – So in our happy days we had a lot in common, we both had my best sexual interests at heart –

I've just re-read the above paragraph. It is disgusting. What am I doing, what do I think I'm doing? Well, trying to recall my feelings when twenty-five, in sexual experience a very young twenty-five – no, trying to recall my inner voice when I was twenty-five but the language above isn't the language of a sexually callow, possessive twenty-five-year-old, it's the language of me, as I am now, which makes me, given that Topsy was seventeen and I'm seventy, a near-paedophile. I'm not sure what the legal age of consent is, these days – going by what I see in ads on television and the newspapers I'd say it's about five years old, but from reports of court cases I come across it could be somewhere in the forties –

Christ, look at the rest of the vocabulary, you can hear the cackle running through it – so Volpone gloating over his gold, or Goethe (also at seventy) fondling Christiane Vulpius (also seventeen) – so I with my Tipsy. No, Topsy, well then, let's try for a more mature note, thus:

Of course I found the idea of arranging myself on or in the bed, waiting for her, very stimulating, although one had to take into account the fact that the British Rail service between Cambridge and London (Liverpool Street or King's Cross) was chaotic, and it could be that having arranged oneself for the early afternoon, one would be still so arranged when she arrived after tea – but patience is a great stimulator, at least it is if one can control oneself – Harold's powers of concentration, for example, are the product of a tightly controlled impatience –

The more often she came down the less complicated the arrangements had to be – during our period of high sexual activity I didn't have to go to the Parker's Piece telephone booth at all, the excitement of it would be that she would turn up when she turned up – it became a routine, one of the happiest of my early adult life, or should I say one of the happiest of one's early adult life, until I and one and all of them, aye, fell out of love with her. In my experience –

In my experience there really is only one thing worse than falling out of love, and that is being fallen out of love with – being fallen out of love with fills you with all the horrors of abandonment, you are contemptible to yourself and therefore, you assume, contemptible to others and consequently even more contemptible to yourself, and really you have no choice but to go away and commit some form of temporary suicide. Well, falling out of love is an altogether grubbier affair, there are no blinding rages or weeping breakdowns to obliterate what is really one long act of procrastination – you look at the only recently adored face, so sweet, so trusting, so vulnerable, and you think to yourself, how could I bring pain to that? And what you also think is, why can't I hurry up and get it over with, get her over with? The longer she's around the more you hate the sight of her – actually, it's worse than that, what you feel above all else is nausea – you are nauseated by her for having fallen in love with you, and by yourself for having fallen in love with her, and terrified of the pain you're going to cause her – how many men have murdered a woman because they couldn't bear to hurt her?

Do women feel the same way? All the women who fell out of love with me seemed to find the pain they were causing quite bearable, though they did say, now and then, that they hated, really hated, seeing me so unhappy, though that didn't stop them seeing me.

A GLIMPSE OF THE FUTURE, A GLARE AT THE PAST

Two odd things happened today. First – when we were crossing the road this morning to post a letter Victoria said, out of nothing, really, as if the thought had suddenly opened itself in her head – 'I think Harold's going to get the Nobel Prize.' This came as a complete surprise to me, because I hadn't realized one was on offer, so to speak – I mean, hadn't realized that it's that time of year, and it is a seasonal thing, I suppose, that Victoria is particularly aware of because a few years ago she went over to Stockholm to see her brother-in-law collect one. 'Well,' I said, 'why not? And he's had such a wretched year . . .' And yes, he's had such a wretched year, the other night at the Belvedere he sat unspeaking, unable to eat or to drink – his only connection to life when he raised his wine glass to his lips and took a kind of phantom sip, although he didn't let the wine into his mouth, it was as if the movement of an old habit stated a fact, however feebly founded – 'Look, I am here, I can do this as I've always done this, now I've put the glass down but perhaps shortly I'll raise it again –' One longs for one of his old rages, one would probably cry from joy at seeing the cheeks turning dark and red, the snarl back in his voice, his eyes glittering with venomous life. It never seems remotely possible that he can make his way into and out of the restaurants, one somehow forgets noticing how he does it, but Antonia I suppose guides him within a loving ambit, he creeps along within it, little steps, resting on his stick, a few more little steps – you assume every dinner will be the last you will have with them, arrangements made a few days or so in advance seem quite fantastical – but there he is, his presence seeming to be beyond a miracle, what can that be but his will and his wife? And his wife is quite simply a marvel – the most lovable, as C.P. Snow would have put it, of women – and on top of that a wonderfully readable historian, and now it turns out an elixir – she deserves to be married to a Nobel winner, just as he deserves to be married to a Nobel winner's wife, furthermore it might be good for his health – So we spake unto each other before we popped the letter through the slot – I can't remember who it was to, or even which of us was sending it – and then we separated, Victoria going back home and I heading up the Avenue for a cup of coffee. On my way I passed a man who reminded me of someone.

He was wearing a trilby with a plastic bag over it, had a spiky grey beard, a yellow mackintosh, baggy blue trousers, white socks and sandals – there was an element of contradiction in his get-up, it was raining, which made sense of the mackintosh and the trilby, but nonsense of the white socks and the sandals. He looked very eccentric, but not poor, all these garments looked as if they'd been selected from a wardrobe, rather than assembled by chance from the tips and dumps that fall in the way of a tramp. He was about my age, I should think, perhaps a tad older, in his early to middle seventies. As we passed each other he turned his face towards me, and gave me a smile, and it was this, the smile, that sent a shiver of recognition through me, and made me stop and look after him. I half expected him to stop, too, I was sure he'd seen something in my face that had given him a momentary glimpse backwards, about forty years backwards, actually, to Cambridge, to a large red-brick house on Station Road where he – or the man I took him to be – and I had taught English to foreigners. The name of the man I took him to be was Manfred Hendow, and he had then exactly the same sort of beard, and – as I've said – the same sort of smile as the elderly man on Holland Park Avenue – a mystical smile, with a hint of a sneer in it. Yes, he was full of contempt, he told me, but most of it was for himself – he'd had a breakdown when an undergraduate at Oxford, an emotional and intellectual breakdown, as a result of which he'd got an inferior degree, but more crucially, had lost his ambition, his will to act in life. He'd read Russian, his family was Russian, and perhaps his fatalism, his depressive taint, that made life in all its manifestations seem futile, was in his genes. On the other hand, he'd been to India for a while, and had learnt there the value of detachment, the withdrawal of the spirit from the ordinary clamours of life. He spoke in a measured, slightly rhythmical voice, and his eyes, dark brown, were usually lifeless, as if willed to be so. Although he was only a few years older than me, he seemed to me vastly more experienced, vastly more complex than I was. It was his loneliness, his calm acceptance of failure, his inert postures – when he wasn't teaching, he would lie on the common room's only sofa, his sandalled feet crossed on the arm at one end, his head resting on the arm at the other, his hands folded across his chest, corpse-like. There

were several middle-aged women teachers, and two or three old men
on the staff, when they came into the common room for their breaks
he would turn his head slightly, and wonder if they wanted the use
of the sofa – they invariably declined, as if acknowledging that it
belonged in some way to him, he had an unchallengeable claim on
it – of course it's quite hard to say to a man who hasn't actually
shifted his body an inch that yes, you'd like him to shift it completely,
you'd like to sit where he was lying, so make way please, and hurry
up about it – but the truth is that I don't think anybody resented his
occupancy, several members of the staff were both forthright and
simmeringly disappointed by life, and quarrelsome with each other,
but Manfred on the sofa, elongated in a melancholy glow, was in
some way out of their reach, like a saint, or half the Arundel tomb.
Occasionally, in the evening, when everyone else had gone, he and
I would go to the students' common room and play a game of ping-
pong. I was naturally quite good at it, and intensely competitive, as
I was at any sport, but it was Manfred's trick to drain any element
of tension or conflict out of the game. He played in a leisurely and
absent fashion, his eye only partially on the ball, and it was difficult
to work out exactly how he managed to beat me on most occasions –
although he did explain to me that he didn't really beat me, rather
he let me beat myself. Well, that can't have been quite true, because
in order to beat myself I had to get the ball to come back at me,
which I couldn't have done without some skilful play by the
seemingly lackadaisical figure on the other side of the net. On the
other hand, I do believe that he didn't care whether he won or not,
although he was mildly amused by my losing. It seemed to satisfy an
abstract sort of malice in him. We didn't exactly develop a
relationship – anyway, not a friendship. We talked quite a lot about
books. He was interested in Buddhism, particularly Zen, and he was
impressively scathing about Christmas Humphreys's Penguin

introduction. I suppose I talked a lot, in my florid manner of the time, about all the novels and poetry I considered to be overrated. I'd come to Cambridge to be a Leavisite. In fact, I was already a fully fledged Leavisite in the sense that I was in possession of all the works of English literature that were hostile to life, 'against life' was the phrase I tended to use of almost anything in, say, the twentieth century that hadn't been written by D.H. Lawrence. So I'd practise my Leavis positions on him, and he would meditate in a weary sort of way, and sometimes in a dreary sort of way, on the uselessness of being, the transcendence of indifference, and so forth. One evening he invited me back to supper, in a cottage he was renting in Little Shelford, a few miles outside Cambridge. We cycled there together, left our bikes at a gate, and walked across the field towards a dimly lit kitchen where I could see, through the window, a young woman doing cooking-like things, with a baby at her hip. He'd never mentioned the existence of a woman in his life, let alone a baby. It had never occurred to me that anyone of roughly my generation could be in possession of either – I was still a virgin, after all, and though I believed that sex would be immediately punished by offspring, I yearned for it, but feared that however long I lived, I'd never be old enough or mature enough to earn it. The woman, small and neat and lively, with a slight but sturdy figure and a squawking but not unattractive voice, was about his age, a few years older than me. He introduced us to each other with a gesture that was like a dismissal, not just for me, but for the other two. 'This is Simon Gray. And that's Donna. The baby's name is Tertius.' And he sat down at the table, folded his hands and closed his eyes, looking as he so often did in the common room, self-excluded. I didn't know what to say, but nevertheless said it. 'Oh. I didn't know you were married.' Donna squawked a laugh, Manfred opened his eyes in amusement.

I wish I could remember the evening, the dinner, the

conversation over it, but I don't really, beyond the fact that apart from eating with us Manfred wasn't really there – he behaved as if he'd effected a substitution, as if he'd brought me along to fill in for him, and I suppose I must have done because I do recall I watched as Tertius was bathed, and then as he was breast-fed, which I took to be an immense privilege from which I mainly averted my eyes, it was such an open and natural act from which I should have been kept away because I brought to it a prurience, I was conscious of the pull on her breasts, the full nipples, the busy, greedy mouth – and Donna's face, her expression calm, her eyes radiant as she rested them on me, and asked me questions in her squawking, abrasive voice but about what I no longer know – she had a direct, uncomplicated way of asking, and I liked it because I could answer her reasonably directly, and didn't feel I had to make the best of myself. Now and then Manfred drawled in and offered her a fact about me that was also for me – 'Simon likes teaching foreigners English. And they seem to like him, the pretty ones. But I don't know whether he likes them. He doesn't do anything about them. He thinks it would be wrong.' He made me feel like one of the students, with too feeble a grasp of English to understand what he was saying about me, but suspecting that it was contemptuous. Yes, I was suspicious. Nothing was right about all this –

I can no longer follow the stages that led to my being ensconced in a flat in Harley Street, on the run from St John's College, Cambridge, which had given me a writing fellowship the main condition of which was that I had to go abroad – but I wasn't abroad, I was in Harley Street and not writing anything, not even replies to sent-on letters from St John's College, Cambridge, asking where I was – the only bits I can remember are the bits I don't want to remember – our first fuck, for instance. Actually, it wasn't her first fuck, obviously, as she had a baby by what was also evidently not her first fuck – she had a long and turbulent history with men, she used to entertain me with it – I think I've put down that she had a slightly quacking voice, but did I mention that she laughed in husky yelps that were almost like screeches – her voice sometimes made me grit my teeth, and yet I fell in love with it, I came to find it attractive and exciting, no young woman I'd met before had a voice like it, so uninhibitedly dissonant, but then I'd never met a young woman who talked about the kind of things she talked about, and in a voice like that. Before Harley Street, before she'd left Manfred, long before our first fuck, so back in Cambridge therefore –

Back in Cambridge she would sit on my one chair in my room in Jesus Lane, and I would sit on the edge of the bed, a double bed oddly enough, as only Trinity students – young, single males – ever occupied this lodging house –

LEN TO THE RESCUE

This lodging house, which was owned by a large, bald Pole with a loud voice. His plump younger wife, sweet-voiced and English, cleaned our rooms and made our breakfast – they were a very kind couple, considerate and helpful, though a bit mean with bathwater unless you took your bath cold, but then gas heating was expensive – and the breakfasts were ample, lots of toast and butter and jam and tea, bacon and eggs – actually the eggs were a problem during my first year, there was sometimes quite a lot of hair underneath and around them, like a rather scanty nest – when I came back for my second year she had taken to wearing a rubber shower cap, so obviously she had a scalp condition, possibly alopecia. One of my co-lodgers was a research student who was writing a history of mathematics, a ten-year project, he would say frequently, not counting the three he'd already spent on it. He was from the north, so much from the north that he really did think that southerners were effete, lazy, corrupt – not far wrong in my case, I suppose, although I was also miserable – yes, effete, lazy, corrupt and miserable is a reasonable thumbnail of my spiritual and/or moral state at the age of twenty, in my first year at Cambridge, while a reasonable if external thumbnail of Len – is Len his real name or do I just think that basically all northerners of that period were called Len, after Len Hutton? – would be dour, hard-working, moralizing and miserable – so really there we were, the pair of us conforming exactly to each other's stereotypes as we bantered miserably away across the breakfast table fifty years ago. Like me he spent every evening at the cinema but, unlike me, he went actively, with an alert eye and a sharp ear and an encyclopaedic knowledge of actors, directors, screenwriters, even editors and cameramen, and yet he seemed to despise every film he saw, or perhaps he only talked about the films he despised, unwilling to contaminate the films he liked, loved even, by discussing them with me – we had many breakfasts together, three years of term-time breakfasts, in fact, and our conversations would go something like this – 'Saw a film you'd like last night,' he'd say, 'yes, you'd like it.' 'Really, which one?' ' The John Ford at the Regent.' 'Oh,' I said, '*The Searchers*. Yes. I've seen it. I liked it very much.' 'There,' he said. 'Knew you would. Knew you would. Said to myself, that's the film for you.' I got his drift, of course. 'And what did you hate about it?' 'Everything,' he said triumphantly. 'Great big phoncy bloated artistic –' artistic was one of his most scathing words, he somehow slipped the hint of an 's' in before the first 't', making it sound almost lavatorial, Arse-Tist-Tuck. 'Absolutely not,' I said. 'Epic, poetic, humane –' etc. – I saw *The Searchers* again, about five years ago, and about halfway through I found myself recalling Len and his judgement, and from then on it was as if I had double vision, one eye mine and the other Len's, completely at odds with each other but both of them true, because actually *The Searchers* did seem simultaneously epic and bloated, humane and phoney, poetic and Arse-Tist-Tuck –

Well, Len got into this because I can't bear, when it comes to it, to struggle my time with Donna back into my life, but having started on it, I can't seem to find a way of not going on with it, either – stalled is what I am, stalled. Try Q & A –

MORE Q THAN A

There's a film called *Q & A*, I came across it on Film Four the other night – no, a year or two ago – about a homicide detective who is also a homicidal detective in that the suspect he is interrogating he ends up killing, he was played by an actor with an odd voice that didn't go with his face, which was saturnine, a beaky nose and dark liquid eyes, altogether an impressive and glamorous figure of the Hispanic-American type until he spoke, or piped rather – he's been in quite a few David Mamet films, all convoluted plot and rhythmic, demotic dialogue, you almost nod your head to it, your poor old head which is befuddled by all the twists and turns and surprises of a plot so complicated –

Did you love her?
I remember anger, bitterness, hopelessness, despair, so yes.
Did she love you?
Yes. Until –
Until?

We had sex.

Bad sex then?

No, worse than that.

Can you be more precise?

Well, actually it was no sex – a lot of physical activity but no actual sex.

Can you be more precise?

It was in a room in Harley Street.

Oh, it was some sort of medical thing then, was it?

No. I was living there. This was after I'd left Cambridge. A flat at the top of the house. It belonged to a surgeon, a very nice man. Donna was working as his receptionist. He let me have this flat for a very small rent. For Donna's sake, I suppose. As I was thought to be her boyfriend.

But you weren't?

I was until –

You had no sex with her?

That's it. Yes.

What form did this no sex take?

When I'd peeled my trousers down to my knees, and rolled my underpants down to my trousers' crotch, I lay on top of her and bucked about, yelping.

Why?

I didn't know what else to do, obviously. I was a virgin.

A twenty-five-year-old virgin?

Right.

Unusual, possibly?

Don't know. This was 1961, remember, before the Beatles' first LP and so forth.

And so you were anatomically ignorant?

Yes.

But you're a doctor's son.

Yes.

Couldn't you have consulted a book?

I did, but it didn't make much sense. I suppose I could have copied a diagram but I could scarcely have held it in my hand when I got on top of her, like a road map.

Was she naked?

Yes. She took all her clothes off, and let down her hair, talking all the while in her slightly quacking voice, brightly and eagerly, how we'd waited long enough, and now Manfred was out of the picture, and as little Tertius – at this stage quite a big Tertius, at four years old – was so happily settled with her parents – and we had the use of this flat and this nice double bed – I wanted her to undress for ever and quack for ever, to put off the moment of reckoning –

She didn't know you were a virgin?

No.

Would it have been better if you'd told her?

I expect so, because the next time she showed me what I was expected to do, and how and where to do it, and after that it got easier and easier, and by the end I would really have enjoyed it if she hadn't hated it so much.

Why did she hate it?

Probably never got over our first time, my first time, to be exact, she never got over my first time. She liked older men, really, older than herself and much older than me – men who took charge and ran the show. Even when I got used to it, I never ran the show, I got into the habit of waiting for instructions.

Why didn't you warn her that you were a virgin?

Too embarrassed, obviously. And also before I met her there was another girl, an undergraduate, who was famous for having slept with a man who was famous for getting sent down for smoking pot.

She came around regularly in the afternoon for tea and conversation. One afternoon, before I'd begun to make the tea on the little gas ring beside the gas fire, she said, 'I keep wondering when you're going to ask me to go to bed with you.' I was very calm, though parts of me stirred. 'Yes,' I said, 'I was wondering that too.' She was a very shapely, round girl, Jewish, sexy and yet maternal, with russet hair and pouty lips – a firm chin withal. Her father was a doctor, with a practice in London, Goldhawk Road, and she was reading History. She had been very much in love, she'd told me, with the chap who'd got sent down for pot smoking – I should point out that pot smoking was at that time very unusual in Cambridge, a truly exotic offence, so he was a legendary figure – undergraduates of both sexes who didn't smoke pot themselves because they didn't want to get sent down liked to have their names linked with his – as did Esther. That was her name. Esther. I think there was something in front of it – Emma Esther – sounds wrong, Anne – or Anesta – yes, Anesta, not sure, though, if that's how it was spelt, but I'll stick with it. Anesta was very proud of having been Pot-boy's lover, she liked to say the word 'lover' in confessional sentences – 'My mother would never have accepted my having . . .' – she always said his name in full, not Ned or Japes or whatever, but Michael Stumpfield, let's say, 'Everybody knew that Michael Stumpfield was my lover,' 'My mother never accepted that I was Michael Stumpfield's lover.' So we had tea and conversations about her being the lover of Michael Stumpfield, of whom of course I was not only jealous for sexual reasons, but envious for life reasons. My body was full of hope but my mind, or wherever the will is lodged, was full of confusion and despair, because it knew that the 'I' of me – what Kant calls 'the synthetic unity of apperception' – was too timid to make even a shy move towards getting what my body wanted – on top of which there was the not completely suppressed suspicion that when it came down to it I didn't really like her very much, not only because there was too much Michael Stumpfield, but also too much breasts, which were prominently covered and gave me a headache until that afternoon when she said, 'I keep wondering when you're going to ask me to go to bed with you.' And I said, 'I was wondering that too' – but what I was really wondering was whether this was a variation on Michael Stumpfield's opening gambit, had he perhaps said, 'I expect you're wondering when I'm going to ask you to go to bed with me' – or more casually, more confidently, more pot-headedly, 'I expect you're wondering when I'm going to take you to bed' – anyway, the way she said it didn't sound right to me, even to me, who'd never heard words like these spoken before, except in films with subtitles – nevertheless she took off her clothes in a modest and stately fashion, as far as I could see, I partly averted my eyes, which I believed to be the polite response, and at some point, before she was completely naked, I explained my – our – situation. I hope I didn't actually say, 'So be gentle with me', but I suppose that was the implication – anyway, as soon as I broke the news she got dressed again.

Didn't she say anything?

Well, she laughed. As I've said, she was quite a big girl, soft and curvy, and when she laughed her breasts seemed to laugh too, bouncing and bobbing to her laughter. She liked my jokes, which I now see was the best thing about her.

Did she think this was one of them?

No, it wasn't that sort of laugh. When she was dressed and having a cup of tea, she explained that she just didn't want the responsibility.

The responsibility of taking your virginity?

Presumably. From then on she let me nuzzle her whoppers.

Which is to say?

That she used to let me sit on her lap like a very large baby and suck her nipples and when I got excited and wanted more she would stroke my head and murmur, 'No, no, I'm still not ready, still not ready, Mr Jumblenose.'

Mr Jumblenose?

A private joke.

Sometimes you wanted to kill her. By the end you were sick to death of her breasts, you associated them with pain, hunger, torment – they were a form of torture, really. Lust aroused and unsatisfied.

That's not a question.

No. It's the answer you might not have given. Tell me –

Mmm?

What aroused your lust in the years of your adolescence and early manhood, before you suckled at Michael Stumpfield's lover's whoppers?

Oh, the usual stuff – a flash of thigh, stocking tops, the curve of a medium-sized breast in profile, a nipple erect in a diaphanous bra, the slope of stomach into a tangle of hair, handcuffs, Hank Janson covers, *The Collected Works of Immanuel Kant.*

Pornographic clichés, you mean?

Absolutely.

Women as objects and pornography?

Ideally. I'm only talking ideally here. Hence Kant.

Are you ready to go back to Donna?

No.

The double bed – you were sitting on the edge of it, as you did with Anesta, and like Anesta, she was sitting on your desk chair –

– and like Anesta she told me about her past, about which I remember nothing except that she'd been at art school for a short time and had been promiscuous. For me, at that time in my life, promiscuous was undoubtedly one of the most exciting words in the language. I was only twenty-one, after all, and so ignorant of sex that its vast vocabulary, of which I had some command, had no proper – i.e. 'lived', as we Leavisites, worshippers of D. H. Lawrence and the dark Gods of the Unconsciousness, used to say – no proper 'lived' content. In the following months, many, many months, about forty-eight of them, in fact, our relationship developed, matured, ripened until it imploded in my first fuck, as reported somewhere above. This was Cambridge just past the middle of the last century – we did things differently there. At least I did.

BILLY AND THE GOLDEN BITCH

Donna, as I've also reported somewhere above, Donna didn't love me. As she was the first person apart from myself with whom I had sex, I was passionately and hopelessly, the more hopelessly the more passionately, in love with her. If that's the right phrase – 'in love'. I've always had a jealous disposition, I think, as well as an envious one – I know that there's a distinction, people are constantly making it over dinner tables, but my feelings for Donna combined them both, I was jealous in the way that Othello is jealous, and could easily imagine writhing about on the floor and jabbering nonsensical obscenities about her friendships with other men, but also I was envious, envious of her, I'm not quite sure that I can get to the core of this, how to explain it, though even as I write this I know exactly what I mean – I mean that I wanted to be her, and envied her for being her when I couldn't be, because I had to be me, instead – I don't believe she was a particularly mysterious or contradictory person, she seemed always to know what she wanted – a proper husband with a proper job, a proper house with a proper garden, another child, possibly two, and eventually an artistic sort of job of her own. She also liked neat clothes, good food, a bottle of wine.

The only contradictory fact in her life was Manfred, that she should have become embroiled with him and found herself living for a time in isolation with an illegitimate child in a village outside Cambridge, but that was in the past, Manfred was gone abroad, I forget where to, and she was in London, in Harley Street, working as a receptionist to a successful surgeon with whom I became friends – he once invited me to watch him at work, he was so confident and calm and full of distinguished stoops and gestures until, dealing with an old woman whose artery burst, he had to hold it down in her stomach to stop the blood spurting but it kept coming up in plumes, and he was suddenly all brute strength and angry exclamations, like a plumber dealing with a burst lavatory pipe. He was a New Zealander, successful and handsome. I wasn't jealous of him, he so clearly wasn't a lover or an ex-lover of Donna's, but fond of her in a paternal kind of way, so as far as I was concerned she was in the right sort of element during the working day. The evenings were more complicated because she had to spend either an unwanted few hours in bed with me, or a few hours thinking up and then defending excuses for not spending them in bed with me, and then had to go home to Wimbledon, to her parents, who were looking after Tertius, and they were both completely mad, she used to say, and not as a figure of speech. She took me there for high tea a few times, at weekends. Her father was a small, middle-aged man with a grey moustache and he had a way of sitting with his ankles neatly crossed and his arms folded – and stood like that, too, although not with crossed ankles – as if he were being photographed. He had a vision of the country crashing and mentioned it often, with irritated satisfaction, in brisk, dark sentences, which he addressed mainly to the television set, even when it wasn't switched on. He made it clear that he didn't like me, or the thought of me, probably placing me among the pinkos and pansies who were conspiring with the unions in the nation's downfall. He had a managerial position in a mowing-machine firm, I think it was, and had a lot of trouble with office dissidents. On one occasion, a sunny evening, and the french windows open, he suddenly left the room, returned with an airgun, shot a pigeon that was plodding aimlessly about on the lawn, then ran to the corpse and booted it into the bushes. It was all so horrible and so unexpected that it made me laugh, and little Tertius laughed with me, in one of our few moments of togetherness, and I think Donna laughed too, pleased perhaps that there was a little fun in the room at last. The mother paid no attention, she was bowed over her knitting, her elbows out to her sides, her needles clicking away, humming lightly. So from that limited experience of them, I would say that she was right, they were slightly mad. And before she went home to her slightly mad parents, she would have to spend a few hours with me, who was also, and not slightly, mad – there were times when I was a fucking loony, actually, from the reasons given above, a combination of sexual jealousy and sexual envy and frequently sexual frustration.

One evening I was waiting for her in the kitchen of the flat at the top of the house, waiting and waiting, until long past the hour she usually finished work, and then going down at last to find her – to find out what she was doing – who she was doing it with – as I say, I didn't suspect the surgeon, I knew that he wasn't particularly attracted to her, in fact I knew that he found my company much more interesting than hers because he liked to talk about literature, and all of Donna's reading had been done under Manfred's auspices, to help her understand him – books about Buddhism and so forth, which she hadn't understood – anyway, the surgeon wasn't interested in Buddhism, he was interested in T. S. Eliot and so forth, which is where I came in. So down I went, pretty certain that I wouldn't find her with the surgeon, or if I did it would be innocently – just as I got to the top of the last flight of stairs I saw a heavily set man wearing a trilby strutting down the hall, then letting himself out. He was framed for a moment in the doorway, as if in a film, his back to me so I couldn't see his face, but I had the impression that something was sticking out of the side of it, a pipe presumably. Well, people were always coming and going, it was a house full of medical specialists, there was nothing particularly surprising or ominous – nevertheless, I knew by the boiling in my blood and the tumult in my brain who this was, he was Donna's – he was hers – hence the strut and the pipe, the trilby, the bulky, confident maleness of him, framed in the doorway. I didn't think it odd then, back there in the spring of 1961, that a man with a trilby, smoking a pipe, was standing on the doorstep, leaving a house full of doctors, though logically he must have put his trilby on his head, lit up his pipe, while still in the house – of course people smoked much more back then, many men smoked pipes – the other day, looking out of a taxi window in Holland Park, I saw a middle-aged man in a sensible suit walking along the pavement, smoking a pipe. It gave me quite a shock, he must have been the first man I'd seen for years smoking a pipe, my instinct was to shout out to him through the window to be careful, there might be a policeman about, then it struck me that he might be the victim of a time accident, he'd walked into his next century without knowing it, go home, go back to where you came from, 1980s, 1970s, whenever, get back there! – and then we were past him, and when I looked through the rear window, to check that he wasn't a hallucination, he was strolling along as real as life, it was the people around him, the young men in ghastly sawn-off trousers, the tops of their knickers showing, tufts of hair on their faces, swilling from cans and bottles, slouching towards Bethlehem etc., that seemed hallucinatory, the chap with the pipe and I were from the same world that wasn't this one, how is it then that he looked so at ease, and I was so anxious on his behalf, and on mine? It must have been the pipe that gave him a sense of solidity and confidence, made him feel at home in any century until he ventured too far forward, when he'd find himself surrounded by men with guns, who'd pick him up on their technological intelligence networks because of his strange costume and the incendiary device in his mouth, a new breed of terrorist, obviously, and so pow! pow! pow! but not so that you could hear it, more like little kisses, and holes right through him that you could see through, no blood because the discharged little missiles somehow absorbed the blood as they passed though the body, cleaned up after themselves, so to speak – well, I would have put holes through my man, Donna's man, exiting the house in Harley Street in the spring of 1961, wouldn't have minded seeing his blood spurt out all over the floor of the hall, to punish him for the pain he caused me, for the panic and bewilderment –

If he'd been facing the other way, about to come down the hall, what would I have felt? He stepped into the sunshine, closing the door behind him, and, I would like to write, out of my life for ever, but I can't be sure of that, because if it was Billy, in insurance, he didn't step out of my life for ever, he probably stepped down the road to a pub, to wait for Donna, with whom candlelit dinner and sex. A trilby hat? The one time I met Billy he had a hat in his hand, but I can't be sure it was a trilby. I was too busy trying to meet his powerful blue gaze to notice the details of his clothing etc., but he had a hat in his hand all right, my money's still on a trilby. The question I have to ask myself, though, is about the man on the doorstep: was my eye inventing the trilby for the man on the doorstep, or is my memory inventing it now? Has my memory taken it out of Billy's hand and placed it on the man's head? Did Billy smoke a pipe, or is my memory shifting it from the man's mouth to Billy's?

The next bit I remember pretty accurately I think, I went to Donna in her little office, more like a cubicle, at the end of the hall. She was curled intimately over the typewriter, taking dictation from a tape-recorder through earphones attached to it – I often caught her like this, sealed off in a private world of the surgeon's voice speaking into her ears, and into hers alone, of his patients and their forthcoming operations. She would type at great speed, with a little frown, occasionally breaking into an inward version of her quacking laugh as the New Zealand surgeon's voice shared a joke with her. Of course she didn't acknowledge me as I loomed ominously away at her desk, although it seemed to me quite impossible that all my boil and tumult should fail to make its presence felt – and I am quite tall and she's quite small, with her neat, strong little legs crossed at the knees, her neat, round little breasts bobbing under her blouse, those hands playing like a pianist's across the keyboard, the frown, the smile, another little quack –

She felt my presence at last, took off her earphones, and gave me too much of a smile, as if I were one of the surgeon's sadder cases. I explained that I had been getting worried, had been waiting for her upstairs in our flat until long after she'd said she'd be finished for the day, normally I wouldn't have dreamt of coming down to interrupt her, just wanted to make sure she was all right, in fact had intended just to listen from the top of the stairs, if I'd caught her voice on the telephone or the sound of her typing, I'd have gone back up again – in fact I'd been about to go back up again and resume my waiting but I'd caught a glimpse of a sinister-looking bloke in the hall – I don't know if I talked trilby and pipe, but at some point early on in this heated exposure of my jealousy and fear cleverly disguised as a farrago of nonsense, she exploded into her quacking laugh, and said something, made a gesture, something, something – I think what I felt most of all was her weary exasperation, an unloving adult to a boring and unlovable child – how it went on from there, the step by step of it that led to my raising my fist – I remember hanging there above her, fist raised, bellowing phrases that I'd never thought of and heard with a kind of bewilderment – where had they come from, these phrases, was it really I who was shouting them in a tone I'd never heard before at a volume I didn't know I had in me, and if so who was this I that spoke so strangely, so exotically, so violently, it certainly wasn't me as I knew him. The words, the three words that astonished me most, and still do, and astonished her most, but no longer do, because she's dead, came at the climax of a sentence the beginning of which I don't remember – 'you golden bitch!' 'YOU GOLDEN BITCH!' What? I look at them now, on the page, and hear myself shouting them, and see her face, her incredulous expression. Neither of us had the slightest idea of what I meant, she was in no understandable respect golden, she was, if anything, a sort of dun colour in her general effect, she wore brownish clothes, had brownish hair, had on her best days a pink complexion – she had a negligible income – golden simply didn't come into it – into any aspect of her –

I am sitting here, it's the dawn following the dawn when I wrote the above, which I've just read through. I am almost in tears, not because of the content of the passage, but because I now remember that while I was in the middle of writing it something very important struck me, a memory of something that happened, that I thought could wait until I'd finished writing what I was writing, and then I'd go back to it and write that down too, but I didn't go back to it, I got to the image of myself threatening her with my raised fist, shouting the incomparable – incomprehensible, I mean of course, words about her being 'a golden bitch', laid down my pen, took a couple of sleeping pills, remembered I hadn't gone back to that other memory and then decided no, it can wait until tomorrow, it's too important to tackle when I'm beginning to feel drowsy, wait until fresh and vigorous, vigorous? Hah! Well, until fresh, fresh? Also hah! Well, until tomorrow, then, and here I am, in the tomorrow, and I can't remember, haven't a clue as to what it was, that important memory, and so my almost tears are of frustration with myself, and contempt for myself, my anger at my stupidity about my memory, that I don't even remember that my memory keeps failing, and always when I most need it – why then does it tantalize me with tit-bits so vivid that they are both unforgettable and forgotten, it's almost as if they have a life of their own, like fish, say, they swim towards the forefront of our consciousness like fish and just before they get there you blink and they're gone – sometimes as you blink you see them going, their tails flicking them into the muzzy waters they came out of –

Well, perhaps if I go back to 'you golden bitch', trembling above her with my fist raised, her incredulous expression – the moment when we both knew that the affair, such as it was, was over. Well, of course, not quite like that over – I didn't turn on my heel, stride down the corridor that Billy in his trilby and pipe had sauntered down just a few minutes before, I went back up to the flat, and she – in her own good time possibly, or possibly as soon as I'd left – either went home or, more likely, went to the pub, where Billy was waiting for her, calm, on a stool by the bar, at their usual table by the window, or in the corner on the phone to his wife – he was married, Billy, at least he had some children – but that wasn't the important thing I was trying to remember. Everyone involved – Billy, the surgeon, Donna, Manfred – had children – except me, of course.

It seems, in fact, that affairs are never over, or I wouldn't be writing about my affair with Donna, which was in its hopeless prime more than forty-five years ago, two marriages ago, two children and four grandchildren ago, and yet here it is, long after her death, vexing me again this mid-October midnight.

I positively made the decision to leave her that night. I would go abroad, to a cheap country, and write a novel. Spain seemed a likely place, a dictatorship, a depressed economy, cheap food and lodgings, I could be a subversive, Republican spirit, with a blighted heart – who knows what damage I could do to the ageing tyrant in the Prado, or is the Prado where they hang the pictures? – well, then, in Madrid, or wherever Franco hung out.

A SALUTARY TALE

We went to dinner with the Dashwoods last night, Jonnie and Sylvia, it was one of those cheerful and funny evenings spent discussing the sheer awfulness of this country, from the condition of its children – educationally, morally, socially the most backward and neglected among the advanced countries – and the lethal nature of our hospitals, where people die of illnesses they didn't bring in with them –

And so forth. And so forth

And then we talked of murder, albeit unrelated.

A couple of friends of theirs, sophisticated, they enjoyed theatre, concerts, exhibitions, all the cultural life of this great city – they went to absolutely everything, though not necessarily together – he was a businessman, a stripper of assets, as far as I could make out – anyway, there they were, a much-liked and distinguished couple who didn't perhaps quite get on – she had something of a temper, could be – our hostess witnessed it on occasions – a bit of what we used to call a nag, or a shrew, but he dealt with any little exhibitions, in public anyway, with dignity and forbearance – he was known as a calm and collected soul, unruffled and kindly in manner, and always impeccably dressed, formally dressed, for his business engagements as for his cultural nights out –

One morning he turned up for his first meeting looking slightly dishevelled, no tie, his collar undone, not serious lapses, but noticeable because uncharacteristic. Nevertheless he went about the day's business in his usual mode, nothing else awry that subsequently anyone remembered, and when he'd worked through all his day's appointments he went to the local police station, and told the officer on duty that last night he'd murdered his wife when she was in bed. She'd told him he was mean, and by way of a response he'd suffocated her with a pillow. 'Mean.' It was the way she said it, I suppose.

The police went to the house and found the body in the bath. He explained he'd put it there because he understood that bodies, after death, sometimes made a mess. He'd also enveloped her in a blanket, presumably for seemliness, or perhaps from an idea that she would be more comfortable. On examination, she was found to be wearing earplugs, which, I was told, was odd – would she be wearing earplugs, it was asked, if they were in the middle of a row? My guess, for what it's worth, is that she put them in immediately after telling him he was 'mean' for punctuation – 'No good your answering back, I can't hear you! Conversation closed! Silence, thank you!' It meant, of course, that she didn't hear herself being murdered, the pillow over her face, her ears blocked – blind, deaf and mute, completely full of herself as she died. Apparently it takes quite a few minutes, four or five, to suffocate someone with a pillow – I wonder how he did it, did he stand over her, pressing his full weight down on it with his hands? Or did he perhaps sit on it? Either way it had to be a prolonged act, with only one conclusion – although you could argue that backwards, and say that given the conclusion it must have been a prolonged act, and it's possible that he was appalled to find her actually dead when he lifted the pillow – but then if he hadn't intended to kill her he would have pleaded manslaughter at his trial, surely, and he didn't.

Although the police charged him with murder, they released him on police bail, thus enabling him to attend her funeral. As the widower his was the privileged position, seated directly in front of the coffin, and only a few feet from it. He sat through the bleak and rapid service with his head bowed very low, his hands clasped in his lap, and remained sitting so when the service was over. People stood, hesitated, began to leave, then a man went over to him, took his hand and shook it. Other men did the same, women came and stooped down to kiss him on the cheek. He received each shake of the hand and kiss with a muttered 'Thank you', his head still bent.

He represented himself at his trial. He was methodical, businesslike and clear-minded in his presentation of his defence, which was that he suffered from a mental defect that had a physiological cause – when he became angry a sort of shutter came down in his brain that separated him from his actions, and he therefore couldn't be held responsible for them. It's possible that if he'd pleaded provocation, or had it pleaded for him professionally, he might have got away with a lesser charge, a lesser sentence – anyway, something less than life imprisonment, although of course these days 'life imprisonment' is a *façon de parler* – having served some seven years, and now nearly eighty years old, he is in the process of being returned to society – on the grounds, presumably, that prison cells, like hospital beds, mustn't be blocked by the elderly.

Did he love her?

If he'd loved her, wouldn't he have pleaded guilty? Wouldn't he have wanted a punishment, if he'd loved her?

But perhaps I'm missing the point. The point is that this murder was a very private business, as intimate and as contradictory as, well, as intimate and contradictory as sex, or as Othello's suffocating of Desdemona, come to think of it –

Only he would know those moments of killing for what they were, knew whether he expected a corpse as their conclusion, or whether the intensity of the explosion, the release of his righteousness and rage, was the complete experience – perhaps he thought that once he'd done it, and at last cleansed their marriage with a sort of giant orgasm, they could then both get on with their lives with a better understanding between them – and if that was impossible because, as it turned out, she was dead, if he'd sat or pressed a minute or two too long, if it turned out that some sort of expiation was needed, well, then that too was a private matter, he'd see to it himself, or in communion with the spirit of his departed – external processes like the police, the courts, the law shouldn't be allowed to interfere in the happenings between a widower and his wife – or perhaps he should have done what Othello did and spared himself as well as us the embarrassment of a trial, of hearing his explanation of how especially funny things happen in a brain like his, etc.

The bit I completely understand is his going to work the next day, going through with all his meetings as normal, because if you can make today normal, then possibly tomorrow will be normal too, more meetings in the morning, lunch with a colleague or to clinch a deal, an opera in the evening, then home to   home to – ?

But just a minute. After he'd killed her, and wrapped her in a blanket, then put her into the bath, he still had that night to get through. What in God's name did he do for the rest of that night? Doesn't bear thinking about –

I suppose he tried to find ways of waiting for the dawn, then for the day to begin, then for his day to begin – went once or twice to the bathroom to make sure he'd actually done what he'd done, apologized – 'I'm sorry, so sorry. Oh darling, darling' – or explained – 'If you'd seen your face when you put the earplugs in, the purse of your mouth, you'd have understood, darling – I know you couldn't help it, but nor could I, you see' – or he might have blamed her – 'You made me do it, damn you, damn you – see what you've done, your fault, your own fault, your own bloody' – very possibly a jumble of all three.

As he was a rich man, and lived at a good address, I assume he had another bathroom at his disposal. But if there was only one, and he had to share it with his dead wife – peeing and crapping, shaving and brushing his teeth, his eyes averted from the bath and its shrouded contents – and of course he couldn't have had a bath or a shower –

Let's assume he had another bathroom, that they each had their own bathroom. His and hers. And that he put her in hers.

So he got through the night, and started the next day, neither the last day of his old life, he'd already had that, nor the first day of his new life, he hadn't got to it yet, so really a hiatus, a pseudo-day, in which he mimicked himself as he had been twenty-four hours earlier, a cultivated asset stripper going about his business with his familiar aplomb, apart from those two details, the unbuttoned shirt collar, the absent tie. No one noticed anything amiss, apart from the collar and tie, which they might well have interpreted as welcome signs of a relaxing of the spirit, a touch carefree and, who knows, a mite sexier.

How did his lunch go? Was it a working lunch, a sandwich grabbed amid the hustle and bustle of some asset-stripping, or did he slip off somewhere, a solitary, meditative meal, or he went without, kept his nose to the grindstone, telephoning, emailing, faxing, strip, strip, strip –

But at the end of the day – at the end of the day he went home – let himself in through the front door, went to the bathroom with the bath with the corpse of his wife in it, and yes, it was there, yes. Perhaps for a short while he tried to think of alternatives – all those scenes from films when a man with a long burden over his shoulder stumbles down the stairs into a garage, gets it into a car, then drives through the night – but where would he go?

There was a story in the papers recently of a man who drove from somewhere in Surrey, I think it was, all the way to somewhere in France with his wife's body in the boot. He stopped eventually at a motel, and found himself phoning one of their children. 'Hi, Dad, where are you? We've been trying to reach Mum. Where is she?' He told them where Mum was, and where he was, and then phoned the local police. He too had killed in a rage, no forward planning, he'd had to make it up as he went along – think of all the luck he'd had, getting through customs and immigration on either side of the Channel with a corpse in his car – But then the more luck he'd had, the more he'd had to keep going, and where to? In the end the luck had worn him out – really, he just wanted to go home.

It was sensible of our own wife-murderer to go to the police and set in motion the next part of his life. I wonder, did he button up his collar and put on his tie before he went? And what did the police think when they saw him come through their door – almost certainly not that this elderly and respectable-looking man had come to confess murder, more likely that he had come as a victim of a crime, which he was, or as a man who had lost something valuable, which he had.

AND A PREDICTION FULFILLED

They're usually among the first to arrive, but on this occasion everybody was there – there were about sixteen of us – at the Ivy before them, the dinner having been arranged as a birthday dinner by Faber, his publisher, some time ago. The day before Harold had been in Dublin, where they've been having a festival of his plays, a week-long festival – at the airport coming back he'd stepped out of his car, slipped, and gashed his head. Antonia had had to get him to a hospital, an emergency ward, to have the wound dressed – fortunately it wasn't a deep wound but all their travel plans had gone awry. I'd last seen him a couple of weeks before, when he had been much as he'd been that night at the Belvedere – that he'd actually made it to Ireland seemed to me beyond belief. I'd heard from our mutual agent, Judy Daish, who'd seen him there, that he'd been very frail, but enjoying himself – had even managed to do some readings, sometimes thin-voiced and husky, but always audible – it had gone well, and he'd seemed to have flourished – and then the calamity at the airport. It struck me that it wouldn't just be the damage to the head but to the whole system, when you fall down after a certain age it's a long, long fall, we are our own precipices etc., so while we all busied ourselves with talking we were also all keeping an eye on the entrance.

They weren't really very late, perhaps twenty minutes or so. It was an almost surreptitious entrance, nobody in the Ivy except those sitting at the table looking out for him seemed to notice him, he looked quite small, actually, slip-slopping softly along in special shoes because his feet hurt, with something oddly nautical about him – a matter of the blue jacket and particularly the cap, pulled rakishly down over one eye to conceal the bandage – he also looked very continental, from the South of France or Sicily,

and distinctly roguish, like a Resistance fighter in an old
Hollywood movie, and though you couldn't say he looked robust
he looked as if he were back on this side of life's frontier. We stood
up and clapped as he took his place at the head of the table, and
would have liked to have done more – thrown our caps into the
air, raised our voices in song, chaired him around the Ivy – to
further honour the man whose birthday we were celebrating, and
who only a few hours before had been awarded the Nobel Prize.
Antonia came and sat at our end of the table. She was almost
solemn with relief and happiness. 'Who would have thought?' she
asked. 'Who could have thought?' looking down the length of the
table to her husband, who raised a glass to her with a pirate's
wink –

PART THREE

A TABLE IN BARBADOS

One of the reasons I was particularly looking forward to Barbados this year is that I thought it would be the perfect place, sun, sea, no stress or strain, just swimming, reading, lolling, sleeping, the perfect place to give up smoking, but now of course –

Consider this: there we were, stepping into our hotel, the hotel we've been coming to for the last fifteen years or so, and in spite of uneasiness during the flight, a sense of being ill-fated, something momentously wrong in the offing, I felt, we both felt, a flood of relief akin to joy to be here again, to see the familiar buildings in the familiar sunshine, the turquoise sea shifting to a nice, gentle rhythm, the staff pleased to see us, as if they shared in our sense of a shared past – and then to be back in the old room, standing on the terrace and looking down at the lawn, the beach-chairs, the bit of the bar where in the evenings Harold and Antonia used to play bridge with two old ladies, when suddenly behind me Victoria's voice – 'What's this!' – she was holding a sort of card, or a sheet of what looked like laminated paper, shiny to bring out the force of the print – SMOKING IS NOT PERMITTED IN THE RESTAURANT.

The hotel is owned by two brothers, both personable young men, one more attractive, the other more intelligent, but hard to tell apart when they're not together. The one who visited our table to welcome us back seemed to be as attractive as he was intelligent, his public school manners in good working order during the annual exchange – how had our year been? Oh good, good – and theirs, how had theirs been? Oh good, oh very good, oh excellent! back and forth for a few minutes, and it would have been quite delightful except that I kept remembering the laminated card on the bedroom table which made me extra-fidgety for a cigarette, and I was about to terminate the conversation and take the several steps to this table at the bar when Victoria with her sweetest smile asked him quite suddenly, it was a non-sequitur really, the reason for the ban. 'Oh well, it's bound to happen, sooner or later,' he said, smiling warmly back at her. 'Like death, you mean,' I said, 'but surely there's no need to grab at it before your time,' and added, 'Presumption is sometimes presumptuous, in my view', which I thought interestingly enigmatic. 'But what about pregnant women?' he said. 'We have to think about the pregnant women, don't we?' 'Praise the Lord for pregnant women, where would we be without them?' I replied, I hope not snarlingly, got up, raised my wife from her chair, and conducted her here, where awaited us our puddings and coffee, over which we had a brief discussion about whether he was the less attractive or the less intelligent brother, and agreed that there was no way of knowing, as his brother wasn't there to help distinguish them. I smoked irritably, stubbing out many cigarettes before I was halfway through.

Nevertheless, having betrayed my intentions and myself in so many ways, I must address the smoking issue four-square on.

Well, not tonight. Tomorrow perhaps, when I am feeling fresh, and without rancour. Tonight it is enough to be sitting scantily dressed by the sea, a cigarette between my fingers and nothing to distract me except Rollicks, the waiter, who like me is a year older, probably to the day, since we last met. Rollicks is laying the tables for breakfast, moving about with brisk, soldierly movements, coming over every now and then to see how I'm doing with my Diet

Coke – if I look up to my left, as I've just done, I can see Victoria on the terrace, standing quite still, looking out towards the sea.

A low wall separates this bar from the sea. All the people on the beach have their backs to me, quite naturally, as they are facing the sea, apart from one small, elderly woman who has her back to the sea and is facing me, and 'facing' really is the right verb here, every time I glance up from my yellow pad and from habit expect my eye to meet the sea, I find it meets instead the face of this woman staring over the wall straight at me, the wall cuts off her body from the waist down, it's quite unsettling, really, she has a turban on her head, swollen cheeks, her mouth is open in a sort of leer, in fact she reminds me of those old seaside postcards, a sinister version of them, instead of a large, disorganized woman's bottom there is a large, disorganized woman's face. She may, of course, merely be trying to get into my writing – everybody in the hotel now knows that I write, and what is more that I write about the people in the hotel. In previous years when they've seen me at this table, they've assumed that I'm engaged on an epic novel, perhaps, or a legal brief, or that I suffer from a compulsive deficit disorder – I'm not sure that that's the correct term, 'compulsive deficit disorder' seems more appropriate to my bank account – anyway, I mean a psychological disorder that compels me to write on and on meaninglessly, or seemingly meaninglessly, but eventually there might emerge a meaningless, or seemingly meaningless masterwork, of the order of *Finnegans Wake*. In previous years I was ignored, being a familiar part of the scenery, nodded to now and then by this and that guest, but always treated with respect by the waiters and other members of the staff, who have an innate reverence for a writing person who is also reputed to be a heavy tipper. Now, though, a lot of what I have scribbled at this table has been published, and what is worse,

a case of really bad planning, the last book was published during the
week that we arrived here, and my face has appeared in the
newspapers that they read, a day late, over their breakfasts – not just
my face but much of the rest of me, in some cases complete with a
cigarette and one of the dogs – usually George, as she's developed
a nose for photographers and flings herself on to my lap whenever
she notices a man pointing a camera at me – it occurs to me that in
the photographs I am almost completely clad, whereas at this table
I am almost completely unclad – so their eyes can go from the
elderly man in their newspaper, posing in distinguished writerly
fashion, a dog in his lap and possibly a cat at his feet, his hand
resting on the lower shelf of an overflowing bookcase, cardigan
hanging loosely and cloakingly over a stomach that expresses itself
in a dignified and graceful slope – their eyes can go from that
photograph to the actual elderly man in flesh and blood and
swimming trunks, the dignified and graceful slope exposed as a
shapeless and pendulous sack, with scary brown nodules growing on
his arms and chest – when I asked my doctor why I had these
nodules that seem to have multiplied every time I count them, he
said they were nothing to worry about, they come with age – my
fear is that they will join up, so that they will eventually cover the
whole of my body like a sort of suit – anyway, these nodules are part
of the package that the people in the hotel, looking up from the
photograph on the table in front of them, take in with a little gulp
of disgust, I expect –

But the point is, as I've said, that not only do they know what I
am doing, but they suspect – with good reason – that I'm doing it
about them. In fact, I'm beginning to get the feeling, confused and
I hope merely the symptom of a short-term mental disorder, that
some of them are posing for my writing, are expanding their
characters, or assuming new ones, in order to be caught and

recorded on my yellow pages. They gesture to me, wave and wink, some actually come over and ask me how it's going, and spindle off into anecdotes about writing relatives, or how they themselves once thought of reporting in a book on their strange and dangerous holiday in Kenya, also how an aunt once met Noël Coward, but I don't get the impression that any of them has actually read one of my books, or seen one of my plays – I'm known to them entirely through appearances, my recent photograph in the newspapers, my posture as I write. My situation is therefore hopeless on two counts – not only can I not spend any more hours this holiday sitting at this table doing this, but we can't come back next year, or ever again – I look at those words 'can't come back' appalled – we've been coming for year after year for more than a dozen years, arriving on the same day and roughly at the same time – at this very table I've written one complete book, and large parts of two others, rewritten and further rewritten scenes from two of my plays, I've had a great deal of happiness at this table, at which I've also mourned, writing about the loss of my closest friends, dreamed of sex and my childhood, remembered my schooldays, loved my mother and failed to love my father all over again, it really should be a sacred place for me, but in the course of the last few minutes it has simply become a table at which I used to write, I notice how uncomfortable the chair is, and that the table itself has an irritating tendency to sway unless a little pack of paper is inserted under one of its feet, and of course I also notice the many people who are seated at nearby tables – quite a few of whom go out of their way to pass close to me, and say, for instance, 'Still smoking, I see! Good for you!' so that I feel I'm putting on an exhibition – the hotel writer at his smoking or the hotel smoker at his writing – a lively blonde lady of some sixty summers, I'd guess, who has a frolicky, friendly manner just came up to me and told me she'd heard my book being read aloud on the radio the day before she left, she'd had such fun identifying the characters, was she right in assuming the one I described as a 'drunken Pan' was – and she pointed her finger across the bar to where the man I had described as a drunken Pan was sprawled across the counter, his arm around the waist of a slender young woman in a bikini so neat and sexless that it looked like a uniform – and what I described as his 'rotting fig of a nose' was where I described seeing it, deep in a glass of something that looked as if it had come out of his nostrils – the last five words are freshly minted, so probably more a mark of my deterioration than his. 'No, no,' I said, 'no, that man over there Pan! No, of course not, I can't remember ever having seen him before.' She said he came here most years, at the same time that she and I did. 'Really,' I said, 'well, last year was the first time I've seen him.' I don't think she took in the implications of this completely reflexive giveaway remark, although I might have helped her by hurrying into 'Not that I saw him last year, as far as I can remember.' I fixed indifferent eyes on Pan, who had dismounted from his bar stool and was rolling unsteadily towards me – the neat girl in the bikini was still at the counter, so perhaps she isn't connected to him except accidentally, perhaps he'd wrapped his arm around her waist as if it were a pillar, for support only – he arrived in front of me and punched me in the stomach. It was by no means a powerful blow, it might have passed for an over-weighted friendly cuff, and his speech was friendly enough. 'Hello, old writer!' he said, in a gust of alcoholic foulness. 'Good to see you back, how's it going, you've been busy, seen you in the papers' – but his small brown eyes had a gleam that gave the punch, which I can still feel, a vindictive or possibly vengeful meaning – 'And you're here too,' he said, his arm curling out and around the lively lady's torso, and drawing her into him, 'come and have a drink, come and have a drink,' and back to the bar he went, she with him, clicking along in her high heels, and throwing me a glance over her shoulder, as if to say, 'What can I do? Here is a man!' Or even, 'Here is a Pan!' And there they are at the bar, he bellowing slurred laughter, she screeching with merriment, she sounds rather like our dog Toto in one of her frenzies. So I'll have to go. That's it. I'll have to go –

It's odd to think that these are the last words I'll ever write at this table – well, it's my own fault, as are most of the things that I don't like about my life.

PART FOUR

ON NOT BEING SIMON CALLOW

We're in Suffolk and I'm just back from our local bookshop, where there was an unpleasant scene that I'm trying not to dwell on. Let me dwell instead on what I've been mainly doing since we came down here, two weeks ago.

Well, I sits and reads, I sits and smokes, and sometimes I just sits, my only physical activity the tonguing of my recently acquired false teeth, lifting them up and resettling them on my gums. They're quite uncomfortable when I leave them alone, twice as uncomfortable when I toy with them, as I am now doing –

Which reminds me, I've got to send Simon Callow an email. Something's been troubling me about my last meeting with him. We had dinner where was it? Oh yes, the Wolseley. And I have a feeling, have had it ever since we parted on the pavement, that I'd been mildly unpleasant in some way. Not unpleasant to him, I hope, he's one of the people I couldn't bear to be unpleasant to – though I realize that not being unpleasant in intent doesn't mean I'm not being unpleasant in effect – but there was an incident involving a clutch of actors, friendly actors, friends almost. One or two came over to our table and offered hugs and cheek-scraping and so forth, which I responded to as best I could, actually managing to clutch them fiercely, if not affectionately, and rub my cheek up and down against their stubbles and beards – one of them was an elderly man, older than me, who I hope will do a tour of one of my plays later in the year, and the other was an actor who was once, years ago, in a play of mine. We stood there talking of old times and new, then went with them to their table, where there were three or so women, wives, mistresses, whatever, whom we hugged and kissed, we sat down for a very few minutes, a very few, before the huggings and kissings, the scrapings and gruntings of our farewells – all well and good so far, all well and good, I'd got intact through one of those little social skirmishes I hate so much without giving anyone offence, as far as I knew, but when we were on the pavement, just as we were about to step into our respective taxis, I heard myself saying: 'A lot of false teeth in there.' 'What?' said Simon, bewildered. 'You know,' I said. 'False teeth.' 'No,' he said, 'I don't know.' I named the two actors, the older and the slightly less old, who'd first come over to our table. 'Oh,' he said, and looked faintly shocked, not at the thought of their having false teeth, but at my having noticed and commented on them. And yes, it is an odd thing to have commented on, I can see that, though not odd to have noticed. One notices what one notices, and the fact is that I'd been intensely aware of their teeth, and had studied them to see whether they were false, and now I suspect that perhaps Simon was upset on their behalf – they'd been so innocently and boisterously friendly and affectionate, and there I was, on the pavement, a few seconds later, making comments about their teeth as if I were talking really about their morals – so I feel I must explain to Simon that what was really on my mind was not their false teeth but mine, which I was either wearing that night for the first time or was going to be wearing the next night – I can't remember whether I had them in my mouth or merely had the thought of them in my mouth. I'll send him an email. I'll compose it here and then transcribe it. I don't want to put a foot wrong:

Dear Simon – I've had some false teeth installed, and have been sitting here (in Suffolk) shifting them with my tongue up and down on my gums, and then suddenly remembered the last time we met, at the Wolseley, when I became acutely conscious of the false teeth in others, who actually may not have false teeth, but as my own were either recently arrived or impending, I was determined to find them in every face. Which made me think of what they mean to someone of my generation. They mean grandpas and other ancients, whose teeth you could note in a glass if you should happen to find yourself in their bedroom, or moving about in their mouths while they were eating – sometimes they would do something, a sort of clicking, with their jaws and the contraption would hang free and then jut forward, giving one a ghastly glimpse into the mechanics of old age. My own are uncomfortable, but at least invisible to others, I think, as they're silicon (can that be right?) molars, right at the back of either side of the jaw, and artificially yellowed to match the nicotine originals in the front of my mouth.

Why am I telling you all this? Not on a need to know basis, surely.

LIBRARIES, BOOKSHOPS, BROTHELS

Why in God's name did I write all that down here, and not on the email, and then zip it off to him? I'm not seriously going to type all that out on the computer, am I? Actually, to tell me the truth, I think I'm in serious trouble, and I'd better start facing up to it, before it's too late and I slip under the waves. Let's try and get it straight.

Start with what's been upsetting you. The scene in the bookshop. So trivial, really, and really not worth –

– to begin with, I hate going into bookshops these days, not a book that isn't whoring after you, slashes of paper across their middle and between their legs like lewd costumes, three of us for the price of one, the publisher their pimp – 'Three of my best girls! Or boys! For the price of one!!'

– and a lot of the novels gave the impression that they were written by the same woman under a variety of similar-sounding pseudonyms, and the faces of these women looked strangely misogynist. I imagine them at parties, praising each other's work with moues and grimaces, or in the literary pages describing each other's plots in coils of deadening prose but with adjectives 'engrossing, enthralling, delicious, delightful' – that the publishers can trowel out and paste all over the paperback edition –

– and there's a new look that the middle-aged male authors have, or the ones conscious of entering middle age (their 'maturity'), their mouths go up in a grin of spiky, or disdainful, imbecility, the dandy as village idiot –

– but to come back to this afternoon –

– the reason I went to the bookshop this afternoon was to buy *Arthur & George*. It's a novel by Julian Barnes about Conan Doyle and the half-Indian, half-Scottish solicitor whose name Conan Doyle cleared of a particularly disgusting offence – slitting open the bellies of horses, as far as I can make out from the reviews, etc. – I have a feeling that I'll enjoy it, not the slitting-horse's-bellies part, needless to say, though I'm sure it's done very engagingly, but the Conan Doyle-on-the-case part, as written by the man who'd written *Flaubert's Parrot*. Furthermore I've taken a fancy to the cover – an olivey-green mottled hard-board cover, with two figures etched into it – Arthur, bulky, and George, schoolboy size, both with hats, seen from behind, in silhouette. It's very beguiling, with a flavour of an old-fashioned book, a turn of the century – whoops! turn of the last century – sort of book. In fact it looks almost as if it belongs in the Chelsea Public Library from sixty-five or so years ago, when I was ten or so, that I would pick from the shelves marked 'Mystery' possibly, or 'Historical', and I would tumble through the pages, looking for a paragraph that would suggest that this was the book for me.

You were allowed to borrow books for two weeks, if you were late you got a fine, and if you were later than that a portly man, middle-aged and jocular, a friendly bailiff figure, would come to your door and collect both the book and a larger fine for the trouble he'd been put to – Mummy would be embarrassed, apologizing again and again for the trouble her dolt of son had put him to, and directed a few lazily aimed cuffs at me after he'd gone – 'Why can't you remember, you little fool, it's so humiliating having him at the door like a debt collector, and you should think about him, he has to trek around Chelsea because of noodles like you!' – I never thought to say, because I didn't know enough, that if noodles like me remembered to return their books he'd have been out of a job –

I've been in many libraries since, though not as many as I should have, but none that gave me as much pleasure as the Chelsea Public Library, where every spine of every book carried the promise of adventure, or laughter, or an erection – the 'Romantic Historical' section, with pulsing titles – *Desert Maiden* might have been one of them. I wish I could remember the title of the fictionalized biography of Katherine the Great. In the first part of the book, when she was the young Katerina, she was tempestuous, rebellious, untameable, consequently frequently half-naked and bound. In the second half her sensual and voluptuous rival, the soft-skinned blonde with the cascading hair, Anna Mons, was stripped naked, fastened in chains at the neck, wrists, waist and ankles, and sent sprawling at the feet of her former lover, Peter the Great – I must have borrowed and returned the book about thirty times in the year

1947, and could hop from passage to passage without checking the page numbers, as if I were blind and working in Braille, a skill I would have needed if our forefathers' predictions about the consequences of filthy practices had turned out to be true. That was the thing about books then, not just the ones that aroused you but also the ones that made you laugh or frightened you – it didn't matter how many times you'd read them they were still incompletely experienced, in fact the recollection of them seemed to freshen and sharpen them, while making you feel secure –

The best stories were the favourite stories, beginning them again made your toes tingle, and your eyes still popped with surprise at revelations that you knew by heart – now, half a century later, I read some books again and again, most particularly Jane Austen, but I don't re-read even *Mansfield Park* as I re-read books I loved when I was twelve – it's that I want to hear Jane Austen's voice, so personal and confidential, that has run through all my adult life, and makes me believe that I have a continuous self – though not one's normal sexual self, because she speaks to you as if you were a woman – her sister, an equal, her confidante.

THE GREAT DICTATOR

Is one ever aware of one's sex when reading fiction that isn't erotic or pornographic? I have an idea that I feel more manly when reading Tolstoy, but what about Henry James? What sex does one feel – do I feel – when reading Henry James? I haven't read him for years, I don't believe I have the powers of concentration any more, at least for the late ones, *The Golden Bowl, The Wings of the Dove, The Ambassadors*, with their endlessly unwinding and rewinding sentences – but of course they were dictated, the late novels, they were dictated to a lady with the name of a spin bowler, Rhodes, no, no, Bosanquet. I can't be making this up, surely?

Assume you aren't. Think it's all true. Then think of Miss Bosanquet sitting there with her pad on her knee – no, Miss Bosanquet took the dictation on a typewriter, the Master liked to hear the noise of the typewriter, the steady clackety-clackety-clackety of Miss Bosanquet's typewriter as she loaded his sentences on to it as if it were a cargo train, chugging and clacking his sentences from the sofa where he lay to the generations beyond, clackety-clackety went Miss Bosanquet's faithful but mortal fingers at the typewriter, clackety-clackety – did his sentences keep time to her fingers, or did her fingers keep time to his sentences? – that's the question that comes to me, as I consider those works of his dictatorship – at the end he thought he was Napoleon, actually signed off one of his deathbed letters with Napoleon's name – but there was something else about Miss Bosanquet. something extraordinary. I'll Google her, what was her Christian name? I've an idea it was Tabitha, Tabitha Bosanquet? No, here it is, Theodora, Theodora Bosanquet, literary editor of *Time and Tide*, etc. etc., and here on Google is the extraordinary thing – she was psychic and a medium. James came back to her in a seance and asked her to take down dictation. Other writers, Galsworthy, Hardy, Meredith also dictated to her from beyond the grave. They explained that they had a great deal of unfinished work and that it was her duty to transcribe it and pass it on to the world. After her death they found notebooks full of their mint-fresh but posthumous work, so really she was a ghostwriter to ghosts –

And here's his Napoleonic letter, quoted in a little article by Leon Edel, with all kinds of copyright warnings underneath. It consists of instructions for the improvement of 'certain apartments' in the palaces of the Louvre and the Tuileries, and though it doesn't actually make much sense, it concludes with an imperial flourish:

> Please understand I regard these plans as fully developed and as having had my last consideration and look forward to no patchings nor perversions, and with no question of modifications either economic or aesthetic. This will be the case with all further projects of your affectionate NAPOLEONE.

Napoleone seems odd to me, as if he were a pasta – ravioli, macaroni, napoleone – but still, one can imagine the Master on the sofa, slipping in and out of consciousness, his mouth moving soundlessly or to inane purpose, Miss Theodora Bosanquet at her typewriter, her fingers following their impulses as if on a ouija board, clackety-clackety-clack –

I've just sent another email to Simon Callow suggesting that I'd like to take over his life – he wrote to me that he was just finishing a television series in which he travels to glamorous European cities and sits in the rooms, sometimes in the chairs and on the beds, of great composers, Sibelius, Haydn, Mozart, the various Strausses, in his capacious briefcase an already well-received script he's written on the relationship between Noël Coward and Gertrude Stein, no, that can't be right, surely Noël Coward and Gertrude Stein couldn't have – oh, Gertrude Lawrence, of course, Gertie, a script on Noël and Gertie, and in a few days' time he begins rehearsing the part of Fatsco, I think it is, in *Women in Whites*, I'm getting all these things wrong deliberately, out of envy, because, yes, there's nothing I'd rather do than take over Simon Callow's life at the moment, well, for the next year or so, and possibly his bank account, too, perhaps not his bank account, nor his body either, come to think of it, it's a body that suits Simon but wouldn't suit me unless I also took over his eating and drinking habits, in which case I'd certainly need his gastric system, I'm not allowed to drink alcohol and I have no appetite for proper food, only savage cravings for disgusting things, cakes, chocolate, cigarettes, Diet Cokes – so my gastric habits wouldn't go with his digestive tract – there'd have to be modifications here and there, in fact I'm beginning to see that the whole thing is impossible unless I take over complete occupancy of Simon Callow and his life, his body, his lover, his appetites, his vices as well as his virtues, tasks, rewards, consciousness, dreams and nightmares, relatives and friends – in which case I would just be Simon Callow, and what would be the point of that, when he's already Simon Callow and there certainly wouldn't be room for two of us – now then, now then, what happened in the bookshop was this, I plucked a copy of Julian Barnes's *Arthur & George* from a table mainly devoted to this one book and took it to the counter, where a girl, more a girl than a young woman, with red hair and businesslike spectacles and a noticeably pretty smile was dealing with another customer and while I was waiting two portly and respectable local matrons came and stood beside me, facing the counter and talking animatedly about something that I enjoyed overhearing at the time but of course have forgotten in the light of – this: the girl finished with the customer, wished her a very good day in a soft Suffolk accent, turned to me, to take the copy of *Arthur & George* along with my held-out credit card, checked herself, looked at the two women who were still chatting and not aware, really, that they were in a sort of queue, then said to me, 'No, I think these ladies came first' and to them, 'Good afternoon, can I help you please?' They glanced with vague reproach in my direction, really I think noticing me for the first time but nevertheless assuming that I'd been justly reprimanded – so I sort of spanked *Arthur & George* with my hand, slap, slap, slap against its cover, threw it back on the table and left. I've an idea that nobody noticed me, particularly.

How sad, though, that I couldn't have said, simply said, 'Well, actually I was here first, I think. Not that it matters, I'm in no rush, after all', because after all I wasn't. I wasn't in any sort of rush. I wasn't feeling impatient, even.

A HOT DOG AND OTHER MEMORIES

Peter Hall rang just now to discuss the future of my new but rapidly ageing play *Little Nell*. He says that he definitely wants it to open his new theatre at Kingston, and then take it to Bath and Birmingham, and then into London. Or he might open it in Bath or Birmingham, then move it to Birmingham or Bath, then on to open his new theatre at Kingston, and so to London. The thing is, though, that he's not sure that he'll have a new theatre in Kingston to open it with or move it to, because he's not sure when, or even whether, he'll have a new theatre in Kingston to be opened by anything. The theatre itself is there already, everything physical is in place apart from the money – I had to stop to dab my eyes, which were running slightly – not from grief over this latest lack of firm news about poor *Little Nell*, I hope – perhaps my eyes are just rheumy, as elderly eyes often are. So – now dabbed, vision clear, back to – well, nothing, really, because actually I'm struggling to fend off a sudden yearning for a hot dog. I really don't understand this at all, because hot dogs are shiny pink and brown rubbery sort of sausages enclosed between two halves of an elongated synthetic bun, with runny red and green sauces over the sausage that leak through the bun into the palm of your hand and when I write it out like this I cannot understand how I could conceivably be yearning for one, and indeed I no longer am – what I must have been yearning for was the sight and the smell of a hot dog as I experienced it when I was six or seven years old in Montreal – certain Sundays were hot-dog Sundays, Grandpa and our aunt Gert would take us to the park, Grandpa would buy hot dogs from a cart attached to a horse, Gert would supervise the putting on of tomato ketchup, French mustard and that green stuff, and then present us with exactly what I've described above, which would make us, my brother Nigel and me, almost swoon with pleasure –

We were sent back to England a year before the war ended, when I was eight, and I remember being haunted by the memory of Montreal hot dogs through the long London years of rationing, when the main feature of food was its absence, especially noticeable to boys who were in the Canadian habit of too much of it, until eventually we fell into the English habit of too little of it. It took a French boy, staying with us 'on exchange' to bring the too little of it back to our attention – his appetite hadn't been reduced by the war and rationing, so he had expectations that Mummy couldn't meet. When she put his first dish in front of him, slivers of cold meat, he consumed it in seconds, almost before we'd picked up our knives and forks, waited for his next course with visible signs of impatience, and when he grasped that there wasn't one, only more of the bread and marge he'd disdained while swallowing his meat, his indignation broke through his limited English – he was fourteen, I think, anyway his voice had broken, unlike mine, and I was very impressed by his gruff aplomb, that he should dare to speak to Mummy like that! Her initial impulse must have been to give him a swipe across the chops, in fact she got to her feet and for an instant she drew herself to her full height, chin in the air, cigarette smouldering, no, she probably wasn't smoking, it's that I always see her smoking whenever I think of her, and then explained in her slapdash French that we English were still, through rationing and other deprivations, fighting the war from which you French had withdrawn before it had scarcely begun, and although *vous français* had had the Germans occupying *votre pays*, you *français* had continued to eat very well – Pierre, I actually do think his name was Pierre, we had two Pierres in successive years – failed to understand much of what she was saying, but he got the essential drift, enough of it anyway to find it worth reporting in a letter to his father, who reported his reporting of it in a letter to my father, which Mummy had translated by someone or other, to her further mortification, because not only did Pierre Numéro Un find the food inadequate, but he also found the house in which he was served it, from which he'd departed a day or so before his papa's letter arrived, to be little better than a slum. A slum! 47 Oakley Gardens, SW3! A slum! Just because there were a few bombed-outs living at the bottom of the street and pre-fabs around the corner in Manresa Road, because of the war, the war that they hadn't even joined in –

And yet she loved all things French, loved being in France. When we went there *en famille* after the war she exclaimed continuously on its marvellous Frenchness, everything was just as French as she remembered it – 'Look,' she said, as we drove away from the boat through Calais, 'the very streets – the cars, a Citroën, James! – oh, a *gendarme*, and there, the little outside lavatory, they're called *pissoires*, and you see the wine shops – James, see the windows! all that wine – and the pavement cafés and there's a *pâtisserie*' – she said the word with such a French flourish – 'you boys have never tasted a real French *pâtisserie* – do stop, James, and we'll all have a *pâtisserie*, the boys can have their first *tarte au pommes*!' James stopped, and she led us to the little shop, its open counter just off the pavement laden with cakes, fruit tarts, etc., the smell of their recent baking hanging in the warm air, and it's certainly true that

Nigel and I had never seen such a display, not even in Montreal, nor smelt such smells – 'peach, pear, apple,' she said, 'apricot, *fraises, framboises* – and that's the one I'll have' – she gestured at it, one of her grand gestures – 'the blackberry!' and a swarm of flies rose up from it, leaving not a blackberry but a plain custard tart – we hurried back to the car, and Nigel and I experienced our first real *pâtisseries* further down the road, deep inside a café off the pavement, where the *pâtisserie* counter had a net over it. 'Of course you have to understand,' she said, 'that the French have never cared much about hygiene. But you get used to it, it's part of the charm.' 'On the other hand,' said our father, still a doctor though on holiday, 'there's dysentery you know, my dear. You don't want them to get dysentery.' Our mother agreed that she didn't want us to get dysentery. 'So do try to be careful what you eat! Make sure it's fresh, if it isn't, send it back!' Easier for her to say than for us to do, as we were being dispatched to our different exchanges, Nigel to one outside Paris, as I remember, and I to one in Valandre-sur-Mer – I can't remember anything about the boy I was exchanging with, or his family, but the sea was full of jellyfish for a whole week, I remember that, and we couldn't swim.

The only exchange I really remember was the second Pierre. He was theoretically Nigel's responsibility, being the same age as Nigel – fifteen and somewhat – but Nigel had gone to spend the summer with an aunt in Ireland, so I was appointed to the position of English boy in his place, and was sent to meet him at Victoria Station. I waited at what I was sure was the right platform, the train arrived at the announced time, disgorged its passengers, there were lots of them, French and English – think of it, Victoria Station in 1950, all those people in drab clothes and hats, so many of them smoking – and all of them gone at last, no one left at all except a man, the very image of middle-aged oddness, wearing not just a hat, but a deer-stalker, like Sherlock Holmes, and like Sherlock Holmes, smoking a pipe – he stood there serenely puffing, waiting for someone that couldn't possibly be me – well, that was the second Pierre, eccentric and charming and with me quite paternal, an older brother without the complications. Mummy adored him and even Daddy, also then a pipe-smoker, quite took to him – they'd sit together in the sitting room, in their armchairs, puffing away but not saying much – well, they didn't need to, Mummy with two maley males in the room could converse with both of them simultaneously and with me lolling beside her on the sofa, in the comfort of her scent and cigarette smoke, for squeezes and cuddles. Pierre's English was serviceable enough to express his admiration for Mummy's cuisine, especially for her versatility with Spam – he thought Spam completely delicious, however it turned up on the plate, covered in batter probably his favourite – I don't know what he and I did together in the daytime, but he always seemed to enjoy himself, and not to mind my being almost two years younger.

I wish I could remember what he looked like. I wished we'd taken photographs. I've always been a lazy and reluctant photographer. The trouble is that the present never seems worth photographing, only the past, when it's too late, which is why I suppose I've so few photographs –

Now of course I wish I'd taken lots and lots, especially of my parents, especially of my mother, my mother in her prime, to block out the memory of her skeletal hand clinging to mine, and I determined not to look at my watch until I did, a swift, casual glance down at my wrist. 'Oh,' she said, in an anxious whisper, 'don't go yet, Si, stay a little while longer.' 'I can't,' I said, 'I have to pick Ben up from his nursery school.' She held her hand out to retain me. I held it to my lips, kissed her quickly on the forehead and left. I had enough time, more than enough time to get to the nursery school, so I walked along Putney towpath, and thought about the kind of son I was, who would deprive his dying mother of a few more minutes, that's all she'd claimed, a few more minutes of his company. I still don't know why I wouldn't stay. It wasn't coldness of the heart or fear of seeing her so extremely ill and dying. There had just been an undeniable impulse to remove myself. Inexplicable that it comes back to me now, as it did one afternoon last summer on Spetses when, drying after a swim, I watched a tiny old lady sitting in the rim of the sea, picking stones out of the water, looking at them, putting them back, not childishly but like a child, and my eyes filled with tears of shame. I am now nearly ten years older than she was when she died, I've had all those years more than she had, and I hadn't given her a few minutes of those years, on an impulse –

HOW TO KILL THE QUEEN

We're in a heatwave, so hot that it's a real effort to cross the garden from my study, which is a slightly dangerous place as it's full of winged insect life, including horseflies and blowflies, which means there's a corpse somewhere about, I suppose. Let's hope it's in the bushes outside, not actually in here, a dead mouse or vole rotting underneath my desk, by my feet, or the corpse of my most recently uncompleted masterpiece rotting away in a drawer. There are also bees, wasps and hornets, not swarms of them, of course, they come in singles, twos and threes, then drift about in the corners of this small room, or become suddenly animated, and beat against the wire mesh I have over the windows, before drifting off again. I try sporadically to usher them out through the door, which I have to have open, in the hope of catching a bit of breeze, any whiff of living air in this inert weight of heat, but even if I succeed they come straight back in, as if their understanding is that they belong here, that my study is really a kind of public nest, like a bus shelter, say, where they can hang out until inclined to return to their private quarters. I wouldn't mind, really, if I didn't hate the thought of blowflies, and weren't nervous of being stung by wasps. The last time I was stung by a wasp, on a small boat in Greek waters about ten years ago, I went into shock, and had to be carried, on the point of death I was subsequently told, in a slow, unresponsive ambulance over mountains and through flocks of goats and herds of wild horses to a hospital which was in its hygienic arrangement more lethal than a wasp sting. Actually, it may not have been the wasp sting that caused me to pass out, simultaneously vomiting and squittering on the deck of the small boat, but the sea urchin I was eating while I was being stung, it had an odd taste. And actually it may not have been the sea urchin or the wasp sting, it may have been alcohol poisoning, which is what one of the doctors claimed in the hospital – gathering his students around him he stabbed his forefinger at me with ill-humoured contempt and gave a lecture, a brief, scathing lecture. I only understood those words we share with them, alcohol being one of them. His students nodded and laughed mutteringly at the old English guy between the tattered and grubby sheets who was dehydrated from being poisoned by let's say the lot, insect and crustacean and alcohol.

Victoria thought she could see a nest in the roof above my door, another of wasps or hornets around the side, and a nest of bees at the back. 'You mean that they all, wasps, hornets and bees, get on with each other!' I exclaimed, sniffing a moral in it, to do with possibly the present situation in the Middle East. 'If wasps, hornets and bees can live in harmony so close to each other – Where are you going?' She said she was going into the house, to telephone pest control. 'What do they do?' I asked. 'Get rid of them, I hope,' she said. So any moral to do with politics and the Middle East would have to find a role for the pest controller.

The pest controller was a very pleasing man, we thought, short, balding and neat, with an academical, almost professorial manner. He spoke in long, easy sentences, rather like an accomplished television expert. He walked quickly around my study, identifying the nests pretty well where Victoria had identified them, then he donned his uniform, a sort of loose helmet with a transparent mask over his face, so that he could see through the cloud of chemical he was about to squirt through a hose attached to a canister. He explained what he was about to do, and sent us, for our own protection, to the kitchen. He joined us there in under five minutes, having destroyed the nests of bees, hornets, wasps. This is how he did it, as far as I could glean, and anything I didn't glean was my failure, because he spoke in the relaxed, confidential manner I've described above, eloquently and informatively – the chemicals he squirted into the wasps' nest would be picked up by the feet of the worker wasps as they went into the nest to groom the queen, so of course when they groomed the queen they'd be grooming her with poisonous feet, she would die, then without a queen they would die partly from the poison partly from redundancy, loss of purpose, I suppose, or grief. He was quite clear about it, but I got a bit confused taking it in, as it involved possibilities that had never occurred to me before. I remember another fragment – he told us that the slow, sluggish wasps we see at the end of summer that we call lazy and think – most of us, anyway – are that way because they've come to the end of their natural time and are dying out with the season, are in fact pregnant wasps, looking for somewhere to lie during the winter, a spot under a tile on the roof of my study, for instance. Come the spring they give birth to the worker wasps who will construct the nest in which they will dwell the summer long – at least until he comes along with his hose and canister and poisons their feet. He also said that one of the extraordinary things about the nests is that they always, every nest ever investigated, contain exactly forty-eight – I think it was forty-eight – anyway, always exactly the same number of chambers, maybe it was forty-nine because the central chamber was the queen's, and an even number of forty-eight chambers would encompass the royal chamber. And he said that the size of the royal chamber was in proportion to the size of the queen, so that every queen, large or small, had precisely the same amount of space at her disposal. He stood there, in the kitchen, drinking water, a hand on the counter sort of propping him, his feet crossed at the ankles, his eyes shiny with the pleasure of imparting information that we both wanted and didn't want – I think I can speak for Victoria here. She looked spellbound but stricken, making polite little sounds of distress because the fact was, and still is, that we had called in this pleasant, well-spoken and balding man to put an end to a complicated scheme of life. Had we the right? Now I think about it, I realize that he didn't describe the fate of the hornets and the bees, would they have been approximately the same as that of the wasps?

'Now,' he said, 'if you want to keep insects out of the kitchen' – all sorts of them were all over the place as he spoke, masses of flies. Flies in kitchens are disgusting, there's no getting away from it. They defecate, urinate, salivate, vomit and probably masturbate over any bit of food they alight on, sometimes as you're raising it to your mouth. So yes, we said, we wanted to keep them out of the kitchen and out of my study, their two favourite places. He said that there were very good systems we should consider, but the one that he advocated, he had one himself at home and it worked perfectly and he went on to describe it – it seemed rather complicated and technological to me. I'm not sure that Victoria grasped it properly either, but we were so completely persuaded by him, he was so meticulous in his manner and so authoritative, that we agreed to have it, two of it, whatever it was, expensive though it was. He said he would arrange to have them delivered in a couple of days, accepted a cheque – included in the amount was a sum for his work on the nests – gathered his equipment and drove off in his van. I had an idea that he would be singing as he drove back through the country lanes, 'Bee-loud glades, loud-bee glades, here I come, here come I.'

The fly-killing contraptions were delivered this morning and are now in place, one on the windowsill by the fridge in the kitchen, the other on a bookshelf in my study. They look somewhat like birdcages, but instead of containing a bird they contain a circular tube, and behind the tube is a sheet of metal. A cable goes from a plug in a socket at the top of the cage to a plug in the wall. When you switch it on the tube turns a luminous blue and the metal sheet behind it is electrified. Insects of all types are attracted by the luminous blue light, fly to it between the bars of the cage, circle around it, settle on the sheet of metal behind it, and are promptly electrocuted. It's quite unsettling, really, because the electrocution makes a sharp, sizzling noise, as of a strip of bacon tossed into a hot frying pan, and is sometimes quite prolonged – So far we've been unable to watch the final moment, averting our eyes as we see a wasp, say, winging its way eagerly towards the cage, and keeping them averted until a little while after the sizzling's stopped, but the animals have been distinctly uneasy, the cats sitting with their backs to the cage, Toto lying curled under the table, growling, and George, the most sensitive of creatures, hurrying about the kitchen, darting in and out through the flap, making whimpering noises. We wondered, in fact, whether she could hear within the sizzling other sounds, screams for instance. Do insects scream? A question for a Moral Sciences paper: 'Do insects scream? Discuss.'

At the bottom of the cage is a tray on to which their corpses drop. When the tray is piled high you slip it out and shake the corpses into the rubbish bag in the kitchen, or cross the garden and shake them over the fence into the field. You can glance down before you do so and take note of the astonishing uniformity of the dead. Moths, mosquitoes, blowflies, wasps, hornets, bees, horseflies, greenfly, grasshoppers, ladybugs, butterflies, almost indistinguishable from each other, dried and frazzled as they are, like toast crumbs.

It's 3.15 a.m. and I've just come back into my study from having a pee. A moth came in behind me, a very large moth, almost the size of a small bird, and with powerfully beating wings. It flapped and flapped around the lamp on my desk while I tried to usher it back out into the garden without touching it, because I have an idea that touching moths, or anyway their wings, kills them – so I waved my hands at it and blew at its arse, then fanned at it with a newspaper – it was pale grey, so pale that it was almost colourless, in fact it would have been ghost-like if it hadn't been in such a tumult, blundering around the light until I fanned it off course towards the door, it actually went out and then banged back in before I could shut the door, it just missed my face, sort of helicoptered over my head and when I turned around it was squeezing its large body through the rails of the electric cage – I got hold of the cage and tried to shake it out, but in fact succeeded in shaking it right into the cage, it went around the blue tube several times, and then it made for the electric plate, there was a small flash, more like a spark, and I turned my head away from the noise that went on and on and on – like Harold's poem of that title, and its content too, come to think of it – on and on and on and on –

Now it's a few minutes later, and I'm sitting at my desk writing this, and as I write I realize that all I had to do to save the moth was to switch the cage off – instead of tipping and tilting the cage to shake it loose, just switch the bloody cage off – Well, I've done that now, I've switched it off, and tried not to see the husk, no longer grey but brown, lying on top of a heap of flies, wasps, other moths and so forth, so forth in the tray – I think I'll keep the cage switched off until I go to bed, and meanwhile let me remind myself that the natural life-span of a moth is very short, possibly only a matter of hours, but then a matter of hours may be a long time if you're a moth – the equivalent for me of, say, seventy years come next October –

I was watching Agassi beating a big chap called Pavel, who looked much older than Agassi – but almost everybody looks older than Agassi, who has the eyes and smile of a very sweet child, or one's best idea of a very sweet child, and is as bald as a baby, shaven bald, one assumes, not alopecia – anyway Pavel, heavily built and lumbering, but with a powerful backhand and marvellous powers of retrieval, is in fact a couple of years younger than Agassi, and was giving him a very hard game, but Agassi, swept along on waves of love from his New York fans, triumphed and blew kisses at us, bowed straight into the camera and blew kisses at me, personally it almost seemed, with McEnroe's voice, over, telling me how much I loved him.

A moth blundered on to the screen, on to Agassi's mouth, then blundered off, towards the insect-killing machine, which I turned off just before it could get through the bars. I tried to usher it out through the door, but it vanished, probably behind the curtains. I left the door open so it could get out, and in came Errol. He went around my feet to the curtains, fished behind them, stuffed the moth in his mouth, then it was down his throat. Bits of the wings hung out. Then down they went.

THOUGHTS, USELESS AND STRAY, AFTER A BOMBING AND A SHOOTING IN LONDON

A policeman who in quieter times likes to discuss his sexuality with the public has just appeared on television and said that the words 'Islam' and 'terrorist' don't belong in the same sentence. But any word can belong with any other word in any sentence – 'It would be wrong to say that every follower of Islam is a terrorist' is an example of a sentence in which the two words belong. 'The words Islam and terrorist do not belong in the same sentence' is another example, as is the sentence 'The words Islam and terrorist occasionally belong in the same sentence.' But of course what he was really saying, and what he intended us to hear, was, 'Do not dare to engage in a discussion in which you associate Islam with acts of terrorism'. He went on to instruct us not to think ill of Islam, these murders are merely criminal acts, to be viewed as non-racist, non-ethnically discriminatory unreligious acts and so forth, as if his first thought was that the population is so imbecilically homicidal that we'll rush out and stone the first Muslim, or approximate Muslim, we see, and then burn down mosques, etc. and so forth. Or does he hope that a man who's packing himself with explosives will hear his words, rip off his psychic camouflage and identify himself to himself as a mere criminal, and defuse himself, resolving henceforth to lead a civically blameless life?

Saying that murderous acts can't by definition be acts of faith only makes sense if you are referring to a specific faith, a clear and basic tenet of which is that murderous acts must not be committed in its name – but there are different faiths, and different gods – I suspect if our cop has any idea of God it's as a mush-headed, compassionate, sexually open cop, just like himself, if marginally outranking him, with whom he can have conversations about their love for each other as they share a joint. OK, it seems less harmful than a view of God as a patriarchal pimp, running a Paradise brothel you can blow yourself up and into, with a portion of girlies for every infidel you take with you –

A god who's lodged himself in someone's psychological and moral system by whatever means – pre-natal trauma, psychosis, hypnosis, divine manifestation, sexual frustration – and who says I Am in You, Through Your Bombs Shall My Will Be Done, is a god in occupation and it's no good thinking you can evict him by denouncing as 'criminal' the works committed in his name and for his sake.

Islam is a beautiful faith, I read or heard somewhere or other just yesterday, possibly from Blair the politician but it might have been from Blair the policeman, but there's no such thing as a 'beautiful' faith – there can be beautiful churches, mosques, synagogues, temples, paintings, icons, prayers, music, all artefacts that can be judged aesthetically, but there can't be a beautiful faith because faith can only be judged morally and logically – and with a faith the logic tends to work backwards, from a deeply held belief to the arguments that confirm it. The only proofs of God's existence I've ever studied are from Thomas Aquinas, and made perfect sense in the way that any perfectly worked out construct is likely to make perfect sense, but I could find nothing in the arguments that would persuade me to believe in the existence of God – inasmuch as God's existence can be proved by logic, He will only exist in logic, man-made –

Almost piecework, really, so many corpses bringing in so many virgins – are these virgins live virgins or dead virgins? Inasmuch as the murderous martyr receives them after his death how can they be alive? But if they're dead too, how can they get to it, carnally speaking? This is fatuous and literal thinking, the point is that they're heavenly virgins, enjoyed in heaven, which is a transcendent but physical place, actually made visible in Hollywood films *circa* 1950, with Tony Curtis in baggy pantaloons and Janet Leigh in diaphanous ones, Paradise as a Hollywood harem, or an adolescent's wet dream, and all you have to do to get there is blow yourself out of where you are now – a poky flat in Birmingham, for instance, with its dismal, seedy, rowdy streets, or – who knows? – a pleasant maisonette in leafy Muswell Hill.

What reward if you take a few co-religionists on the side? It's a scatter-bomb approach, after all. Say that though you get ten infidels you also get four Muslims, two of whom had planned to back-pack themselves to Paradise next week. Well, from one point of view it doesn't matter, they were Paradise-bound anyway, from another point of view they might feel aggrieved that they will now miss out on the virgins. Well, they'll just have to put it down to the disadvantages of a multicultural society, in which you're unlikely to get a bus- or tube-load that is 100 per cent infidel –

As I light yet another cigarette I swore not to smoke, I find myself wondering about the Muslim fundamentalist attitude to smoking. Is it OK for them to smoke as they back-pack lethally along crowded Oxford Street? Could they be encouraged to use cigarettes as their next weapons, dishing out packets for free, seeing them as long-term weapons of mass destruction? They have endless patience, centuries of patience, they bore their ancient grudge secretly, in silence, until everybody forgot that they had one, and then here they are, looking almost exactly as they looked when the West last thought about them, in flowing garments, bushy beards, bundles on their heads, and something in their hands, a book, a hook, a bomb, a throat –

A man who saw him in the tube said he was crouched on the floor, quivering with terror, then a man in jeans ran to him, pushed him down flat and shot him through the mouth and through the head, eight times – finally, when there were no alternatives, the truth – terribly sorry, not a Muslim terrorist on his way to Paradise but a Brazilian electrician on his way to work – yes, terribly sorry, but still, aren't we lucky to have such brave and highly trained policemen who will run up to a man crouched quivering with terror on the floor of a tube and push him down flat, and shoot him eight times through the mouth and head –

A few days after the bombings a friend of mine was on a London bus, on the very crowded top deck, sitting beside a man who from his complexion was possibly from the Middle East, and was wearing baggy trousers, a baggy shirt, and holding on his lap a lumpy carrier bag. His face was very tense, and he made little noises, like mutterings, that could have been prayers. He suddenly shouted out something that sounded like a name, whereupon a man several rows up turned around and shouted something back. Then the man sitting next to him shouted the word 'Basri'. The man in front repeated it, 'Basri', and held up two fingers. My friend rose, went down the stairs, got off at the next stop, walked rapidly around the nearest corner and lit a cigarette, and then – actually I don't know what he did next – but what he didn't do was phone the police, from fear of having to explain the stereotyping nature of his thought processes – dusky hue, loose garments, carrier bags, sudden exclamations to a friend in an unrecognized tongue, etc. Now let me ask myself what I would have done in his place. Would I have done as he did? Or would I have alerted the police? Or would I have risen to my feet and shouted, 'Listen, everyone! There's a possibility that this bus is going to be blown up! I might be wrong. It's up to you. I'm leaving. Goodbye and good luck!' I hope so, but I doubt it.

PART FIVE

TURBULENCE IN THE AIR

The captain has just informed us that there is no impediment to our taking off, we're running a mere ten minutes late, for which he wanted to offer his personal apologies, he hoped we would enjoy our flight as much as he would enjoy flying us.

He's just spoken again to explain that we're about to experience a bit of a delay, a passenger has failed to turn up and claim his seat, therefore they're going to remove his baggage from the hold 'because we can't be too careful in the present environment', as he is sure we will understand. He said that if we look out of our portholes, those of us on the appropriate side will be able to watch the missing passenger's baggage being taken off. I don't know whether I'm on the appropriate side, but I haven't looked through the porthole, being unable to imagine a less interesting spectacle than baggage being taken out of a hold and driven off – though I do wonder a bit about the person the baggage belongs to – how come he's checked in both his luggage and himself, but hasn't taken up his seat? Has he been blocked at security and carried off for interrogation, or is he asleep in one of the departure bars, or too involved in purchasing duty-free to notice his flight being called, or suddenly decided to call it off, go home to the wife and kiddies? Is he a terrorist or a loser? Or both – after all, what could be more of a loser than a terrorist who is nabbed going through security, it would be a first, even the shoe-bomber who couldn't ignite his shoe managed to get on the plane, Christ, he's an irritating bugger, whoever he is, delaying the flight by not turning up to be on it, irritating of BA too, etc. –

*

We're in the air, an hour late. I have on the tray in front of me the third volume of Mahfouz's Cairo trilogy, which I've been keeping especially for the plane, having read the first two volumes last week, but I don't think I can concentrate on it – the fact is that I have a bit of a stomach problem, a euphemism for irritable bowel syndrome, itself a euphemism for, among other things, feeling a need to go to the lavatory, itself a euphemism for something I can't think of another euphemism for, and can't bear to be forthright about, I find the word when written even more offensive than when I hear it spoken, put this down to the hyper-sensitivity of an over-educated but not especially well-taught man who has been embroiled in many of the unsavoury aspects of gastric life – thus it was that I was on my feet as soon as the fasten seat belts sign was off – on my feet and patrolling the aisles between the two sets of lavatories, keeping an angry eye on who went in and out, occasionally slipping in myself to no avail. I hung around for a good half-hour outside the economy lavatories at the bottom of the plane. It's a very full plane, not an empty seat in business or economy, and it strikes me – firstly, so where is the empty seat of the passenger who failed to come aboard? Secondly, that all the passengers, several hundred of them, have good strong bladders and bowels, as the only one to show any interest in the lavatories is me.

I stayed there, down by the economy lavatories, too long, when I wanted to return to my seat at the top of the plane I found both aisles blocked by stewards and stewardesses with trolleys of beverages, and the only place I could stand and wait for them to pass through was, of course, outside the lavatories – I'm beginning to worry that I'll be suspected of having an agenda, a sexual one, that I'm trying to pick up a fellow passenger, perhaps squeeze into the lavatory with him or her.

There was an interval between the passing of the drinks trolley and the arrival of the lunch trolley, and so I got back to my seat in time for a tray of food, which I'd been dreading because I knew I would eat it, whatever it was, and that as soon as I'd eaten it I'd be back on my feet, up the aisle, hovering outside the now familiar doors – It was lamb curry, they'd run out of chicken curry, the malignantly beaming stewardess explained, as if guessing at the explosive effect a curry of whatever animal would have on my stomach – I got it down in no time, followed it with a bread roll that I stuffed with cheese, then sent down a thick-textured pudding and two cups of black coffee, thus placing myself by mine own hand in an emergency situation. I tried to clamber to my feet but lost my balance and tipped sideways into the aisle. I had a glimpse as I fell of an elderly i.e. my sort of age woman in a green blouse who is seated a row up from me on the other aisle getting to her feet, obviously lavatory-bound. I raced ahead along my parallel aisle, but she must have spotted me, her mind working to the same pattern of competitive urgency as mine – her seemingly heavy trudge was in fact quite speedy, and she kept her lead, a bulky figure whose mauve trousers contrasted uneasily with the green blouse, there was something about the bunch of her shoulders, the bundle of ginger and grey hair that hung down her neck. I could sense her satisfaction as she closed the lavatory door, having noticed, as I had, that the facing lavatory was occupied – so down the further aisle to the depths of economy I bustled, assuming a scholarly air because I couldn't bear to think that these people should know where I was going. How come this atavistic modesty in an age in which you can see on your television the frankest, not to say grossest, ads for diarrhoea cures, irritable bowel syndrome, constipation, as well as lavatory paper. The other night, racing on my Sky+ through the commercials between the overs of a test match I'd recorded, I glimpsed a young woman holding up something I couldn't believe she was holding up while sitting on something I couldn't believe she was sitting on, so I tracked backwards and froze on it. Yes, she was sitting on the lavatory (toilet) holding up a toilet (lavatory) roll, and she was smiling, no, almost laughing, with joy. I wondered whether anyone else looked at her with the same outraged disgust that I did – certainly not the green-bloused, mauve-trousered bulky woman with gingerish hair who made it to the lavatory before me. She might be of my generation, but she was open and matter-of-fact about her mission, triumphant in her victory, while I tried to persuade interested spectators – what spectators? – that nothing was further from my intentions, that I am a man of strange impulses and sudden distractions, who could guess what business he has outside any door, let alone a lavatory door?

Then at last we were rolling down the runway of Athens airport, and then we were slickly and efficiently through immigration and on to the baggage collection. Baggage was already rolling smoothly through the flaps and around the track. While we waited Victoria confirmed on her mobile that our driver was in the correct place in the arrivals lounge, waiting to drive us to Porto Heli, where we'd take a little water-taxi over the sea to Spetses.

AND TURBULENCE ON THE GROUND

There were only half a dozen people waiting, increasingly restlessly, when our black suitcase came through, and the conveyor belt stopped for a few minutes. When it started again we began to recognize a few pieces of unclaimed luggage because they'd already passed before us several times. Then they too were seized by grateful hands and the little cluster of us saw it in each other's eyes – the dull recognition that now we knew whose luggage they'd taken off at Heathrow. The black bag, the one they hadn't taken off, contains almost everything we don't need. The other bag, beige and missing, contained almost everything that we do need – all Victoria's clothes, my sponge bag in which I'd put the only nail clippers – they're toenail clippers actually – that work on my fingernails, and a carrier bag full of my pills, a load of books, and finally, most crucially, Victoria's Filofax, which she'd been forced to transfer to the now missing bag at Heathrow check-in, and which is probably her most cherished possession, apart from me.

A very polite and therefore appropriately gloomy chap in an official uniform came up and said, with great clarity and force, as if they were the only words of English he knew, 'Is finished the baggid. No more. Is happen often in BA! Go there!' and pointed us to the counter which dealt with lost luggage. We went there, and engaged in a miserable jostling and hustling to get to the head of the queue – the trouble was that there were several attendants behind the counter, several queues, therefore several choices. When we joined a queue the one beside it shortened dramatically, but when we shifted across to join it several people came out of nowhere discernible and added themselves to the front, then when we turned back to our original queue a couple of couples had got into our previous places, so by the time we reached a very pleasant young woman with fetchingly sympathetic eyes and fluent English, had filled out forms etc., given our address and mobile numbers, we were the last at the counter, the last off the plane, so to speak, and over two hours late.

The driver who met us was Soros, the charming but ill-fated driver who picked us up last year, and was arrested twice in the half-hour trip from the airport to Piraeus. This time we had a four-hour drive ahead of us, so the opportunity for calamity was increased eightfold. There was only one calamity, though, and it was me, my stomach, swollen and inflamed by BA's incompetence.

Sometimes it's as if my bowels are carrying a weight of guilt – load of guilt – I can't work it out. Try again. A moral man's

conscience must feel like this, heavy with undischarged guilt –
enough. Leave it alone. Let's just say that it heaved and groaned
through the darkness, around the hairpin bends, up and down the
mountains. I sat at times almost bent double with the pain, the
dread. Whenever we passed a remote outpost, a taverna or a garage,
I wanted to cry out, 'Stop! Here there must be a lavatory! Stop, I
say!' but I didn't cry out because Soros wouldn't have understood,
as he has no English at all, relying on a natural sympathy to
interpret our wishes, and very few people are in sympathy with
other people's bowels and bladders. And I was too shy to find an
alternative means of communicating, for example tapping him on
the shoulder and miming. What would I have mimed? I could have
asked Victoria, who knows a little Greek, but I thought that would
be unfair. I don't understand it at all, really, why I should revert to
childhood timidity on such a matter when I pride myself on my
forthrightness in most of my life-dealings.

So on and on and on and on through the darkness except for one
stop at a large bar in a car park, just after we'd got outside Athens,
where I managed a dribbling pee, and then, dare-devil that I am,
poured a Diet Coke and a large espresso diluted by hot water into
a bladder that already felt more like a boil. Then on and on and on
and on through the darkness. At one point I asked Victoria how
much longer, did she think? She said she thought about half an
hour, and when half an hour later by my bladder I saw a signpost
which said Porto Heli 48km I did actually let out a throbbing kind
of moan that must have made the hair stand on the back of Soros's
neck, but still he drove, steadily, imperturbably, implacably through
the darkness, on and on, on and on, on and on and on. Yes, there
had definitely been car journeys like it in childhood, 'Why didn't
you go before you left?' 'Because I didn't need to go before I left.'
'Well, then, it serves you right, you little fool.' 'But it's not my fault

I didn't want to go.' 'But it happens every time, every time!' 'But I can't help it!' 'Well, try and hold on a bit longer, just a bit longer, there's a good boy!' 'How long, how much longer!?' I yearned for a conversation like that, one in which the responsibility was shared with an impatient but loving adult who knew everything worth knowing about all one's physical states, and was sure to get you to where you needed to go in good time, if only just in time, which was the best time of all.

We got to Porto Heli at about 11 p.m., and as is the body's way it immediately ceased making its demands. Relaxed and easy, I lounged casually on the quay, one arm supporting itself on the roof of the car, the other wrapped around the wife's waist, the bowels and bladder lapsed into genial passivity, all of me in harmony with the smooth, unruffled sea as I played out the familiar and comfortable role of your run-of-the mill BA passenger, angry, contemptuous, despairing, etc., no hint in the voice and gestures of the recent physical agonies that could also, of course, be attributed to BA.

And so we crossed the sea to Spetses, where Alex was waiting for us with her motorized tricycle, which had a small cart attached for our bags, and within five minutes we were at the house. I am now in its garden, writing these last words before I go to bed.

PETALS, MICE, CATS

Again in the garden and again at night, our second night in Spetses. I'd planned to read the third volume of Mahfouz's Cairo trilogy, but can't because there's nowhere in this maddeningly disagreeable house with enough light to read by. In fact there's not really enough light to read by during the daytime either. It is a large garden full of nooks and crannies, with chairs and tables in them, but wherever you sit the foliage is so thick around you and over your head that the light scarcely gets through – and though you're sitting in shade it doesn't feel like shade, in the sense of being protected from the sun, because the atmosphere is heavy and fetid and gives you a headache which is intensified by the strain on your eyes as you struggle to make out the print. I like Mahfouz's trilogy too much to attempt it in these conditions, so there it is, the third volume, marked at page 6, probably to be so marked until we're on the plane home.

This horrible house is entirely my own fault. Last year we had a house high up on the hillside, overlooking the sea. It was a lovely thing at night to sit at the long table on the terrace and gaze down at the bright specks of sea-taxis zipping across the darkness, seemingly so haphazard in movement, but full of purpose – I remember sitting at that table in a white plastic chair, looking out and writing the scene down – but the steps up to the house from the side of the beach were so steep and rough-hewn that it was a real labour to make it to the top, my heart would be pounding, my face covered in sweat, my breathing short and raspy, I had to take short breaks with a cigarette to recover myself, then onwards, upwards, almost collapsing when I got to the door. That was the part I most remembered when we thought about where to stay when we decided to come back for a fortnight this year. I remembered the steps and the exhaustion, not the terrace and looking down at the cool blue sea in daytime, the speeding, winking boats at night, which is why I am crouched in the fetid and oppressive darkness of the courtyard outside our bedroom, scribbling this down with my right hand while with my left, which should be holding a cigarette, I scratch at my ankles, bitten every few seconds by midges, mosquitoes, etc., interrupting myself only to stare at the wild cats that peer back at me through the foliage or leap down from the roof or the wall and arch their backs and spit hissingly at me. Of course the other house had cats too. A mother, two adolescent sons, and three kittens, they were dark ginger and white, with small, alert, intelligent heads on long necks, with long, thin bodies and long, prancing legs. They were exceptionally agile, high jumpers, sometimes leaping through the kitchen window, and sometimes through the living-room window, and one of them or even some of them came in one day and crapped all over the sofa, but there was no doubting their pedigree. They were royalty. While these cats, these cats are like rats, at least I respond to them as if they were rats, and believe I would actually kick at one if it came near me, which would be most unfair as their behaviour is scarcely their fault. The people of Spetses have a history of dealing badly with cats, and one year wiped them all out by poisoning, clubbing, drowning them, then were astonished to find the island overrun by rats. They had to bring cats back. But I suppose the distinction between cat and rat is now a fine one in Spetses. The inhabitants would treat the cats like rats if there were no rats, and perhaps many of the cats behave accordingly.

A lost bag gets more and more lost as one tells off the contents – Victoria's Filofax, my sponge bag containing the only nail clippers, all my summer shirts, my iPod – my seven pairs of espadrilles, why did I pack them all, I thought, even as I put them in, you can't possibly need seven pairs of espadrilles, and then I thought, but they're new, you haven't tried them on, perhaps only two or three pairs will fit, besides it's not BA's business how many pairs of espadrilles you take, your taking a surplus doesn't entitle them to confiscate them, and on top of it all, all my medication, again why did you have to bring six weeks' supply when you're only planning to be away for two weeks, again I cannot answer the question except to say that it's easier to pour the whole lot into a carrier bag and stuff it in your suitcase than to count the requisite number of pills, furthermore I must have thought it's better to be safe than sorry – hah! – but you're travelling BA should have been my next thought, BA may or may not make you safe, they'll almost certainly make you sorry – now there'll be days or anyway hours of endless phone calls, visits to Spetses chemists, how long can I survive on one pair of trousers, two shirts, one pair of espadrilles –

I have just finished the third volume of the Cairo trilogy under the glare of a lamp I've rigged up in an overhanging bush. A light wind has shaken petals off the bush. I've no idea what the flower is. I'll ask Victoria in the morning. They're very big petals and they're scampering about like mice under the table I'm writing on – I keep catching them out of the corner of my eye, the petals and their shadow, and though I know them for what they are, and therefore know that they're not mice, my feet twitch nervously every time a petal brushes against them, but even if my feet think the petals are mice, what are they afraid of? Mice don't bite, do they? No, but they scamper up your trouser leg if frightened, will you be able to assure your trouser leg that it's a petal and not a mouse, which anyway wouldn't bite you? But if the petal got to your crotch, would it find teeth and sink them into you? There's no doubt that I'm quite spooked out here at 4 a.m., now a few minutes past 4 a.m., out here in this dank, unwholesome night air, compressed almost into the bush from the branches of which sharp-toothed petals are tumbling, tumbling –

It's time I went to bed, but I'm afraid that the damp has got into the wiring of my lamp, and that when I switch it off I'll electrocute myself. On the other hand if I don't switch it off, what then? But I can't bear to think of it glaring on into the dawn, though in this garden it would be a dark dawn – I really hate it here, on the other hand, again on the other hand, I'm glad I've read Mahfouz – almost all the first volume, and sections of the two other volumes, have the transparency of a great novel, you seem to go straight into the characters without being conscious of the words that take you there – and this in translation, as with Tolstoy – and you feel the alien world of Cairo during the First World War becoming utterly familiar to you, habits and customs that would be disgusting when reported to you out of the context he creates come to seem quite natural, so that one accepts, for instance, the prosperous merchant's attitude towards his wife and daughters even when shocked by it. He's a wonderfully sympathetic creature, this merchant, majestic, epicene, wise, intolerant, devout, unfaithful. When he behaves badly, which he does quite often, we find ourselves wishing quite simply that he wouldn't, as we do with our friends, the close ones that we can't allow other people to judge, and when we judge them ourselves it's with the proviso that the judgement should carry no penalties. Very few novelists can do this, it seems to me, make us make close friends with characters we wouldn't hope, or even want, to understand if we came across them outside the novel. Mahfouz brings comfort – for which my gratitude and blessings here in this uncomfortable garden, with dawn possibly approaching above the incarcerating foliage, how would I know? – bed, bed, bed, bed, bed with you.

LOST IN TRAFFIC

It's five in the afternoon. See that half-naked elderly man sitting in the outside bar of the Klimis hotel. He's half naked because he has taken off his sopping shirt and hung it over the top of his basket, which contains a wet towel, wet swimming trunks, two packets of purple Silk Cut, a mobile phone, some money in a strange woollen wallet (local produce) that he purchased this morning, and also in this wallet are his false teeth. The swimming trunks he is wearing are cold and damp, as is his stomach, which hangs down over the top of his trunks. His sodden espadrilles are on the floor beside his feet. He is smoking, sipping coffee, spooning down lumps of chocolate cake – altogether a poignant and grotesque spectacle to both tourists and people indigenous to the island, they avert their eyes from him as they pass by, as did the slovenly young waiter who served him. He is in this condition because he has just returned in a small sea-taxi from Zogheria, his favourite beach in the whole world – about halfway back the seas became tumultuous, pitching the little taxi up and down, sheets of spray slapping over the body, face and hair of the elderly man who likes to sit outside the cabin, on a bench beside the one-eyed helmsman, Michaelis, rather than inside the cabin with Victoria, his silly little goose of a wife, who prefers to be warm, safe and dry – he was smoking, of course, as the first large wave rose up against him, pasting his cigarette across his lips and almost washing it down his throat before he managed to gag it back into the water – when they were about five minutes from port a voice blared urgently out at Michaelis from his radio, and he swung the boat around in an arc, heading back to Zogheria, or so the elderly man thought, but then Michaelis bounced over some particularly high waves to a cement promontory on which a cluster of people were failing to get into a sea-taxi, which was listing sideways and clearly had something wrong with it – Michaelis swerved towards them, lined his boat up, helped aboard a group of four, led by a fat and furry young man in bathing trunks and sandals, with inward-slanting teeth and enormous glasses – the elderly man rose with his customary courtesy from his bench to let the group pass easily into the cabin, whereupon the furry young man sat down in the elderly man's place, leaving the elderly man the bench on the windward side it might be called nautically, anyway the side facing the open sea, which lashed furiously at him, sending its spray into his face and over his shirt as the boat rocked unsteadily off towards the harbour –

So now, safe on land, he sits, dilapidated, looking washed up and out, gobbling down the cake for the sugar to restore his strength, gulping down black coffee and cigarette smoke to restore his nerves, waiting for his wife Victoria to return from the shops with fresh fruit, yogurt and honey for tomorrow's breakfast. The waiter is pulling down sheets of plastic to protect the café from the waves that are beginning to come up over the seawall and are rushing across the pavement. The wind is strong, it's quite cold now, but the sun is shining, here comes his wife Victoria, holding three heavy plastic shopping bags, and really it was a marvellous afternoon in Zogheria, the water calm there, glowing in the sun, the taverna and the family just as when last seen – so the old guy, cold and wet, victim of a callous man in furry skin with inward-sloping teeth, can still consider himself among the blessed.

Sitting in the *amaxi*, the horse cantering along, the carriage rocking and swinging, my arm around Victoria, I had the feeling I've had so often in Spetses, of regality and freedom, jaunty, debonair, my straw hat in my hand, when suddenly, and quite unaccountably, the memory of the dead from all the summers here – Piers. Alan. Roger. Peter Payne. Roxannie. Joanna.

I've become frightened of almost everything on this small island where I am used to being at my ease. At night enormous motorbikes roar up and down the narrow alleys, driven by extra-large young men with boisterous thighs – they seem Brobdingnagian, and I, shredded by nervousness, a Gulliver, no, a Lilliputian – when I hear a motorbike's noise from afar, or from a distant alley, I jump and clutch at Victoria's arm, but if it actually appears in the alley we're walking down, coming at us from behind or its headlights like golden fists as it bears down at us, it being a combination of the large man on the large machine, with a bundle behind him that usually turns out to be a girl, her slim legs raised, with her knees clamped against his hips, her arms wrapped around the monster's usually enormous stomach. Likely as not he's bald-headed, he wears a black string vest and trunks but never a crash helmet. I assume there is no law forcing him to, so I ask myself – so careless of his own life, how can he be careful of ours?

This morning along the front rode a paterfamilias on a motor-bike at a terrific speed, on his handlebars a child, on his lap another child, on his pillion a woman with a child in her lap –

ILLUMINATIONS

Just back from dinner at the house of a friend of Alex, on a large terrace overlooking the sea. We had a magnificent view of the annual pageant, in which is re-enacted the destruction of a Turkish warship by a host of locals in their fishing boats. The Turkish boat is dragged into the middle of the harbour and the small boats encircle it, setting light to it. As it bursts into flames fireworks go off in the harbour, magnificent explosions of colour that hang in the air then fade down, then more magnificent explosions, plumes, haloes, stars, dragons of lights. As we were watching this, at about midnight, awe-struck and exclaiming, Victoria's mobile rang. Andie from BA to say that our bags had been found and would be in Spetses at midday tomorrow – so, with all that splendour in the sky, we felt a rush of gratitude, love in fact, for good old BA, dear old BA, who had got our bags back from themselves and were returning them to us. I'd be getting my toenail clippers back, the only clippers

I've ever had that worked on my fingernails. Something exotic in purple, orange and green flowered above us, and down in the harbour everybody suddenly burst out singing, and we were filled with such delight –

In previous Spetses summers, when the water was warmer or the body-heat younger, we would swim for hours off Zogheria – well, two, sometimes three hours, out across the small bay to the line of rocks that runs beneath the pine wood, then swim around the point into the large bay where lay the water-boat, a long, broken-backed half-sunk vessel, painted grey-green, like a battleship – we would swim past it, it wasn't really swimming it was a kind of strolling on our sides or on our backs through water that was so soft and velvety and warm. We would swim to the end of the bay, roll around, and swim back, sometimes stopping at a small cove with a church above it, climb up to the church and walk back through the pines to the taverna, or we would swim back to our beach. There seemed no difference in temperature when in the water and when out of it, almost no change in our sense of the elements. But now – now the water isn't cold precisely, but it has a cold edge to it.

This evening, after it had stopped raining, we went down to the harbour and took an *amaxi* to Nata's for dinner. I used to love riding in an *amaxi* – the wonderful strength and agility of the horses pulling us along, the clip-clop of their hooves, the regal swing of the carriage – in early years in Spetses, when I had a very bad back and walked with a stick, I took them extravagantly – I would doff my straw hat to familiar and even unfamiliar faces in way of celebration as I bounced and swayed, clip-clop, clop clop clop, on the road that runs along the sea's edge, the roguish majesty of it. But this evening when we set out and surged through the streets all I could think about was the motorbikes, the Vespas, the motorized tricycles accelerating around us to pass us or coming straight at us with a last-second swerve. How could the horse, a lovely white creature with a high head and a swinging mane, but all flesh and blood, sinews, nerves, muscles, sensitivity – how could it bear the noise, the brightness, the constant relentless assault, the threat. There was a moment when a furious and enormous motorbike came straight at us, then bullied past us on one side, while a Vespa with two middle-aged men overtook us on the other side. Our driver paid no attention, sitting slouched with his whip resting above his horse, which trotted steadily on, clip-clop, clop clop, head held high, mane swinging, but I became frightened – pathetic, I thought – but when the horse slipped and buckled at the knees and the carriage dipped, I gripped Victoria's knee and shrank in terror, and I didn't think my reaction was at all pathetic, it seemed to be the most natural reaction in the world – the three humans thrown on to the cobbles, the horse rearing and shying, the wheels running over us as the hooves came down on our heads, faces, our lives ended in the cold damp of this September evening in Spetses –

It was warm in Nata's dining room and I felt ill. I went out on to the terrace, sat with my feet against the low wall and listened to their voices, Victoria's mingling in the laughter, and I worried about my future, would my currently shaky limbs be strong enough to carry me into it, would I be continent when I got there – home? home? where is home? and went quite blank, as if the metaphorical and rhetorical question had become a particular one, and I didn't know where my home was for that night, where I was to lay my head. Victoria came out and smiled down at me, so there I could see quite clearly where I would be laying my head that night, and for all the nights of my life to come, I hoped. She led me home, a slow journey through the dark, as we went down passages too narrow for motorbikes.

I PRACTISE MY PROFESSION

I keep failing to mention the bulletins I receive by email every night from New York, sent after the rehearsals of *Butley*, and signed by one Michael McGoff, the stage manager. We receive them on a kind of combined computer-mobile phone sort of device, called a BlackBerry, that somehow collects all the emails sent to both Victoria and myself in London, and to which, on this same BlackBerry, we reply – at least Victoria does, as I can't really manage the keyboard, it is too cramped and fiddly for my fingers, which are not contorted by arthritis, as they might well be at my age, but are so plump – overweight, really – from under-use and from lack of exercise that when I try to pick out the letters I invariably hit two or three of them at the same time. So now every night before Victoria goes to bed, we have a little session – it's become a ritual, really – in the garden or in the bedroom, depending on the weather. I light a cigarette and sit comfortably, a glass of Diet Coke in my hand, while she summons up the day's emails and reads out those addressed to me, and some of those addressed to her.

Sometimes I have to reply, and I admit I rather enjoy the lordliness of it, dictating a few sentences as if she were my secretary – it makes me feel as if I'm on a yacht, for some reason – I suppose from scenes in films, a fat elderly man, generally a mobster, reclines on the deck of a yacht anchored off Cuba. He has a cigar in his mouth, there are two or three of his lieutenants, minor hoods who are usually wearing suits – he of course is wearing swimming trunks and a cap and between his legs there is a fishing rod, its line going over the stern, so he has half an eye out for the swirl of a fin, a big fish, a tuna, and half an eye on the girl in a bikini, who has a notepad on her knee – I'm not sure I've ever seen a film with that exact scene in it, and now, when I try to visualize it, the man I see is familiar, not a mobster, and not at all like myself – he is burly with a lot of thick grey hair on his chest, he has the cigar but it's clamped between his jaws, which are stretched in a grin, he has a grey beard, a square, bullish face, something stupid about it, and aggressive, and his posture is also aggressive, he is standing with his legs apart and the hint of sucked-in bloat about the stomach, and the fishing rod held out as if it were a weapon – the memory of this image, which I know I have seen in newspapers or books, is somehow distressing. I think it's because I think it's phoney in some way. Who is it, who is it? Someone famous. A film star, probably. Clark Gable? Who ever talks about Clark Gable these days?

Well, back to the BlackBerry, and opening and answering emails from Michael McGoff, the stage manager of *Butley*. Usually I enjoy his emails, they invariably contain titbits of interesting information – for example, a week or so ago we learnt that one of the actors wanted to wear the shoes that he or she – I'm not specifying the sex of the actor, as I want to conceal his or her identity – on the other hand I don't want to write he or she, his or hers every time I mention him or her by pronoun, so from now on I shall write she and her on the strict understanding that I might really mean he and his – anyway she wanted to wear in rehearsal the shoes that she'd be wearing in performance, to give her feet a chance to get used to them – she has awkward feet, apparently, and wanted to be sure that she would be able to move easily about the stage when it mattered i.e. in front of a paying audience – so for the following couple of nights Michael McGoff would include in his bulletins a sub-bulletin on how the actor was getting on with his shoes, which had been specially, and at great expense, made for him. It was quickly apparent that these specially made and expensive shoes were causing her a lot of pain, and having a crippling effect on her acting, would have to be dumped, and a new pair cobbled – and then came the news that she was going back to her own, old shoes, the shoes that he'd been wearing in the first days of rehearsal, he would continue wearing them through rehearsals, and then wear them in performance. Then the day before yesterday came a brief sentence to the effect that the management had negotiated a weekly rate for the rental of her shoes in performance – so the management will be paying him for wearing her own shoes, which would certainly turn out to be far more expensive than buying him custom-made shoes – which, of course, the management has already done, and discarded. Now what, I wonder, has happened to those shoes? On whose feet will they end up? Would they fit me if they are a man's, or Victoria, if they are a wife's?

Hemingway! The man with the beard, the cigar, the stupid grin and the belly, fishing on a boat off Cuba for tuna is Ernest Hemingway! And that's who I reminded myself of when I was dictating to Victoria on her BlackBerry. Odd, because I don't think I have anything at all in common with him, not even the belly – his thrusts, mine droops.

Well, as I've said, when the emails are a stage manager's reports about an actor making money out of the use of her own shoes, that sort of thing, they're amusing, and also make me feel that I'm a part of what's going on over there, in New York, that I'm valued, in other words, and important, but don't actually have to do anything – what could be nicer for a man on holiday? But the last few nights the emails have become slightly ominous, furthermore they're not general rehearsal reports, they're addressed specifically to me. One of the actors, the young actor playing the part of Gardner, who has a single scene at the very end of the play, which makes it an important scene, is having trouble mastering an English accent, is there any chance, the slightest chance, that I can figure out a way to help him? In the latest email Michael McGoff says that Nicholas Martin, the director, will be phoning me to discuss this problem further.

I TELL MY WIFE TO RUN ALONG

The director, Nicholas Martin, phoned this afternoon our time, early morning his time, to discuss the problem and to propose a solution, which he said was simplicity itself. That we, or rather I, should rewrite the scene, turning Gardner from an English undergraduate into an American exchange student. In fact, we could make Gardner come from anywhere in the States that suited us, we could give him any accent we liked, including the accent that he actually has – Midwestern, I think Nicholas Martin said – if we made him an exchange student. The actor playing Gardner – let me call him Eric – Eric is a really gifted and charming young actor, Nicholas Martin said, who has a touch of 'something special' about him, he was sure I would see the point of casting him when I met him and saw him in action, it was just that when I heard him I would also see the point of the phone call, the English dialect coach had worked really hard with him, in every rehearsal he'd shown a marked improvement, but not marked enough to make him convincing and – and – and well, he, Nicholas Martin, and our leading actor, Nathan Lane, and all the rest of the company along with the producers, and no doubt the stage management and the man on the street, were deeply fond of this delightful and – and – to cut it short, nobody could bear the thought of having to let him go, he was sure I would understand.

I did understand, I said, I really did, but I also really didn't think rewriting the scene, which had been written almost forty years ago and not been tampered with since, would come easily to me. I wasn't the same chap that had written the play. Nowadays I saw myself more as the chap who collected and spent the royalties on behalf of that other, almost forty years ago chap who'd written the play. I did actually say all this, in an even more roundabout way, because I was wondering if I had it in me to say what I suspected I really needed to say, which was: 'No, no, on no account will I tamper with this venerable old scene! Fire the delightful young actor from the Midwest now! Recast the part and have done with it – the longer you leave it etc. etc. – and above all, please, please have it done with before I come over there, so I won't have to have anything to do with it!' That's really what I needed to say, complete with exclamation marks!! What I said instead was, yes, I said, yes of course I'll have a go at rewriting, couldn't bear to think of the alternative, of course I couldn't, why the very idea of replacing this fine young man who was so very, very talented, Good God, of course we mustn't etc. – He thanked me profusely on behalf of everybody, including the stage management, man on the street etc. – and we hung up in a salvo of loving farewells, speak soons etc. – The thing is I like Nicholas Martin very much, and think he did a very good job on *Butley* in Boston three years ago, and have every confidence in him, his judgement on such matters, but –

I gave Victoria the gist of the conversation, rather grimly, I expect, said the least I could do was to have a crack at it, and then realized I didn't have a copy of the play with me, and couldn't possibly remember the scene apart from the central fact of it, which is that Butley, who is a self-destructive lecturer in English Literature, hands Gardner T. S. Eliot's *Four Quartets*, and asks him to read out loud a passage from the second quartet, *East Coker*, the passage that begins – 'In that open field/ If you do not come too close, if you do not come too close,/ On a summer midnight, you can hear the music/ Of the weak pipe and the little drum' – one of my favourite passages in the whole of English poetry. I hope, I said to Victoria, that I wasn't expected to translate this passage into an American accent, and I suddenly became very indignant and quite noisy at having agreed to tamper with the scene, a scene that had always worked very well, it was a shocking suggestion, unprofessional, why had I let him talk me into it? Why had I given in and agreed? – on I went, and on a bit, with shameful phrases like 'bloody Americans' thrown in – though of course, now I come to think of it, Eliot was an American until he got himself naturalized – and though I can't remember whether he was legally American or legally English when he wrote *Four Quartets*, I don't believe it matters whether it's read in an English or an American accent as long as it's read with understanding and feeling, and as they insist that Eric is a fine young actor I'm sure he'll find the understanding and feeling for the poetry if he's allowed to do it American – so all I have to do is to get them to send over the dialogue, the very little dialogue before and after the passage from *East Coker*, change a few words in his lines so that they sound American – so what was I making all the fuss about? Why all those dark feelings and indignation about the venerable old scene, I won't be compromising the venerable old scene here, certainly not sufficiently to justify all the fuss and nonsense – is it a symptom of the ageing process, or have I always made this sort of fuss and nonsense over this sort of thing?

I got Victoria to BlackBerry the stage manager, Michael McGoff, requesting that he email the scene over, not omitting the passage from *East Coker*, as I haven't brought *Four Quartets* with me, in fact the only poetry I've brought to Spetses is some Wyatt and some Coleridge, how stupid not to bring a decent anthology. As soon as the scene arrives I'll get to work, if altering a few words can be called work.

Victoria is out in the town, doing some essential shopping – fruit, cold ham, bread and most importantly, bars of chocolate to help me through my addiction, spasms that start at two in the morning, that I defy until about 2.30, and then defeat by cramming bar after bar in my mouth until about 2.45, when I sit slumped, satiated, bloated, here, where I'm sitting now, except it will be in the moonlight, what there is of it when filtered through the heavy foliage, as opposed to the feeble twilight, what there is of it now, as filtered through the heavy foliage dripping with dew. But by then, by cramps-in-the-stomach chocolate time, I hope I will have completed my task of Americanizing the young English character Gardner for the sake of the young American actor whose name I keep forgetting, oh yes, I decided to call him Eric, after little by little – it has turned out to be a more complicated business than I imagined, not simply a matter of Americanizing a few words and phrases. I did that in five minutes flat, in fact before Victoria went out to shop, in fact she was heading towards the gate with her basket on her arm, wearing her straw hat aslant over one eye and her gypsy smile, as if eager for an expedition into the heart of Spetses town at its most bustly period, and I was just about to say, 'Hey wait a minute! Why don't you BlackBerry this off to New York before you go?' In fact I got the first bit out, 'Hey, wait a minute' – so that she turned, her hand on the gate latch, and she smiled and waited, reminding me of Eliot's 'La Figlia che Piange' – 'so I would have had her turn and smile', no, that's not the line, I always mess the line up when I try to remember it, anyway I was looking at her standing at the gate, and misremembering the line from 'La Figlia che Piange' when the thought struck me, sometimes thoughts do actually seem to strike one like a fist, thwack! In the middle of the brain's solar plexus. 'No, no,' I said. 'It's all right,' I said. 'You run along!'

'Run along?' she said.

So we had a brief conversation about what I meant by telling her to 'run along', and off she went, with the high, prancing gait of a fiery steed just untethered – actually she just walked with her usual grace around the gate, her hat atilt, and out of sight – leaving me to deal with the thought that struck me right in the middle of the brain's solar plexus – that Gardner is talked about by other characters regularly throughout the play, and now that I'd Americanized him he'd have to be talked about quite differently – not as a bolshie, troublemaking English undergraduate, but as a bolshie, troublemaking American exchange student, which, at London University in 1970, when American exchange students were famously humble and shy (i.e. educationally retarded) was almost a contradiction in terms, and would certainly require from the playwright a modicum of explanation. In other words I couldn't just have him come on at the end and be American, I had to have him American before he comes on, when first referred to, and have his American-ness alive whenever he is discussed, which will involve backtracking through the whole play.

The whole bloody play was there this morning when Victoria checked, it was actually there, in the BlackBerry, not just the scene I asked for, but the whole bloody play, in microscopic print. For some reason – oh yes, the computer was down in the rehearsal room, the stage manager, McGoff, had had to phone the producer's office and have them do the scan and email and all that stuff, and it had been impossible – here's where we get to the 'for some reason' – a technological reason, I assume, but it might have been a human one, laziness, inattention or malice perhaps, it had been impossible to scan and email just the relevant passage, they'd had to send the whole bloody play, and in almost invisible writing – Victoria set to work reading the instructions for the BlackBerry and fiddling with the keyboard and finally succeeded – she has some of the magical powers I associate with the older woman, though in reality, in years as well as in other ways that really count, she's much younger than me – she succeeded so brilliantly that she initially over-magnified, instead of having several microscopic unreadable pages, we had half a word – three or four gigantic letters filling the screen – so more fiddling, peering, fiddling, until finally the whole play became readable, but only at four or so lines on the screen at a time, she couldn't get it any smaller without reducing it back to microscopic.

It was an interminable business, scrolling backwards and forwards three or four lines at a time to find the places where Gardner was referred to, but not as interminable as trying to think of new lines for the other characters, because of course – something else I hadn't anticipated but should have – new lines demanded different responses, and so whole patches of dialogue, even though quite short, had to be changed, and this in its turn had a knock-on, and sometimes knock-backward, effect – a changed small patch of dialogue in a scene in the middle of the play involved looking again at, and slightly changing, a small patch at the beginning of the play, and that, when slightly changed, made me look again at the small patch in the middle and change it slightly, and then to a small patch towards the end of the play, just before Gardner enters, and a slight change there. So back and forth, forth and back I went, until I began to fear that at any moment I would start in on other, unrelated scenes, and in no time I'd be performing major and almost certainly life-threatening surgery on this venerable old play that had been resting neglected in attics and basements for nigh on forty years, and resting quietly in my writer's soul for nigh on forty-two years. I've done such stupid things before, rewritten old plays until they become not-quite new ones, sort of Frankenstein mutants really, that are unproduceable in themselves because they're reminiscent of the play that they're derived from, and also prevent the revival of the play they're derived from because producers read one and then the other and think about them in relation to each other until they're not sure which characters belong in which play and so move on to a play with no siblings or half-siblings and not written by me – I believe that Michelangelo had the same problem, or was it Leonardo? Whichever it was, it is generally now considered to be the consequence of his botched sexuality, or his anal retentiveness, anyway something like that, which prevented him from letting go, never considering a piece finished and done with and so forth – I also share the problem with many lesser figures, I suspect axe murderers might suffer from a version of it, the swing of the axe being the desperate, but deeply satisfying last step in letting go, or making let go. Simon Gray, Axe Murderer, has a convincing ring to it, as a potential headline, though probably of a small item on an inner page. I've often, when trapped in the mire of writing a play, with drafts on drafts half done or phonily completed and totally hopeless therefore, longed to murder myself, and violently, but I don't see how one could do it with an axe, how get the leverage and balance required to swing the heavy blade in on oneself – except for the crotch, that would be the only easy target area – no, I've just tried it, stood with my legs apart and head down like a golfer, then swung a phantom axe upwards, and it turns out that the easiest slice would be right between the buttocks, and how would one guarantee that it would be fatal, and how attempt to explain it if one survived it? One would end up not in a headline but in one of those can-you-believe-it columns that report real-life misadventures, like the cross-dressing burglar who couldn't shed the high-heeled boots while fleeing from the police, he was also impeded by the tight skirt and constricting undergarments, or the flasher who stepped out of a dark doorway and found himself pointing his penis at his female boss – he subsequently claimed that he was tendering his resignation by cocking a snoot, or perhaps snooting his cock at her – you can follow him into the future with your imagination, the sex offenders' register, unemployment, alcoholism, homelessness, or of course rehab on television, acclaim and a fortune to waste –

You can never tell whether these stories are true, or whether someone like me is making them up, as a way of avoiding the issue, which for me, this evening, in an insalubrious garden in Spetses, is the suspicion that I have probably messed up my play by Americanizing one of the characters in it, and all to save the job of Eric, which isn't even the real name of a young actor I've never met, and am already hoping I shall never have to meet, or if I do meet him, it will be as a perfectly acceptable English undergraduate, circa 1970 – him, I mean, not me – how treacherous grammar is, if you don't keep an eye on it. But where is Victoria, is the question? Where is my wife, is the big question? She's been gone for hours, it seems to me – where is she?

She is lying on the bed, reading. I went in on the off chance, and there she was, looking surprised to see me looking surprised, she came back some time ago, didn't I remember, we'd had a brief conversation about where we'd go for dinner, surely I remembered? I said I did, now that she'd reminded me, but the truth is I didn't remember, I have no idea where we're going for dinner, but when we come back I shall have her BlackBerry the new lines to New York, about twenty of them there must be, and only a few of them spoken by Eric (Gardner), the rest spoken by the other characters about him.

A RASPBERRY ON A BLACKBERRY

We had dinner in the old port. The restaurant is set on a concrete and narrow promontory that stretches out to sea – we had a table at the end, there was a high wind and – actually I don't really want to go into it much, the food and the service, because it's owned by a good friend, he's been kind to us over the years, taking me up to and from his restaurant on the back of his motorbike when I had a bad back and could scarcely walk ten yards without having to sit – this was about fifteen years ago, when he had a different restaurant, up in the hills. He's much younger than me, shares a birthday with Victoria in fact, and looks like Yves Montand, some years like a rather fleshy Yves Montand, other years like a rather lean Yves Montand. He has a very troubled relationship with women, especially Scandinavians, who find him immensely attractive – they're always very attractive themselves, and intelligent, and well educated, and sophisticated – they are all these things to a slightly higher degree – honesty compels me to say it – than he is, but they are also doting and motherly and want to look after him and settle down with him, yes, willing to give up good jobs as teachers or solicitors back in Copenhagen or Oslo, and settle down with him in Spetses, help him run his restaurant and no doubt bear his children, and then they're gone, and when we ask him, let's call him Luka – he speaks very good English, by the way, as do his girlfriends, they speak to him in English – hey, Luka, we say, where

is Ingrid? although by now we know the answer – and he smiles
sheepishly but radiantly, it's actually a rather boastful smile, and he
spreads his hands and says that it's very sad, she wanted more than
he could give, he is very sorry, he misses her – but now there is
another girl, she comes from Norway, he met her while holidaying
in Rome at Christmas, she's arriving next week, he's looking forward
to showing her to us, she's very, very nice – but really his tone is
much the same when a new girlfriend is about to arrive as when an
old one has just left, already rueful and regretful, with a sparkle in
the eye that could be a kind of contempt, when you review his
history – Odd how I don't mind writing all this down about Luka,
but wouldn't dream of writing down what I think about the food
and the service in his restaurant, because I would feel disloyal,
although I suppose I've just done that, too, at least by inference.

As soon as we were back from dinner we set about BlackBerrying,
but there was simply too much, far too much, for Victoria to tap out,
especially as there were little bits of stage direction that had also
occurred to me when rewriting and adding the dialogue, so finally I
waited until 3 a.m. our time, and did it the old-fashioned way, by
telephone. Thank God I had the sense, for once, to get Nicholas
Martin to phone me straight back, so that the producers will have to
pay for the call – the Spetses–New York rates are very high, our friends
here tell us. It took me an hour or so to dictate the twenty or so new
lines that I had made up in the complicated process of Americanizing
Gardner as played by Eric. Nicholas Martin was excited, above all
relieved. He said he was convinced that it would work out very well.
I said I was worried that the other actors might not like having their
lines changed, and he agreed that there might be a little trouble there,
but on the whole everybody was so keen not to damage this young
man at so early a stage in his career, they were determined that he
should keep the part – and that spoke eloquently for the company

spirit, did it not? I said yes, I supposed it did. We ended in a burst of anecdotes, gossip and laughter, and finally on the goodbyes appropriate to each other's different time zones, I wishing him a good morning's work, he wishing me a good night's sleep. But I'm too restless to go to bed tonight, the conversation with Nicholas Martin, hearing his voice, has made the whole prospect of going to New York likely and I wish it weren't. I wish we were going from Spetses to our cottage in Suffolk for our usual few weeks instead of just a few days. A few days in Suffolk, a few days in London, then to New York for five weeks. Five weeks in New York. Christ!

This is the next morning, and on the BlackBerry there is a message from Michael McGoff, on behalf of all the actors as well as from the stage management and the man in the street, thanking me for my prompt and helpful response to a young colleague in distress. However, the new lines I'd provided for the Americanizing of Gardner had seemed to threaten and confuse Eric, furthermore the new lines for the other actors really rather – I forget what word he used for what the new lines did to them, but it was something like 'irritate' – anyway a word with that sort of feel to it – and they didn't think they should spend rehearsal time on unlearning lines that had seemed to work perfectly well, in order to learn lines that came strangely off the tongue and didn't seem to make much sense – those weren't his precise words, but that was his gist. Well, yes, I said to Victoria, hadn't I said! Hadn't I guessed! Hadn't I known! Yes, she said, you had, and you had, and you had – but here is the odd thing, I felt mortified, yes, really a touch mortified that the lines I'd worked on so hard, and for so many characters, along with my new thinking about stage directions, had been turned down by the actors, rather as if I'd been submitting a new play, and there flashed into my mind the actors' comments as they tried my new lines out – hey, this doesn't work, why does he make me say this, this is crap, crap! and so forth – he, she, all of them, aye, joining in to denounce me for expecting them to work on this crap – no doubt even Eric, who in the manner of actors everywhere, especially insecure ones, would speak from a profound understanding, gained through the strange new mystical attachment he's developed to his character – yes, his would be the loudest, the most dismissive voice – I managed to muffle the throb of shame that went through me, that always accompanies this sort of rebuff, and managed to dictate a reply in which I said I was glad and most relieved to get their message, no good could come of changing lines at this stage of rehearsal, no good could come of firing an actor at this stage of rehearsal either, it would upset the whole company, but now that the whole company – he, she, all of them aye! – knew to what lengths the director and playwright were prepared to go to prevent the dismissal – so please give Gardner, a.k.a. Eric, my best wishes and the best of luck – as Victoria sent this message off, she noticed that she'd earlier failed to notice a PS to the stage manager's last message – that they were happy to let us know that Eric has suddenly taken a massive leap forward in his Englishness, thanks to some further intensive sessions with the dialect coach, he is now quite on top of the poetry – the crisis is over, they looked forward to seeing us in New York. So I can console myself with the thought that if my freshly minted American lines appalled him so much that with the help of his dialect coach he's made a gigantic leap into true Englishness, then what does it matter that I've been wounded in my writer's vanity, all that matters is that rehearsals were back on track, a delightful youth's career has been saved – so we went down to the town beach light of heart, though I scowling slightly.

Home tomorrow and I'm coming to the end of this pad. I won't start a new one, I'll just sit here and smoke. To think that last year

I came to Spetses intending to give up smoking, and here I am, in Spetses almost exactly a year later, still smoking. Well, perhaps next year in Spetses. Or next week in New York. Yes, in New York, where they've banned smoking in bars, restaurants, offices, and no doubt rehearsal rooms, it should be easier, more natural –

BUTLEY – ITS PLACE IN MY FUTURE, ITS PLACE IN MY PAST

In a few hours' time we set off for New York for the first previews, that's its place in my future, my immediate future. Its place in my long-term future, if I have one, will depend on whether it's a success or a failure – the truth is that it's possibly my last chance to make enough money to see me through until – see you through until what? Why, see you through until either you need more money again, or will never again need more money, indeed any money at all. As for the past, the man who once wrote *Butley*, where is he now? Well, he's here, writing this, that's where he is, but if I look back –

Sometimes I see him as if he were framed, like a figure in a composition, a man in his very early thirties, with a round Welsh sort of face, a prominent nose that his mother was always certain he would one day 'grow into', small hazel eyes that look smaller than they actually are because of his over-bushy eyebrows, and a chin that usually had a few small red holes in it, razors then being not what they are now, you had to throw away the blades after at the most five shaves, and some seemed to go blunt as you were shaving with them for the first time. I have no idea what sort of character his face expressed or suggested then, as I have no idea what sort of character my face expresses or suggests now. All I know about my face now is that it's a successful liar because it doesn't announce in any aspect, or when all those aspects are viewed together as one countenance, all the sins of commission and of omission, all the forgetfulnesses, unkindnesses, small acts of deliberate let alone accidental cruelty along with the larger acts of cowardice and evasion that it would have to express or suggest if you could see the soul's history in the face – but it's also an honest face now and therefore most likely was so then, to this limited extent at least, that it's quite obviously not the face of a gentleman in whom you would put an absolute trust – there is a furtiveness to the small hazel eyes, it seems to me, whenever I meet them – or try to meet them in the mirror – yes, that's my point, my eyes can't meet my eyes in the mirror unless I will myself to stare unblinkingly at myself, and even so, however hard I stare, the eyes in the mirror are always edging away from the eyes I'm looking at them with – and there's something not quite *comme il faut* about my hair, it looked unnaturally black and glossy back then, when he shampooed it every other day, and is still as black and as glossy now, when I don't shampoo it at all, and only wash it, or rather let it wash itself, when I swim in the sea – it has been unnaturally natural-looking all my adult life – there's a gesture that I make regularly as I sit here, trundling my pen over the page, that he used to make just as regularly when he worked on his Olympia portable typewriter, clackety-clackety, clackety-clackety, sweeping back with the right hand a lock of hair that flops over the left eye – I imagine him doing it then as I do it now – both of us simultaneously, I trundling, he clacketing – clackety-clackety –

But the important thing for me now, at seventy, peering back to that man in his early thirties, is that the man in his early thirties is pounding, stabbing and beating out on his Olympia portable typewriter the play that is going to take me to New York in a few hours' time. All those hours in that little room – such physical hours, drinking, smoking, pushing the hair back, clackity-clackity, and the then wife – who is now seventy years old – asleep, and the son who was then not yet two years old and is now thirty-nine, thirty-nine years old and – and –

Well. Our beginnings never know our ends, as Butley says once or twice in the play, quoting T. S. Eliot – and it seems to me that it's probably also true that our ends never know our beginnings – well, how can we? As we can never know when our beginnings began. I don't mean just the seminal fuck, which is often the end of something else, a vile row or a stretch of leisurely wooing, or something that neither party remembers happening because it happened when they were both virtually asleep and one rolled into the other for comfort during a bad dream, I mean the years before that, when one thing led to another and conclusions were somehow reached before choices were made, when you became a man in an altered condition as a result of a slip of the tongue, or a moment of inattention. They felt more like lapses than choices – one lapsed into the future as possibly one lapses into infidelity, or into bankruptcy, or into death –

PART SIX

AND THERE WAS TINY TIM AT THE ALCOTT

Today, our first full day in New York, we went for a walk. Our intention was to make it a short one, to get our bearings while buying a couple of cellphones, as they're called over here, because our mobiles, as we call them over there, don't work too well. No, that's not right, they do work perfectly well, but they're enormously expensive because every time I want to phone Victoria, say, when I'm, say, on 45th Street, where the Booth Theatre is, and she's on, say, 63rd Street, where our hotel is, the signal goes all the way from 45th Street to England, bounces itself off some mast or other there back to 63rd Street, in other words crosses the Atlantic twice in order to reach its destination a few blocks away – I'm writing all this down in order to persuade myself that it's true – I know it's true, several people have explained it to me, but I still don't quite believe it. But then I don't believe that mobile phones, cellphones, whichever you choose to call them, actually work. It defies reason and common sense, though obviously not science, just as it defies reason and common sense that if you use a mobile phone rather than a cellphone in New York, it will cost you fifty dollars rather than ten cents to phone somebody almost within shouting distance.

We got our cellphones from a shop where a very understanding and pretty Hispanic girl fixed them so that they would work immediately.

We noticed how Sunday morningish New York seemed, it brought back memories of long-ago Sunday mornings in New York, with the sun shining and everything moving at an idle, easy pace. We were suddenly pleased to be where we were, and felt mildly adventurous. Where we were, by the way, when we were outside the shop, was on 65th and Broadway. 'I know,' I said. 'I know what we'll do, let's go up to the Promenade, and see what's on there.' The Promenade is the theatre that had housed my greatest success in New York, *The Common Pursuit*, which I had directed myself, and then a few years later had housed my biggest flop in New York, *The Holy Terror*, which I'd also directed myself. I suppose I ought to have mixed feeling about it, therefore, but I don't, I've always loved the memory of the Promenade, such a neat, unassuming little off-Broadway theatre – off-Broadway signifying its status, not its location, because actually it's on Broadway, but with 499 seats – one more seat would have made it on Broadway, and everything, including the tickets, would have cost much more.

So we strolled up Broadway to 74th Street, or 75th, anyway whichever street the Promenade is on the corner of, except it isn't any more, it's gone – not yet physically gone but in the process of being transformed, so a notice on the wall told us, into dance studios. What was strange was that though the façade and the architecture haven't yet been destroyed, or even seriously disturbed, the spirit of the building was quite different, it used to have a timid lustre about it, a withdrawn grandeur, it knew its place along the avenue, it was the Promenade, both off Broadway and on it, a theatre the playwright and the actors were proud to be in, the audiences too – but the lobby had no atmosphere, no ghosts, you couldn't imagine the theatre audiences that had once buzzed, buzzed, buzzed about in it, it was seedy and desolate, with small, handwritten notices tacked up on the walls – the sort of place that people went into to get out of the rain for a few minutes, or to do quick deals with packages – Well, no doubt in due course it will be remodelled and reshaped, just right for dancers who lead cheerless and ascetic lives and prefer stark workplaces until the music begins – and one day years from now an elderly couple who used to dance in the studios will stand where Victoria and I stood, and look around in dismay, saying the sort of things that we said – 'How could they have let it—!' and 'But what can have happened—!' It won't occur to them that it had a history before theirs, just as it didn't occur to us that before we knew it the Promenade might have been – what? What could it have been, but the theatre that put on notable triumphs, like *The Common Pursuit*, and notable flops, like *The Holy Terror*.

It was quite a blow, really, quite a blow. You expect things to change all the time, you think you're used to it, you approach every remembered and once-loved building with an almost deliberately cultivated dread, in anticipation that it will have been knocked down or made into something else, but you're never sufficiently prepared, besides it's always the ones that you've taken for granted, that it doesn't even occur to you to fear for, that are gone.

Well, look, I said to Victoria, while we're in the neighbourhood, why don't we check out the Alcott, I didn't say 'the dear old Alcott' though that was my tone. The Alcott was the hotel in which we'd lived for about two months when I was directing *The Holy Terror*. It was the strangest hotel either of us had ever been in – its foyer was grand, magnificent, and dilapidated, like the abandoned set of a film made in the 1950s, a Busby Berkeley musical, possibly, although it had too an atmosphere of violence, not small personal violence, muggings etc., but lavish, old-fashioned violence, as if men on horseback might canter into it, swords or pistols in their hand, or from the film of *War and Peace*, King Vidor directing, was that his real name, King Vidor? A Czech, I suppose – there must have been a reception desk, but I don't remember it, or any of the management, come to that, but I remember our suite – five rooms, plus two bathrooms, plus a large kitchen, and cheaper than any single room I'd stayed in previously in New York. From the room I made into my study there was a view of rooftops, charmingly domestic, tubs of flowers and garden furniture – more Paris than New York. Most of the time the Alcott seemed to be uninhabited, apart from ourselves and Tiny Tim, a once upon a time pop star, who introduced himself to us in the elevator, which was big enough for cattle – Tiny Tim, and an actor, a very fine actor whose name I forget but he was the private detective in *Psycho*, the one who is tiptoeing confidently up the stairs when the little old lady who is Anthony Perkins pretending to be his own mother comes screeching at him from nowhere and stabs him to death. He was also in *Twelve Angry Men*, playing the slow, serious one with a frown. Any film he was in was a classy film, he made it so, and the thing about him, the thing we were told about him, was that he had come to the Alcott from an apartment just around the corner where he'd lived happily with his wife but – but he was an alcoholic and he was drinking himself to death, and he'd decided that there was nothing he could do to stop himself, it was out of his hands, but he didn't want his wife to endure the witnessing of it. So he set up in the Alcott and proceeded to do what he couldn't help doing, or so he believed. Does this count as suicide? Not really very different from my brother Piers's story, in its bare bones. He too set up around the corner from his loved ones, and calmly drank himself into his early grave. I've often thought of it as a kind of suicide. Although I don't think that death was consciously part of his plan, I do think he was consciously relinquishing his grip on life, on every aspect of his life but his drinking life. Does that count as suicide? Does it matter what word we give to it? If you don't believe in an afterlife then all judgements stay in the here and now, in which case how we behave, whether well or ill, doesn't matter very much – except, of course, in the here and now. But what judgement can I possibly make on Piers, whom I loved? If I hadn't loved him I might have judged him with confident indifference. He drank his life away, silly bugger! Or – converting it to a general principle – people haven't the right to drink their lives away. Why not? I can't think why not, other than that they wound the people they leave behind, who also suffer because they miss them. So it always comes back to the same thing – if no God and no afterlife, no afterlife and no God, then no judgement. Judging is simply another form of grieving, and all you really mean is: he shouldn't have done it because it's not fair on me. Izaak Walton described Donne, after the death of his wife, as being like the pelican in the wilderness – pelicans being thought to tear at and rend themselves from grief – and yet Donne was a man of God who triumphed in the thought of his own death because 'Then Thou hast done!' – 'hast Donne' – how is it then that he couldn't triumph in the thought of his wife's death? Surely he should have exclaimed triumphantly, 'Then Thou hast Mary!' Mary? Why do I think her name was Mary? It was Anne, surely? Anne Donne? He wrote it on the kitchen door, on the day of his marriage. 'John Donne, Anne Donne, Undonne.'

All this stuff about death, Piers, judgement and grieving – yet all I meant to say was that when we got to the Alcott, it too, like the Promenade, had gone – or rather it too, like the Promenade, was in the process of becoming something else – in its case, one of the workmen told us, an apartment block – which would be an excellent commercial move, I should imagine, certainly make more sense than a hotel vacant except for an alcoholic actor and Tiny Tim, the decaying pop star. Oh and – I suddenly remember – a bridge club. No, two bridge clubs. Another eccentricity of the Alcott, that its top floor was reserved for two bridge clubs. The members didn't live in the Alcott, they just played bridge there once or twice a week. Like the Promenade, its lobby was so far undisturbed, though scattered about its floor were sinister humps of tarpaulin, under which presumably the drills, mechanical hammers, small bundles of explosives, whatever, needed for destruction – well, partial demolition.

MY LIVES ON BROADWAY

There we were then, on a Sunday morning in New York, in the bright New York sunshine, wondering if we dare risk a visit to any other building that still survived intact in our memories.

We ambled down Broadway, ambled and ambled, without much sense of purpose, past our hotel on 63rd, and then we were into the 50s, I ambling less and less fluently as my feet began to ache and my legs to weary. In fact I had my arm hooked around Victoria's and was leaning on her slightly, and moaning not entirely under my breath. Around 50th Street, as we stood waiting at the traffic lights, she wondered whether I was sure I wanted to go on, and I nearly said no, I didn't want to go on, I wanted to go back to the hotel and lie down, but instead I said yes, yes, I did want to go on, there was something I wanted to look at, and wanted her to look at, although it had only really occurred to me as I spoke – I was suddenly full of purpose, because I did, in fact, know where we were going, though I still needed her arm to get us there.

Broadway from 48th Street on was Broadway almost as I remembered it, from my first visit nearly forty years ago, the same garish and seedy façades, seemingly the very same bars and doughnut and hamburger joints, the same sort of people standing around in clusters shouting to each other in Italian, Spanish and unidentifiable tongues, and the same sense of milling – people milling about, almost aimlessly, it seemed – but really it wasn't the same at all. In the old days, the days of my youngish manhood, the millers-about always seemed to have an end in view, and were threatening – you walked carefully, in case you jostled a man with a temper or a cause or a head full of drugs and bad dreams, it was a dangerous place, and if you hung around there at night, in Times Square at one or two in the morning, dipping into a bar or a sleazy movie house or a pornographic bookshop on the lookout for Miss Goodbar or whatever might come your way, you knew that something very bad was also likely to come your way, a terminal mugging, for instance – Of course I was usually drunk, no, I should say that I was always drunk late at night in New York, in those days, drunk and full of contradictory desires and an underlying restlessness that was like desperation – what was it I wanted? I couldn't have put a name to it, it had no exact form, possibly what I wanted was what I had, fear, excitement, anticipation – also the sense of being quite alone, without attachments or responsibilities, available. That was how I spent many nights in New York, from my late twenties to my late forties, every time I came back I brought with me more attachments and responsibilities, but I shed them as easily as ever, after a certain hour, when I'd had enough to drink, in Times Square.

Times Square this afternoon, when I ambled into it, limping and supported by my wife, was only dangerous in that it was crowded. It was like Leicester Square, perhaps, in the mass of bodies moving along the pavements and across the streets, but not at all like in that nobody was drunk, nobody shouted, if you bumped into somebody, which you did constantly, because they were rather clumsy and not very aware, they apologized immediately, with anxious, eager smiles, and they all seemed to be Americans or tourists, but they mostly seemed to be American tourists, out-of-towners with children, babies in prams, elderly relatives attached to zimmer frames, or like me to their spouses' arms. So many of them in the sunshine, so good-humoured and slow of movement and almost passive as they trudged around and around, as if being there were the sole point of being there, a bit like the closing scene of *The Invasion of the Body Snatchers*, or was it *The Night of the Living Dead*? – no, that's not right, they seemed to be alive within, if sweetly and passively, so more like cattle, perhaps, with Times Square their pen, and the police placed at various strategic points, visible and watching, to protect and control them, their shepherds and herdsmen. I couldn't remember seeing police in Times Square before except once, on one of my first visits, two of them handcuffing a middle-aged black man in a red dress and a silver wig, while a third rummaged through his handbag. I remember being struck by the casual, almost lackadaisical manner of it, as if it was something all of them did on a regular basis, also I remember the wig fell off, and one of the policemen picked it up and patted it back on the black man's head, but inaccurately, so that it slipped over one eye –

It took an age to jostle around the square to Shubert Alley. I wasn't sure of my bearings, and we kept finding ourselves back on the corner of 45th Street, waiting for the lights to change, and then it came to me that we had to go towards Eighth Avenue, along 45th Street between Times Square and Eighth Avenue lay our destination – some several thousands appeared to have the same destination in mind, though doubtless without the same reason, in fact among all those thousands and thousands of zombies, mutants, cattle-people, decent American souls I was the only one – I hoped – who could reasonably expect to see his name on placards and hoardings, on the walls of a theatre and even – if my agent had done a proper job – above the theatre. In lights! In lights! On Broadway! My name!

We stood in Shubert Alley, where a strange cold wind appeared to have arisen. It was still a sunny day, quite warm in all the other parts of New York we'd visited, including the small stretch on 45th, between Eighth and Times Square, but in the little arc of an alley between 45th and 44th there was a wind. I suppose the alley itself must have formed a wind tunnel, but if there wasn't wind anywhere else where did it come from to be tunnelled by Shubert Alley?

Nevertheless I stood and pointed, Napoleonically.

'There!' I said.

'What?' She was half turned against the wind and had trouble hearing me.

'There! There!' I heaved her around to face the façade of the Booth Theatre, the bit of it that's in Shubert Alley.

'There!' I said. 'Look!' I pointed at the row of posters on the wall. They were for quite a few shows, *Chicago*, *A Chorus Line*, *Spamalot* – actually I'm not sure there was one for *Chicago*, it just popped into my head as a likely candidate, but I am sure about *A Chorus Line* and *Spamalot*, and there were other posters, presumably for the plays in all the other theatres owned by the Shuberts outside their personal alley, in other spots on Broadway – but two of the posters were for *Butley*, my name distinctly where it ought to be, under the title of the play, and almost a half, well almost a quarter the size of Nathan's. A bit less than a quarter, possibly –

'Yes!' she said. 'Wow!'

I pointed above the theatre, where there was a gigantic sort of frame, in which light bulbs could be screwed, is how I imagined that the electrical side of it was done. 'And in a few days, up there. In lights.'

'Wow!' she said again. 'Your name in lights! Wow!'

We looked up at it for a short while, hunched there in the wind, our heads at an unnatural angle, trying to imagine it, my name in lights,

winking, glittering, sparkling, towering over Broadway, possibly visible
from the extreme edges of the city, or across the water in New Jersey –
all the way to New Hampshire, Connecticut, New Orleans, Los
Angeles – from London, with one of those new AstroAge telescopes
it could almost certainly be picked out – really the wind should have
dropped, the orchestra struck up, and she and I, and I and she, we and
me, and she and he, have hoofed our way down Shubert Alley, along
45th into Times Square – to what tune though? What tune?

We took a cab back to our hotel, and I went straight to bed. It was
nearly five in the afternoon, well past my usual daytime bedtime.

When I woke up we went for a meal at a large Chinese restaurant
we'd taken note of on our walk. We'd both eaten there, separately
and together, in our previous lives in New York, and from the look
of it and the feel of it I'd say that nothing much had changed – not
that either of us remembered it very well, it was just that it felt and
looked as if nothing much had changed in it for many decades –
that the same waiters, at the same ages then as they were now had
served us – or for the stretch of about an hour, failed to serve us.
This is a characteristic of Chinese restaurants, I think, that they give
the impression of being rooted and permanent until one day you go
along as usual and it's simply not there, even if it was there last week,
and you were, or thought you were, a familiar, indeed favoured
customer who would be kept informed of any changes in its
circumstances. Of course, as has been well known in the West for
centuries, the Chinese are an enigmatic people, who talk in riddles
and pass messages about in cookies, but they're also capable of
searing and salutary frankness, as was experienced by friends of ours,
a family of four, two distinguished adults and two comparatively
placid sons under ten, who went regularly to a restaurant some
distance from their home because they enjoyed both the delicious
food and the speed of service. They were nonetheless slightly

puzzled by the gravity of the management's and waiters' demeanours – though they were never rude, they never smiled, or even greeted them as if they'd ever seen them before. Finally, after several years of this, the man, a distinguished lawyer then, and now a judge, let's call him Cravenwood, decided to unravel what had come to seem to the whole family a bit of a mystery. On their way out on what would prove to be their last visit, Cravenwood stopped at the door where the head waiter was loitering, and put it to him: 'Look', he said, 'look, we really, really like your restaurant, the food is excellent, and the service so efficient, and yet you, none of you, give us as much as a smile or a hello, not once in all these years, not even to the boys,' gesturing to them, 'so we can't help wondering, is there any particular reason?' The manager thought for a moment, then said, 'We don't like you.' There's not much you can say to that, really, all you can do is wish you hadn't asked – and not go back, of course. But now I've put it down and given it a little thought, it occurs to me that I wasn't that keen on the Cravenwoods myself, although not being inscrutable, it would never occur to me to tell them so. Besides, it may be illegal these days not to like people, or to say to their faces that you don't like them.

The waiters at the Chinese restaurant we went to tonight would never say they didn't like you, not to your face, they were exceptionally merry, patting me on the back soothingly when I asked if there was any chance of getting soon the dish we'd ordered well over half an hour before – which when it finally arrived wasn't up to much. So perhaps that's the way it works, you can either have good food and speedy service without smiles and hellos, or poor food and virtually no service, but lots of hellos and smiles.

Victoria's gone to bed. She'll be fast asleep. If I listened hard I'd hear low voices, or low music, or possibly low gunfire coming from the television set that's suspended above the foot of our bed. Perhaps they'll mingle into her dreams, become comforting, to make up for the absence of George and Toto on either side of her. In a moment I shall go in and turn the television off, kiss her on the brow, then take a sleeping pill, maybe two, as it's our first night in New York, and tomorrow I have to go to the Booth to watch the dress rehearsal.

On the other hand I might come back in here and write for a while, to keep my mind off various problems, the most pressing of which is what to do about this hotel we're in. If it is a hotel.

GUNFIGHT AT BARNES AND NOBLE

The dress rehearsal was only mildly depressing. I went down to it in a cab with the director, Nicholas Martin. He is a small man, a very short man, a year or so younger than myself, probably. He has spectacles, and a lot of grey hair that is swept back but often gives the impression of standing straight up, partly because he has an air of constant surprise – something to do with his eyebrows, which are naturally on the lift. He is a non-smoking teetotaller, which I assume indicates a rich and varied, possibly even tumultuous past, and we get on very well – at least I get on very well with him, it's almost impossible not to, as not only is he intelligent and funny, he is also very sociable – so sociable, in fact, that you can't always keep a hold on him, one moment you're engaged in close conversation and there is a sudden blur, you blink and look around, and there he is, you spot him over there, engaged in close conversation with someone else, and when you next look he's with someone else, and then somebody else, and suddenly he's back with you, picking up where he left off – whenever I have anything urgent to discuss I

make a point of resting a hand on his shoulder or elbow, as a way
of restraining him, but he's so quick and agile that you could only
be sure of keeping him if you could clamp him – When I discussed
this aspect of his behaviour with him, he explained that it was a
skill, political really, that he'd developed during his time as artistic
director of the Huntington Theatre in Boston, one of the most
comfortable and beautiful theatres I've ever been in, designed by the
man who designed the London Haymarket but requiring for its
survival the support of the good and the great of Boston, who in
their turn require a great deal of attention, especially at functions
like first nights, where so many of them turn up and stand about in
singles, pairs and small clusters, waiting to be noticed – if not
noticed offence might be taken, financial contributions cancelled,
obstacles raised at board meetings, etc. I expect that this explanation
is true, but I also suspect that there is a something in his nature, a
kind of from-flower-to-flower bumblebee something that takes over
whenever he finds himself in company – it's in its way very
engaging, and can also be quite infuriating, especially on those
occasions when, like the bumblebee on a particularly balmy day,
one flower leads to another flower, and one garden to another, and
he doesn't come back to pick up where you left off, and you have
to phone him on your mobile – actually, this can be quite fun, you
watch him as you punch in his number, he is smiling into someone's
face, his arm around their shoulder, then he stiffens, his hand shoots
to his pocket because it can't help itself, he clasps the mobile to his
ear, so that you can see his expression as you whisper, 'As we were
saying about the Edna scene—' and he throws back his head and
laughs, and keeps the conversation going on the mobile as he bustles
over to you.

I learnt all this when Nicholas directed *Butley* at the Huntington
three years ago. Nathan was quite extraordinary and I thought the

play was almost perfectly cast, no, perfectly cast, even the actor who had trouble remembering the lines, and would fall into fleeting vacancies, was otherwise quite perfect – in other words I loved the production, as did much of Boston – and it played there for a limited run of six weeks, and was packed every night, with standing at the back etc. – and was reviewed so favourably, as was the play itself, as above all was Nathan – the *New York Times* said it was a perfect meeting of actor and part, that Nathan was the rightful successor to Alan Bates – and *Variety* said much the same – that a Broadway production became inevitable. It might have been best if it had moved straight away, just as it was, but Nathan had previous commitments – the film of *The Producers* immediately, and then when that got under way something else popped up – as I remember he stepped into a play written by a friend when an actor dropped out unexpectedly, and then was seduced into doing a revival of *The Odd Couple*, with Matthew Broderick his other half – and so three years passed, and here we are, about to open on Broadway, with only Nathan and Pamela Gray (no relation) in the part of Anne, his wife, from the original Boston cast.

Nicholas is staying at the same hotel, in rooms identical to ours on the floor below. He likes his rooms, which he says suit him perfectly – as why shouldn't they, as he is a small man and on his own, while I am quite a large man with a normal-sized wife, which is why our rooms don't suit me. Furthermore – no, the hotel can wait, this is about the dress rehearsal, which was, as I said, only mildly depressing – I've never been to a dress rehearsal that wasn't depressing, the only question being to what degree depressing – mildly is somewhere near the top, absolute top is 'encouraging' followed by 'OK', for the bottom you find yourself rummaging through your vocabulary for words like 'grisly' or 'ghastly' or 'catastrophic' – I was going to describe the dress rehearsal, that's what I sat down to do, in fact, but you know I can't be bothered – tomorrow there's a dress rehearsal in front of an invited audience, and then we're into previews, and I simply haven't got it in me to chart the course of the previews night after night right up to the first night, it's as if – this is quite an odd thought, and would be worrying if I were worried by it – as if I didn't care very much. There. It's out. I want the play to be a success because I want the money, nay, need the money and I love Nathan and don't want him to fail, but beyond that it doesn't matter very much, I really don't care –

I wrote that before we went out to dinner, over which I talked relentlessly to Victoria about the dress rehearsal, then back we came, I still talking about the dress rehearsal, then as we entered this room I was still talking about the dress rehearsal, talking about it when my eye caught this pad on the table and talking about it as I picked the pad up and talking about it as my eye took in the last sentence 'I really don't care –', to which my behaviour all evening has given the lie. So given that I do care, here is the gist of what I said to Victoria, more than several many times – from the dress rehearsal I could see that there was nothing much wrong with the production that a few sackings wouldn't put right. No, only joking etc., not a few sackings, just one – it's Eric, of course. Eric, the fine young actor who plays Gardner and whose career I thought I'd saved by sending in from Spetses new lines of American dialogue so ghastly that he'd virtually transformed himself – with the help of a dialect coach – into an Englishman born and bred, to avoid saying them. If only he didn't come on in the last scene of the play – in fact if he came on anywhere else you wouldn't think there was much wrong with him, rather you wouldn't notice that there was anything wrong with him, you would just assume that the drop in dramatic temperature –

assuming it was reasonably high – was because you, you being a normal member of the audience, had lost interest, as you often tend to do during the course of a play, or that the play had become less interesting – as all plays tend to do here and there over a two-hour or so stretch. The truth is that audiences don't really know miscasting when they see it, why should they, as they have no idea how the part should be cast, not knowing the play, so if this actor, the one I've got so used to thinking of as Eric – in fact the name slipped out when I was having a very pleasant chat with him at the interval, outside the stage door, where we'd both gone for a smoke – he corrected me the first time with a gently wrinkled brow and a puzzled smile, the second time with a rather worried laugh – 'Yes, I'm sorry, I don't know why I keep calling you Eric,' I said. 'I don't know any Erics' – I almost said 'any other Erics' – if Eric had turned up anywhere else in the play, he would have slipped past you, to be forgotten until he turned up at the curtain to take his bow, and even then you might not have placed him clearly, because his would have been a brief and early bow, and almost at once the more prominent actors would have been flowing in from either wing to bow and curtsy big-time – and he wouldn't, in short, have had to be sacked. But as I say, and kept saying to Victoria in Spetses, he comes on in the last scene, which automatically makes him important, and furthermore we've heard a great deal about him at regular intervals during the play, how he behaves, even what sort of clothes he wears and we know that Butley is, or says he is, intensely interested in him, so we want to know what effect he has on Butley – we sense that the direction of the rest of Butley's life, the life he's going to lead after the curtain comes down, so to speak, is going to depend on what transpires between the two of them – particularly when he reads out the lines from *Four Quartets* – 'In that open field/ If you do not come too close' – but I went into all this in Spetses, before

I'd met him – now that I have I can confirm as accurate everything that Nicholas said in that long conversation on the telephone about his talent and his charm, but the point about Eric is not that he isn't a good actor, nor that he isn't charming – he has an exceptionally sweet and easy manner, a sympathetic face – but he is wrong for the part. His sweetness, easiness and charm, indeed his talent, are all rendered irrelevant by the simple fact of his not being able to be, in speech or gesture, a student at an English university in 1970. Every other actor in the play can assume the necessary Englishness, and assume it naturally – anyway, so that it seems natural – but Eric is modern, American, anomalous – and made more anomalous with every line of verse he reads out – he can't make sense of it, not only because his accent is ineradicable – apparently it's still being much worked on by the English dialect coach – but because his sensibility is almost visibly at odds with it – the words are coming out of the wrong sort of mouth, and it's unfair, unfair to Eliot, because his great lines sound feeble and enwizened, unfair to the play, because it comes to a halt just as it should be reaching its climax, unfair to Nathan, who doesn't know how to play the scene with an actor who isn't there as the character, and unfair to Eric, who shouldn't have been there as Gardner, should never have been offered the part.

The windows of our hotel suite's tiny sitting room and tiny bedroom are enormous, and through them, directly across the street, I can see into the vast windows of a vast Barnes and Noble, I can see the customers going up and down the escalators, walking between the shelves, if you have excellent eyesight you could probably make out the titles on the covers of the larger books, well, the titles on the posters anyway, and there's a cafeteria, I can see people at tables, making gestures – I like this aspect of our suite, to be a spectator of so much lively movement, the colours of the clothes, people's heads vanishing and reappearing, it's almost as if one were seeing into a city, or a human hive. But there lurks the thought that if we can see into the human hive, we can be seen into from the human hive –

Of course Barnes and Noble is brightly lit, its contents highly visible, and I am sitting in a corner of our sitting room in darkness, for modesty's sake, as I am wearing only my vest and underpants, so I hope that if any part of me can be seen from Barnes and Noble it is only the tip of my cigarette. I shall sit like this writing rancorous thoughts and glancing through the windows, until midnight, when the shop closes. After that there will be only a few people moving about, cleaning and clearing up . . .

I am now looking at a completely empty shop, the lights have been lowered but not turned off, and it seems to ride there, on the other side of the street, like a great ship, abandoned and ghostly – and here are two figures come into view, walking towards each other from opposite ends, many racks of books between them, I wonder if they can see each other, from here it looks as if they must, but there's something about the way they move and keep turning their heads, as if they have no sense of another presence, or perhaps they're so used to each other – yes, that's probably it, they're wearing blue uniforms and one has a cap on, so they're security guards – do they have guns in holsters, I must look the next time we're in the shop. If they came across each other unexpectedly, would they go for their guns and shoot, die in a hail of bullets, there among the books?

I looked in on Victoria, who's tucked up in bed watching television on a plasma screen – it gives a wonderfully clear picture, she said, but the commercials interrupt every few minutes, and it's difficult therefore to grasp a narrative that's really just made up of bits – we wondered if this means that Americans have had to develop formidable powers of concentration in order to keep all the bits in mind and connect and then reconnect them, or is it that their powers of concentration have rotted away, so they no longer care whether they have a consecutive narrative – we talked crap like that for a short while, while we put off discussing what was really on our minds: can we spend five weeks – now four and half – in these tiny quarters, or should we find somewhere else? We agreed that either tomorrow I'd phone the producers and make a fuss, or I wouldn't.

We've moved into a hotel further downtown. When we arrived the lobby was full of people sitting on their luggage, there were a lot of children, some of them crying, others running around in that meaningless way common to children – they looked as if they were waiting to be evacuated but I suppose they were either departing guests waiting for their transport, or arriving guests waiting for their rooms –

Our rooms were ready. We're on the 110th floor, and thus have some fine views towards the river from one set of windows, towards downtown from the other set. There is a very large sitting room with a television, a decent-sized bedroom with a television, a kitchen and eating area, and two bathrooms, and though it's somewhat tacky in its furnishing and underlit and neither television works properly and the armchairs and sofa are uncomfortable, it's fine, fine, and not to be written about because today –

A LUCKY MAN

Tom Stoppard is in New York, for rehearsals of his play *Rock 'n' Roll*. No, for his trilogy *The Coast of Utopia* – *Rock 'n' Roll* is coming over later. He phoned this morning to say he had some important news, he'd found a restaurant which I mustn't name for legal reasons where you can smoke – not in the main part of the restaurant, but in a small room off, where – if they think you're OK – they'll bring out ashtrays and give you the nod. I told him about the various places I'd found, not much use to him as they're all in this area where he's very unlikely to have business, and anyway they're all legal because they're outside – so his discovery of what is in fact a smoke-easy is an altogether different kettle of fish, as Harold might have put it in the days when he a) smoked and b) came to New York – we agreed to meet up at the restaurant this evening, after *Butley* comes down – It'll be nice to see him – it's always nice to see him, but it'll be particularly nice to see him in a restaurant with a small room in which we can smoke.

The restaurant is stylish and comfortable, with two kinds of waiters, one lot young and pretty and eager to please, the other old and creaky but not unwilling to serve, and the food was very good, or so Victoria says, I have no judgement on food, thinking if I can chew it and it slips down my throat it will do – altogether we liked it very much, although it's irritatingly close to our previous hotel, about a three-minute walk, in fact, so we kept saying 'If we'd known'. The only problem was the little room Tom Stoppard had spoken of, or rather its absence, and also the absence of Tom Stoppard, so that it struck us that perhaps we'd come to the wrong address, and were in this charming restaurant entirely by accident. I got up and went to the lavatory by a very circuitous route, allowing myself to misunderstand the directions offered by several waiters, but couldn't see in any corner that I visited a little room, or even a door, except the door to the lavatory, and surely he can't have meant 'little room' as a euphemism for lavatory, that he'd found a restaurant where we could have a smoke in the lavatory – I visited the lavatory, which was certainly very little, especially by New York standards, with two urinals, one cubicle, and no visible ashtray, I couldn't imagine the two of us standing there like a couple of ancient schoolboys – I went back and was reporting to Victoria when my mobile went off, I had one of those awful lurches in the stomach, my first thought that it was tragic news from London, my second that it was bad news from the Booth Theatre, my third that it was Tom Stoppard because there was his name on the little screen of my mobile – 'I was just wondering how long you're going to be,' he said, 'because I don't think I'm going to hang about much longer' – I asked him where he was. 'Well, waiting in the restaurant,' he said, which he then named, and was the restaurant that we were in. 'I'm in the little room,' although he wasn't, he was now coming through the restaurant with his slightly floppy walk, putting his mobile into his pocket, smiling rather mysteriously, as if he'd performed a sort of vanishing act in reverse – but in fact it was all quite simple, the little room he'd come from wasn't in the actual restaurant, it was in the lobby, quite easy to find if you knew where to find it, he said, but he realized now that he should have explained. As we hadn't finished our meal he stayed at the table and we talked about his rehearsals, my previews. I find his calm in these situations almost preternatural, as if, a benevolent man himself, he has become used to benevolent outcomes in his journey through life. I remember asking him, a few months ago in London, whether he thought he was a lucky man. He thought quite hard about the question, considered it properly, in fact, and decided that yes, he thought he was – not had been, but was – let me put that in clarifying tenses, direct speech therefore – 'Tom, do you think you're a lucky man?' Pause for consideration. 'Yes, I think I am.' Not 'I have been', is my point, but 'I am', which somehow includes the future tense – 'I am in a continuous state or condition of being lucky' – this seems to me, from the superstitious point of view, a very sensible answer – if he feels that he is lucky but denies it, as most lucky people probably would, the Fates might take offence and decide that a reversal or two might be good for his soul, while a frank declaration of his debt – yes, I am successful, lovable, rich, talented, and lucky therefore – would endear him to them even more, and they would feel inclined to reward him with a further clutch of honours, although it's hard to think what honours are left for them to give him – he has a knighthood and an OM and doubtless countless honorary degrees – well then, reward him with a further clutch of rave reviews, and a map showing the location of every smoke-easy in New York, and one for London next year, when the ban comes into effect – it is actually one of Tom's achievements that one envies him nothing, except possibly his looks, his talents, his money and his luck. To be so enviable without being envied is pretty enviable, when you think about it.

On the way out Tom showed us the little room, tucked discreetly, as he'd said, into the opposite side of the lobby. He opened the door with a sweeping gesture, as if upon a personal treasure trove, and there indeed, to feast our eyes on, were two large men sitting at a small table smoking cigars, and three women at another small table smoking cigarettes – it looked and smelt extremely unwholesome, one's eyes watered and stung, one scarcely dared breathe, and one certainly couldn't help wondering whether this sort of thing shouldn't be banned. We walked Tom halfway back to his apartment, which, as he described it, was an apartment suitable to a man of his luck and talents, then got a cab back to where we are now, I at the table writing this, Victoria in bed, asleep.

Oh. One thing suddenly comes back from the dinner with Tom the other night, he asked me how I was getting on with my producer, by which he meant the single, active, on-the-job producer, as opposed to the many merely money-contributing producers, and I said, 'Oh you know what it's like with American producers,' and he said yes, he did know, which one was it? And I couldn't remember – not only the name, but the face, anything, really, except the gender – but it did come to me after a moment or two of foolish gestures and mumbles – 'McCann,' I was able to declare triumphantly, 'Liz McCann.' I think the reason I forgot her was that, as yet, I hadn't put down anything about her, and still haven't, and so –

A BARING OF BREASTS

I first met her in about 1976, when she produced *Otherwise Engaged* on Broadway, with her then partner, Nell Nugent. Liz was plump and curly blonde, Nell curly dark and plump, they were in their early forties I suppose, a bit older than me and a bit younger than Harold (who was directing), and seemed, or anyway were thought of as, inseparable, being known about town as 'the girls'. They were also known for their roguish charm by some, and as a pretty tough couple of cookies by others, though there's no reason I can think of for their not being both – there was an incident that I always remember when I think about them in those days that was a fair example of their modus operandi – there is a scene in *Otherwise Engaged* in which an ambitious and intellectual young woman has a drink thrown over her by her lover, who then departs, leaving her alone on stage with the character played in London by Alan Bates and here in New York by Tom Courtenay – she peels off her soaking blouse and for the rest of the scene, for about twenty minutes in fact, she struts and stalks about the stage bare-breasted, speaking with an unattractive cogency of her literary ambitions and her sex life. It was her casual matter-of-factness that shocked and amused audiences back in 1975 (oddly enough, audiences seemed more shocked, and laughed less freely, in fact slightly furtively, in a recent revival at the Criterion Theatre in London a couple of years ago). Now we – that is the playwright and the director, both men of fierce good taste and astringent judgement – were determined that the scene shouldn't become a sort of vulgar treat in what was intended to be a rather classy comedy of manners, and had insisted in London, and now insisted again in New York, that it mustn't be used for publicity purposes, and never, under any circumstances, photographed. 'Absolutely not!' Harold said to the girls, when they raised the possibility, 'Absolutely on no account!' in a tone that they might have felt was almost insultingly emphatic, 'Under no circumstances!' and he made it clear that he didn't intend to discuss it further, and they made it clear that he didn't need to – 'We won't say another word about it,' they said, or words to that effect – and they didn't, until they had to explain why half a dozen or so photographers were found loitering behind pillars and crouching behind seats at the dress rehearsal, just before the topless scene – it was one of the most exhilarating passages of my life, when Harold and I seized and smashed their cameras, ran the rascals out of the theatre by the seats of their trousers and the napes of their necks – two girl photographers we treated more circumspectly, the hand for their neck's napes went around their titty-pops – whoppers, whoops, whoa there, here I am, an old man in a dry month etc. – the fact is that I don't remember what happened after we found the photographers – I know that they didn't get their pictures, I suppose somebody – presumably the stage manager – got them to leave, and we then got on with the dress rehearsal. I do remember a meeting with the girls that evening, though it might only have been one of them, ice and contempt from Harold, but not that much grovelling from the girl or girls, indeed there was a touch of contempt in their own manner, not for themselves, but for the over-fastidious director and his sidekick playwright – although actually I suspect from what I know of him the sidekick playwright wouldn't have minded his play being publicized by photographs of a bare-breasted girl smoking a cigarette –

Strange to think that when I began writing the scene I had no idea that Davina was going to take her blouse off, nor that when she did she'd have nothing underneath it but her breasts. It just popped into my head after I had Jeff throw his drink over her, and I think I had Jeff throw his drink because I couldn't think of anything for him to say in response to a withering paragraph from her – so one thing led to another, within a matter of seconds I went from a fully clothed to a half-clothed Davina on the page, and a few months later there was a half-naked Davina on the stage – I met a middle-aged man not long ago who told me that he was taken to *Otherwise Engaged* by his mother when he was thirteen, and that the Davina scene had given him twenty of the most difficult minutes of his life, he had never been quite so conscious of his mother, at the interval he didn't know where to look and hoped his mother didn't either, it remained one of his life's most vivid memories – to think that I did that to a thirteen-year-old, just by rattling off a few sentences on my typewriter. That was over three decades ago, when boys were boys, and went to theatres with their mummies. Nowadays – nowadays – but what do I know about nowadays?

PICK-UP IN THE BAR OF THE MERIDIEN HOTEL

I don't think I saw Liz McCann again after *Otherwise Engaged* until a few months ago, when I met her in the bar of the Meridien Hotel,

Piccadilly, to discuss the forthcoming production of *Butley* – really it wasn't so much a discussion as a reintroduction – 'Here I am again, Liz, after all these years!' and 'Here I am again, Simon!' I don't know what she expected to see, but probably not me – I mean, people don't change in our memories, we can't add on the changes that life has wrought on them during all the years we haven't seen them, and even if we could it wouldn't be any good, they'd be the wrong changes – we'd look for wrinkles and the skin would be shinier, we'd expect eyes dulled by fatigue and defeat (a dire marriage, troublesome children) and find instead (an unexpected widowing, delightful grandchildren) a sparkle in the eye, a strut in the step; and there are dewlaps, and there are wattles, which I never bargain for – well, who sees in one's thirty-year-old friend intimations of the pouches to come – we seem to take our imagining of ageing from literature or films – whitened hair, wrinkles around the eyes, a stoop or even a shuffle, linear and almost childish ageing, while, well to take the obvious case, the case from which I started, in the bar of the Meridien, in Piccadilly, where I anticipated, vaguely anticipated, a woman who had only aged by being slightly worn down from staying roughly the same for over thirty years, plump and blondely curly, with a frisky manner and bright blue eyes, one half of 'the girls' –

The Meridien bar off Piccadilly is rather like the New York bars I remember from my early visits, very comfortably furnished but dimly lit, so if you come down to it from a bright outside, you find it difficult to see anyone distinctly, at least at first, but my eyes went straight to the nearest unaccompanied elderly female. 'Hello, Liz,' I said to the rather slovenly and mountainous heap that was stretched out in an armchair that looked too small for her, in fact it looked as if she'd clipped it on to the underneath part of herself, a prosthetic addition to her buttocks, to save her the trouble of finding a seat when she wanted one. Her short legs stuck out in front of her, her heels resting on a leather stool. So it was to this rather formless and shapeless being that I said, 'Hello, Liz.'

'Hello?' she said in that American way, 'hello?' like a question. I sat down beside her, thinking that I always thought of her, though perhaps incorrectly, perhaps it was Nell I thought of, as a bit of a dresser – feminine, floral dresses kind of thing – and here she was, in a shirt and trousers that produced an odd and contradictory effect, they seemed loose and baggy and far too big for her, and yet she also seemed to be spilling out of them, folds of flesh visible at the waist and around the armpits, and elsewhere one suspected, if one cared to look. 'Nice to see you – it's been a long time,' I said. 'Well,' she said, 'I don't know about that.' 'More than thirty years,' I said, trying to examine her face for a something that would make her familiar to me, but really in that light her face was almost without features, just a white blob with a white blob of a nose and dents for eyes and mouth, and I couldn't say anything about her hair except that she might have had some on her head, some of which might have been hanging down the sides of her cheeks, though that might have been a scarf. 'Yes, more than thirty years,' I repeated, smiling and nodding at her and trying to be a little romantic by resting my hand lightly on what I hoped was her knee – well, what harm in a little show of caring, of *tendresse*, this was my producer, after all –

It turned out that this wasn't my producer after all, my producer was sitting deeper into the bar's shadows with my agent, Judy Daish, who has sharp eyes and hailed me before I got any further in my seduction of this somewhat bloated and elderly American lady, to whom, of course, I apologized. 'So sorry,' I said, 'I thought you were the lady over there, sitting with – the other lady over there, so sorry.' 'No, that's OK,' she said, 'I was getting quite interested. Gonna ask ya if ya wanted my room number.' And she gave me a charmingly husky cough of a laugh – a fifty-a-day laugh, I'd say, and quite a lot of gin to go with them.

Now the irritating thing is that this encounter with the elderly American lady who wasn't Liz McCann has become my memory of meeting Liz McCann, she usurped the experience so completely that the trifling business of going over to join Judy Daish and the genuine Liz McCann is blocked by it, as is the ensuing conversation apart from a little patch in which she said how much she was looking forward to producing *Butley* on Broadway and then said something else that suggested that she hadn't yet read the play, which pleased me. I have an innate faith in producers who don't read my plays, it means that they're putting their faith in something that's probably more reliable – in this case in the star, Nathan Lane, which makes complete sense – but that's really all I remember of the meeting, I suppose she turned out to be so completely appropriate to the Liz of my memory or my curiosity about her was completely used up by the lady who wasn't her – Supposing Judy hadn't called out, would she really have given me her room number? Well, I suppose I could have passed it on to someone in need.

What about Liz McCann now, here, in New York, the currently active producer of my play, what do you make of her? Not much, not much to make. I see that she's been active, in that everything that should have happened has happened, Nathan Lane's in lights, his face and his name dominate the ads, the previews have been running smoothly enough, though there's trouble from the next-door theatre, which spills its audience into Shubert Alley before our show has ended, and they shout and even sing and sometimes swear and reel about, of course the swearers and reelers-about may be revellers from the nearby bars, but if they're not, if they're actually coming out of the theatre shouting and swearing and reeling about, then that must be quite a show they have next door to *Butley*, I must make a note of what it is, it might be worth a visit – I have an idea it's *A Chorus Line*, does that seem likely? Anyway, the point is that Liz is responsible for preventing these people, whoever they are, from disturbing our previews, and I have no doubt that she will find some way of doing it, by re-routing them, or bringing in the police, or perhaps coming to speak to them herself, with the full force of her personality – no, no, she can't do that, unless she's brought along in her wheelchair, oh yes, that's what I've forgotten to mention, Liz McCann has been physically absent as a producer because she damaged her leg just as *Butley* was going into rehearsals – apparently she was somewhere in the Caribbean, resting up, preparing herself mentally and emotionally for the stress of a Broadway production, when there was an incident of some sort, I don't think I've been told the details, just in general terms that she slipped and overturned herself, but the good news is that she is making a rapid recovery, and should shortly be visiting the theatre in person, rather than through her representatives, who are, I have to say, about as prepossessing as – no, I don't have to say, so I won't.

CRUEL AND USUAL BEHAVIOUR
ON BROADWAY

Let me go through today as quickly as possible, because it's been quite unpleasant, and will in a sense still be going on while I'm writing it down, until I've written it down, when I suppose I can count it as over at last. The nub of it is that the young actor I think of as Eric has been sacked at last – or rather, it has at last been decided that he is to be sacked, although he himself won't learn of it until we've found a replacement – the plan, as far as I can make it out, is to search out potential Gardners, arrange for their auditions, choose one, rehearse him a few times, and while this is being done continue with the already posthumous Gardner, paying him compliments when he comes off stage, issuing him with notes before he goes on stage, as if he were an abiding member of the company – if the new one isn't ready by next Tuesday, the current one, his head still stuffed with reassurances, as he's constantly in need of them, and asking for them – 'How did I do tonight? Is my reading the poem better? Am I doing that bit where I sit down right? And when I stand up again? – Oh, really? Oh, thanks, I was a bit worried about that – Gee, great, thanks, well, see you tomorrow' – is the type of exchange that follows his every appearance – will be sacked on Thursday, I think it's agreed, Thursday or Friday, one of those, immediately after the performance, so when he approaches the stage manager or Nathan or whoever relevant is to hand – 'Hey, how did I do? What about the poem?' – Nicky will manifest himself between them, so to speak, lay a compassionate hand on his shoulder and say something like, 'I think you did really great tonight, under the circumstances, the circumstances being that you're completely wrong for the part, sorry, my mistake in casting you, you're a fine young actor, one of the finest, as you know I know, because we've worked together before, that's why I cast you, and will cast you again some time in a part that we both hope you'll turn out to be right for, but as for your immediate future, you won't be going on tomorrow, could you clear your dressing room tonight, our love goes with you, your agent has been notified.' And if his replacement is still not ready, then the understudy will go on until he is. Anyway, we'll have a new Gardner quite a few performances before opening night if the plan goes according to plan, as I'm sure it will, as it's been used so often, in so many Broadway productions, and it's always worked. It always works.

At least as far as the shows are concerned. One has no idea how it works for the dismissed actor, who has to explain to all the people he's told – parents and brothers and sisters and friends – 'Yeah, that's right. Broadway. I'm gonna be on Broadway – Booth Theatre – with Nathan Lane! We open Oct 25th. Yeah, Oct 25th! How about that! All right!' – that in fact, come Oct 25th, he himself won't after all – won't after all – all the phone calls he'll have to make, or won't be able to face making, all the familiar bars he'll have to go into, the eager faces, the smiling enquiries – will it be a consolation to know that he's one in an endless line, to the crack o' doom and back again, the ghosts of sacked actors, living and dead –

It came about like this, the decision to sack Eric. They were rehearsing his scene, the last – as I keep noting – scene in the play. So there was Eric, as Gardner, on the stage, Nathan as Butley up there on the stage with him, and there, in about the fourth row of the stalls, were the director, Nicholas Martin, his assistant, Michael – a tall, easygoing young fellow who stays close to Nicholas Martin, writing his muttered observations and asides down in a notepad – he reads them back to him at the end of the day's work – almost as useful as a memory, when you think about it, and far less effort than working with your own pad and pen, furthermore a vital means of blocking people from talking to you, when the playwright wants to have a word with you, for instance, all you have to do when he approaches is swing your head towards your assistant, who begins to write, and the playwright, ever deferential, returns to his place at the back of the stalls – but let this pass, let this pass, on with the sacking of Eric – So Nicholas Martin in the fourth row – beside him, his body arched with super-attentiveness towards him, pad and pen at the ready, was his assistant, Michael, and all kinds of supernumeraries, God knows who they were, really, assistant thises and thats to the stage manager, the lighting designer, the costume designer, who knows who, a large pack of them, and then yet other figures scattered out in the darkness of the stalls, probably some of them producers – there are about twenty producers, as far as I can make out, twenty producers scattered into the darkness! – and me, standing at the very back, with my elbows on the balustrade, my hands wrapped over my ears, as a way of supporting my head, which felt both very heavy and completely empty, and also as a way of making it difficult, and if possible impossible, to hear Eric's reading from *East Coker* – 'In that open field/ If you do not come too close, if you do not come too close' – and though it was difficult it wasn't impossible, not nearly impossible enough, in fact, as is often the way, the more I squeezed my hands against my ears, the more sensitive to the spoken word they seemed to become.

They got to the end of the scene and they went back and started it again, which I'd hoped they weren't going to do, but I took it as a portent – they were going to go on doing the scene again and again until I paid it proper attention – I don't think this was a conscious plan, I don't think Nicholas Martin put it to himself that he'd go on and on doing the scene until finally someone, the playwright, for instance, was forced to look at it properly, and then, having looked at it properly, was in duty bound to object. I expect he hoped that if he went on doing it again and again it would somehow right itself, although it can be taken as a rule on the stage, as in life, that the more often you do something wrong the more difficult it becomes to accept that you're doing something wrong, even if you go on sensing that it's somehow not quite right. Well, what struck me on seeing it this second time around was that there were two scenes going on, in two different areas of the stage – centre stage, by the desk, was Eric, frail, feeble and charming, doing the scene as he always did it, out towards Nicholas Martin, and Nicholas Martin's assistant, and all the supernumerary assistants and producers scattered through the stalls, and there in a space on the stage only a few feet away from Eric was Nathan, who'd turned his back physically as well as metaphorically on Gardner and was addressing the lines he should have been giving to him to an empty bit of the stage, thus giving the impression that he was either talking to himself or to a ghost – this was not without a certain emotional effect, quite a powerful one, if surreal, particularly when he declaimed the Beatrix Potter nursery rhyme:

> 'Ninny Nanny Netticoat,
> In a white petticoat,
> With a red nose, –
> The longer he stands
> The shorter he grows.'

Thus he describes Gardner to Gardner, not just as a candle, but a candle of clownish aspect, dwindling before his very eyes, it's quite a violent insult, really, and of course, must be spoken straight at Gardner, not with his back to him, or it won't seem like an insult, it will seem like a nursery rhyme, summoned with no clear intention, out of affectation or whimsy –

So it is again, only in reverse, when Eric/Gardner reads from *East Coker*, so thinly and ineptly, with so little sense of what it's about, that we assume that Butley cuts him off because of the offence to T. S. Eliot, and not – as is intended to be the case – because he can't bear the weight of feeling in the lines. In the final moments of the scene, when Butley dismisses Gardner in language that is uncompromisingly brutal, Nathan had found a way of doing it, gulpingly and sorrowfully, and without meeting Eric's eye, so that we know that in his heart he isn't really telling Gardner just to fuck off, he's really calling out to Joey, his ex-protégé, who during the course of the play has been defecting as his flat-mate, his office-mate, his play-mate – to come back, come back! is Nathan's inaudible but visible cry to the absent Joey, as he stands with his back to a therefore dramatically absent Gardner –

I can see now, and could even see at the time, that this was a difficult situation for both Eric and Nathan to be in, but it also seemed to me then, and still does now, a pretty disgusting situation for the playwright to be in, confronted with either having to watch Nathan playing the scene against its grain, and so having the curtain fall on Butley as a self-pitying wreck, or coercing Nathan into playing the scene as if with the grain but without its spirit, and so having the curtain fall on Butley as a self-pitying bully. Both curtains false, and equally unattractive.

I'm only going on about this because I can't face putting down what happened this afternoon after the scene had been rehearsed several times, to no evident purpose. Finally there came a hiatus, with everyone frozen – no, that puts it too dramatically – they weren't frozen but they went quiet and still, as if fallen into a stupor. I seized the moment, I'd felt it welling up inside me, and now I seized it, or it seized me, and there I was, tramping down the aisle towards the stage, coughing and making the little retching noises that I tend to make in times of crisis, which are audible only to myself – when I had got to the aisle at the end of which Nicholas and his assistant were sitting, their heads together but not quite touching, as if each were waiting for the other to propose something helpful – marriage, or a mug of hemlock – I bent down and whispered – 'The thing is,' I said, 'the thing is, can we go somewhere quiet and talk?'

'Sure,' said Nicholas, 'sure. But what do you want to say?'

'I don't want to say it here,' I whispered.

Nathan pattered lightly down the steps from the stage, and joined us. Nicholas moved along a couple of seats, his assistant moved along a couple of seats, I sat down in one of the vacated seats, Nathan sat down next to me. The four of us were in a line, going from left at the end of the aisle – leading man, playwright, director, assistant to the director. There was a bustling and hustling sound from behind, as all the other assistants, and the numerous producers, moved forward to sit directly around and behind us. Eric/Gardner stood alone on the stage, facing us, smiling wistfully – he made me think suddenly of a stricken colt, though I've never seen a stricken colt, probably he wouldn't look at all like Eric/Gardner, he'd have four legs, for one thing, though Eric/Gardner probably wished he had another two just at the moment, to help him stay upright while being the observed of all observers.

'Simon wants to say something,' Nicholas said to Nathan, leaning across me.

'Yes, but not here!' I whispered.

'What?' said Nathan. 'What does he want to say?' Then turning to me, 'What do you want to say?'

'Well, not here.'

Eventually it was agreed that I didn't want to say what I had to say there, in front of the actor that I was going to propose that we sacked, with the rest of the company plus producers and assistants and surplus assistants sitting around and behind us, and we went somewhere else –

First, to the back of the stalls, and then to a bar across the road from Shubert Alley. What I said was pretty well what I've written above, although leaving out the bit about sacking Eric.

'Well, what do you think we should do?' Nicholas asked.

I put in the bit about sacking Eric.

They both knew, of course, that it was going to come to this, and said so. They'd just been waiting, really, for someone to come along and say it out loud. How lucky, we all agreed, that I'd come along and said it out loud.

I wish I'd said it out loud down the telephone in Spetses, instead of wasting hours working up some bogus Americanized dialogue and emailing it across on that bloody thing, what was it, the blueberry thing – but then I couldn't say it out loud until I'd seen the performance, could I? And how would I have seemed – the elderly and malevolent English playwright sunning himself on a Greek isle while blueberrying requests for the dismissal of some desperate, hard-working and lovable young American actor I hadn't even seen? On the other hand the desperate, hard-working and lovable young actor would have been gone by the time I arrived, he would have been gone and long forgotten, nobody would have blamed me for something they wouldn't have remembered – There is a moral in all this, quite an obvious one, that may serve me well when I get into my eighties, and a similar situation arises – but then a similar situation never arises, there's always an element in it that makes all the difference and – in other words you can learn nothing from experience, at least in my experience.

TOM AND JERRY – BUT WHICH IS WHICH?

Although this hotel is geographically closer to the Booth Theatre than our last hotel was, it takes longer to get there, because the traffic is worse – from the other hotel the cab could go straight downtown, it took on average ten minutes, from this hotel the cab has first to go across town, and then downtown, and it takes, it can take – well, last night, for instance, when I wanted to get to the theatre a little earlier than usual for a meeting with Nicholas Martin, it took me forty minutes to get within a ten-minute walk of the Booth – it would be a one-minute walk if it weren't for the people, most of whom look like immigrants and tourists from the land of the Fattipuffs, there are thousands and thousands of them, they're slow and fat and wheezy, they waddle along right in front of you and right beside you, waddle waddle waddle, hemming you in on all sides, and then it strikes you – at least it does if you're me – that you're just like them, you too are overweight, you're slow and you wheeze, and if you didn't have a limp you too would waddle – but I do have a limp, my legs have become very odd these last few days, almost as if they were disjointed, my left one more than my right one, so I sort of list – yes, there I was yesterday evening, dragging myself down Broadway, listing to the left, reminding myself of a character in a gangster film I once saw, waddle-limping to his death by gunfire. Unlike me, he wore a trilby.

When I got to Shubert Alley there was an enormous queue at the box office, always a gratifying sight for a playwright, and restorative, at least for a moment or two – I sidled further down the alley, to my favourite spot opposite the stage door, with my back to the wall, and a hamburgery sort of place on one side, and a small store that seems to specialize in bottled water on the other. This is where I stand, smoking, before the curtain goes up, and then in the interval – and then sometimes for a few minutes after the curtain's come down. I feel anonymous there, and almost invisible except to those who know me, who also know where to look for me – the director, for instance, comes over to join me as soon as he's seen me arrive. The flaw in this scheme is that those who don't know me feel free to speak freely if they happen to veer out a little as they leave the theatre – a few nights ago, at the third or fourth preview, a middle-aged woman came out of the theatre backwards, and kept coming backwards in my direction

until she swung, still going backwards, away from me, down Shubert
Alley. A little mob of other women with an elderly man mixed in was
following as she instructed them, in a fierce, honking voice, what they
were to feel about my play. 'You can't care about those people, you
can't care a single heartbeat about people like that! Horrible,
disgusting people!' She was still walking backwards as she spoke,
backwards down Shubert Alley, and they were still walking forwards,
towards her, people coming in the opposite direction had to step out
of their way. 'Didn't you just hate the lot of them!' she honked, as she
pedalled backwards, and voices called out from her followers, her
pursuers, 'Hated them, just hated them!' – I kept my eye on the
elderly man, but he didn't speak, just made vaguely belligerent
gestures with his arm – There was something faintly sinister about it,
probably because it looked simultaneously spontaneous and
organized, like the very first stage of a political demo, I suppose, or
of a lynch mob – but I expect they were one of those preview theatre
study groups – and there was another night – but that was my fault
for not getting out of the theatre quickly enough, a small man of
about fifty, I should think, in a grey sweater with a long scarf and a
blue cap which I thought had the word Crap on it, just above the
peak, but it can't have been Crap, perhaps it was Gap, I have a blue
cap at home that has Gap on it, so let's assume I misread it, to make
it conform to what he was saying, or rather chanting, 'Bor-ing, bor-
ing, bor-ing' was what he was chanting, low and to himself. That was
the worst part of it, that not only did he not intend the playwright to
hear, he didn't intend anyone to hear, he was obviously and simply
overwhelmed by the need to express himself, it was his true and
heartfelt judgement on the evening therefore – and there was
something about him, the schoolboy aspect of his behaviour, that was
undoubtedly sympathetic, and I thought that if we'd met at a party,
for instance, I'd probably have liked him.

I should put in here that I've heard some very nice things, too, but compliments never seem to stick in quite the same way, they become generalized in the memory, as pleasant experiences tend to do, while unpleasant experiences never seem to slip their particularity – so of the woman who actually spotted me, recognizing me from the programme and came up to me and said, 'Mr Gray, I just wanted to tell you that *Butley*'s one of my favourite plays of all time,' I remember nothing more than that she was a woman, and was quite big, and might have been my sort of age, perhaps a decade or two younger.

But to get back to last night, and my firstly admiring the long queue at the box office, and secondly going to my special spot between the hamburger type of place and the water-selling store, and lurking there with a cigarette, anonymously and invisibly. Well, it soon became apparent that tonight not only was I anonymous and invisible to strangers, but also to people who knew me quite well – Nicholas Martin, the director, among them. He was standing by the stage door, sort of sideways on to me, talking to his tall young assistant. I saw his alert and agreeable eye take me in from around his tall young assistant's elbow, then he reached up and put his hands on his tall young assistant's shoulders and swivelled him around, blocking my view of him – and probably more to the point, blocking his view of me. I took a few steps sideways, until I had him in my sights again, and again his hands went up to his tall young assistant's shoulders, and he readjusted their positions. I told myself that this couldn't be what it seemed to be, waited a few minutes, took out my mobile and phoned him. I heard the phone ring, and ring some more, then it stopped. 'This is Nicholas Martin, why don't you leave me a message?' his voice said, with a hopeful, upward inflection on 'message'. I left him a message bidding him good evening and informing him that I was a few yards away, and at his service with my thoughts about that scene that we'd arranged to meet and discuss. I was watching the assistant's back, waiting to see if Nicholas Martin would emerge from behind it. Nothing happened for a moment and then the assistant walked quickly towards the stage door and went inside, and there was absolutely nobody where Nicholas Martin ought, by all known rules of nature etc., to have been. I wondered for a moment whether he'd somehow attached himself to the front of his assistant's body, and thus been smuggled by him through the stage door, it was just possible, he was short enough, the assistant's spine long enough – but then I saw him much further along the alley, up at the box-office end, wedged in between a young couple that he turned into a kind of human tunnel that he scaled, like an old-fashioned chimney-sweep, so that he could hug them simultaneously around the neck, then he shinned down and was into the box office where I knew there was a door to take him backstage. I thought of going through the stage door in the alley, trapping him in the corridor as he came down the stairs, but he might whip past me, or turn around and run back up the stairs, what would it look like if the large – elderly, but large – playwright were seen chasing the younger – small but younger – director around the insides of the theatre, and what would I say to him? 'Nicky, Nicky, why are you running away from me?' in that tone Marlon Brando adopts in the back of the car with Rod Steiger in *On the Waterfront*, when Rod Steiger – who is his brother – pulls a gun on him. It's a lovely and sorrowful moment, but I didn't think it would work with Nicholas Martin unless he pulled a gun on me, and if he did, I'm not sure I would get the tone right, I'd turn and run, and we'd be off again in reverse, cinematically more Tom and Jerry or the Marx Brothers than Brando and Steiger –

MR POOLE REVISITING

So I went in and stood in my usual spot at the back of the stalls, and when all the audience was in and the curtain was going up, Nicholas Martin slipped in and stood some way down from me, by the door, through which he shot just under an hour later as the curtain came down. I went out and hung around in my usual spot, smoking, at the interval, not really expecting him, and feeling distinctly unwanted and unpopular – people who have been saluting me, well, they don't actually salute, but they wave with kindliness and respect, come in and out of the stage door quite clearly refraining from looking to where they know I'm to be seen at the interval, it was as if I were someone both shameful and shaming. Now what distinction am I making here? What is the difference between being shameful and being shaming? I must have assumed a difference or I wouldn't have said I was both. The suffix -ful and the suffix -ing, think of other uses. Well, hateful and hating – if someone is hateful it's because they fill other people with hate, whereas hating, it's difficult to think of an ordinary use, except by Apu in *The Simpsons*, who might well say, 'We are hating all the noise Mr Simpson is making', otherwise it turns up mainly as a gerund, isn't that what it's called, when a verb is made into a noun? 'He couldn't abide all the hating that went on between Apu and Simpson etc.', though Apu isn't much of a hater – none of this is helping me to distinguish between being 'shameful' and being 'shaming' but there was a time when I understood, or understood for a brief moment – when Mr Poole, at Portsmouth Grammar School – I was about nine years old, in the infirmary with flu. I had to pee, and the nearest lavatory was corridors on corridors away, it seemed endless, the wavering totter down these cold corridors in my pyjamas, my bladder bursting and thinking that I was going to fall over any second because my legs were wobbly and I was shivering. But I made it, and oh the relief, the joy of it, in spite of the cold and also feeling so hot. When I finished and opened the door there was Mr Poole standing there, tall and bald-headed and looking down at me through his glasses with his usual irritation. He stepped aside to let me pass, then went into the lavatory, and back I went, along the corridors on corridors to the infirmary, and climbed into bed. There were three or four other boys in the infirmary, so it must have been one of the flu epidemics – how appalling, though, that there wasn't a lavatory in the room, or just off it – but there must have been an OK matron, because I don't remember her, just as I don't remember who the other boys were, or whether they were younger or older, in fact, all I remember is being back in bed, so glad to be back in bed with an empty bladder, and shivering, and then there was Mr Poole there standing over me, looking down at me with considered and thoughtful anger – he spoke at me from the foot of the bed in a voice that, though it was conversational, he intended to carry to the other beds, and no doubt to matron. He said it had been disgusting to follow after me in the lavatory, there was wet on the floor and on the seat – I still remember now that I couldn't remember then having peed on the floor and on the seat, but I expect I did, he wouldn't have been making it up, after all, Mr Poole never made things up, and his disgust was 'real' and 'felt', to use a Leavisite vocabulary, 'felt' and 'real', and it was in this context that I first came across the use of 'both shameful and shaming', he said that it was both shameful and shaming that a boy in the boarding house of Portsmouth Grammar School should have so little consideration for others, should be so lazy and disgusting in his personal habits, should be so this and that, that and this, shameful, shaming, should be ashamed, disgusting, it seemed to have no end, his peroration – well, that's anger for you, it quickly becomes addictive, one angry sentence leads into another and then into paragraphs, it becomes exhilarating, and difficult to bring to a conclusion. It's very possible, though, that Mr Poole only spoke for a very brief time, but at the time – and in memory – it was interminable, lying there at attention under the covers, head straight on the pillow, staring obediently at Mr Poole's implacably disgusted and contemptuous face. When he'd done I burrowed under the bedclothes and hoped I'd never have to meet the gaze of any of the other boys in the san, or of the matron. But I have an idea now that nobody said anything about it – and it was a tough enough school, where you were likely to be held to loud and sneering account, with descriptive nicknames and so forth, if you were at the centre of an incident considered unsavoury.

Well, I'm not saying that I felt last night as I felt sixty-odd years ago when I hid under the bedclothes, in fact the fact is that though I can identify such feelings, mortification, embarrassment etc., they're not really feelings in the old sense of the word, in the days when I had feelings I could feel, they're more like reminiscences of feelings, they're so faint and thinned out, and I cared far more about having my cigarette than I did about my shame.

ALL'S WELL THAT ENDS

I went back in for the second act and in he slipped as the curtain went up, and out he slipped an hour later as it was coming down. I stayed for the applause because there was so much of it, some of it even being for the play, and for Nathan there were bravos. Bravo, bravo, bravo! they cried, yippee, yippee! as if he were taking his bows on a horse in a rodeo. Then I went backstage and spent half an hour with Nathan in his dressing room. He was hot and shiny from his shower, and looked terribly young, like a boy almost, his eyes very bright, but his eyebrows were lifted and his voice growly and drawly, which meant that he was worried, and wanted notes – I've never known him not worried after a performance, not wanting notes. I thought of asking him about Nicholas Martin, was there something he knew which would explain his reluctance to have contact with me, but thought I'd better not, thought I'd better not worry him with it. So I came back here and worried Victoria with it, over a supper we had sent up from room service – a perfectly edible supper, brought up by very pleasant whatdoyoucallems, not bellhops, waiters I suppose, one of each sex, male for the main course, female for the pudding, or can you still say waitress, in which case a young South American waiter and a young black New York waitress, both very charming and wearing easy smiles – a pleasant meal with the New York night glittering below us, and I fretting and fretting on about Nicholas Martin, why was he avoiding me or was it my usual paranoia? Victoria thought it might be both – that he was probably avoiding me, and that I was paranoid about it, which seemed to me reasonable, and still does. But still – Victoria's gone to bed, and I'm sitting in a corner of the couch, with a portable music player playing Mozart piano sonatas and writing this on a pad on my lap, and as it's all about Nicholas Martin avoiding me, I must be still worrying about it. Well, actually, I wasn't worrying about it while I was writing it down. Now that seems to me important, that writing down my worry was a completely unworrying experience, and not because it was therapy, that sort of crap, but because it was fun. Yes, I had fun writing down all my worry. I wonder how far one could take that. If one were due to be hanged in the morning could one conceivably find any fun in the writing about it – Chidiock Tichborne was very young when he wrote the poem on the eve of his execution, which was not just a hanging affair but a drawing and a quartering affair too – it's no good pretending his poem is fun to read, it isn't, it's a

desolate lament, very much on one note – 'And now I live, and now
my life is done' is pretty well the whole content, the burden of his
song – there are nine cigarette ends in the ashtray, all since Victoria
went to bed –

Spent a harmonious if sometimes excitable afternoon here, in the
apartment, going through the play scene by scene with Nicholas
Martin. By excitable I mean that we both enjoyed it, and laughed a
great deal. He has a hooting and highly contagious laugh, he's also
very observant, and remembers and is good at describing gestures
and expressions. Although I love things that make me laugh, I rather
wish I didn't actually have to laugh, the physical part of it has become
quite difficult, no doubt because of my smoking – the noise I make
is a wheeze, that I try to keep shallow – the moment it goes deep into
my lungs I begin to cough, the cough goes on and on, then I become
dizzy, light-headed and I think I'm going to faint. Anyone who
wanted to murder me would simply have to say three funny things
in a row, so that I couldn't get my breath back long enough. Or
perhaps I'd go into a coma, and stay in it for years, somehow that
would be more ignominious than actually dying of laughter, and far
worse for Victoria, who would find herself having to explain to
people how it had come about that I was lying there alive but to all
intents and purposes quite dead – 'It happened because he laughed
too much at something that Nicholas Martin said' – and supposing
they found the nerve to ask what Nicholas Martin had said, and
supposing she'd actually been there and had heard the jokes and
witticisms and seen me laugh, then collapse laughing, then lapse into
unconsciousness, making dreadful little gasping-wheezing-laughing
noises, and then supposing that she told them what he'd said – what
would they do? They could scarcely rock with robust, healthy-lunged
laughter, it would be unseemly, surely, but they couldn't not laugh,

it would make my coma even more pathetic if it had been caused by
my laughing at something that other people didn't find at all funny.
I imagine they'd have to laugh politely while nodding sombrely, quite
a difficult trick to pull off. Probably Victoria would suggest, without
actually lying, that I'd become comatose from an excess of thought
for others, or from worrying about the state of the world.

Anyway it's good to be back on terms with Nicholas Martin – at
least not to feel that he'd scale any nearby person just to avoid
talking to me. I accompanied him down in the elevator and saw
him into a cab. Just as I was closing the door on him he said
something very quickly to the effect that he was sorry he'd been
'mad' at me, and then the cab sped off. I went to the smoking alley
beside the hotel, and sat at the table I always sit at, opposite the side
door into the hotel, with a Diet Coke, wondering whether I would
ask him this evening why he'd been 'mad' at me, or would it be
better to leave it? It was very pleasant sitting in the alley, it was mild
with a light breeze, and people were coming up and down, they
were all colours, shapes, sizes, such a variety that would once have
struck me as typical of New York and one of the things about it that
I most loved, but now of course it's also typical of London, it was
just as if I were sitting at my usual table on Holland Park Avenue.
I felt the same sort of mood, that suspended mood when you know
there's much to worry about but you can't quite remember what it
is – not exactly serenity, more a gentle vacancy of spirit.

UP IN LIGHTS AND FURTHERMORE

We went downtown together, Victoria and I, though we were going
to different theatres – I to the Booth to see *Butley* for the sixth or
seventh preview, she to a neighbouring theatre, just around the

corner from the Booth, to see the new production of *A Chorus Line*. We got off at the corner of Eighth and 45th, and stood there, quite still, holding each other by the hand as we stared up at the frame that towered from the roof of the Booth that was infinitely more imposing even than the last time we'd gazed at it and had tried to imagine how it would look when lit up, my name in lights – because now at last it was actually lit up, and there, glittering and sparkling, were the words NATHAN LANE, and underneath that the word IN, and underneath that the word BUTLEY. 'So,' I said calmly, trying not to squeeze my wife's hand more savagely than was absolutely necessary, 'so. There you have it. My name not up in lights, after all.' 'Still, the play's in lights,' she pointed out. 'Although,' she added, 'they could scarcely just put Nathan Lane. They'd have to put that he's in something.' I admit that I was childishly disappointed. I really had longed to see my name in lights. But why 'childishly' come to think about it? It seems to me a perfectly proper and adult disappointment. In fact, I can't imagine children wanting to see their names in lights, well, not normal children, anyway, by which I mean of course children of my generation. Children of today, who are brought up almost from birth to crave celebrity, and are mostly abnormal by the standards of my day, would no doubt love to see their names in lights, although whether they would be able to recognize their names without having them read out is another matter. Anyway, I've decided not to be ashamed of wanting to see my name in lights, although I must try to get over being ashamed of not seeing it in lights. It seems to me, however I look at it, that I must have failed somewhere along the line, that I'm caught in a kind of vicious circle – my name doesn't go up in lights because, quite frankly, I'm not famous enough, and therefore not worthy of the bulbs, electricity, space, etc. But the reason I'm not famous enough is because my name never goes into lights. I'm convinced that if people got used to seeing my name in lights they would begin to recognize it in other spheres of life. In fact, their eyes would light up from the memory of a lit-up name when I was being introduced to them, and we would be spared, on both sides, the kind of ghastly conversation that proceeds from my having to identify myself as a playwright – 'Might I have seen anything you've written?' someone will ask, which forces me to offer a list of plays – and with each title they dip their heads in embarrassment at not recognizing it, or occasionally exclaim – 'Oh yes, I think I saw that one, it had Peter O'Toole in it, didn't it?' and no, I say, no, no, it didn't have Peter O'Toole in it – and if I name the actor who was in it, they might say, 'Oh, how odd that I missed it – I generally make a point of seeing anything with him in it, one of my favourite actors!' and with luck we can move on to remembering all the plays the famous actor has been in.

Victoria went off to see *A Chorus Line*, I stood between the hamburgers and the bottled water and talked to Nicholas Martin – really going over the conversation of the afternoon, reminding ourselves of the moments we wanted to pay particular attention to. We stood companionably near each other during the first act, which went well – or well enough, given that three mobile phones went off in the stalls that I could hear. It's a pretty good rule of thumb or whatever that twice as many mobile phones go off than I hear, as there are parts of the stalls, in the front to the far left and right, which are inaudible to those of us standing in the back. If I wrote about my feelings about every mobile phone I heard during a performance – how dark, bloody, murderous my thoughts – the most appalling thing about the people responsible is that they're not even embarrassed – one man, fleshily into his fifties with a thick mop of yellowish hair and a lissom young man beside him who might have been his nephew, in as much as he bore a resemblance – Fleshily's mobile went off just as the Edna scene was getting under way, it made a piercing chirruping noise, like a mad bird – he extracted it in leisurely fashion from his inner breast pocket, and handed it, without glancing at it, to Lissom, who looked at the screen, fiddled coolly, then muttered something to Fleshily as he handed it back to him. But apart from that – this was the thing – they seemed quite involved in what was going on on the stage, laughing and looking towards each other in appreciation. In other words I wouldn't have minded a whole theatre full of Fleshilies and Lissoms, minus their mobiles – cellphones, they're called here, don't forget. Or just cells. I sometimes wonder whether members of the audience cell each other during the performance to discuss the jokes, or the meaning of a line, or perhaps to remind each other of where they're going to have dinner.

In the interval we went to a nearby bar whose name I can never remember as it's too complicated, both a Christian name and a surname, and both of them quite ordinary. I can't say I like it much as it's generally crowded, every table full and everybody at every table shouting and laughing at the tops of their voices, with people also standing between the tables, also shouting and laughing at the tops of their voices – or it's completely empty apart from, say, a couple of tables, and another couple sitting at the bar, and a surplus of waiters, all talking in low voices, so that you feel that you have to talk in a low voice too, otherwise you will be overheard by showbiz journalists, who like, or so it's rumoured, to sit on the fringes of the rooms, in the shadows, hoping to pick up bits and pieces of conversations that they can publish to embarrassing effect – but in fact this evening it was, for once, just right – just enough people to ensure that you could speak at a normal level. I think we both felt very comfortable as we sat over our Diet Cokes and traded cellphone experiences, then discussed a few patches of Act One that needed attention, then aspects of Nathan's performance and then rose to go back to the theatre and then sat down again instead. We'd both, I think, had enough of previews for a while – or at least for this evening – or at least for the very next bit of it, because we agreed we'd go back sort of halfway through the second act, avoid the tension of waiting with the audience for the curtain to go up while overhearing things we didn't want to hear – It seemed like a good opportunity, if there's ever really a good opportunity for such matters – and so I said, 'You said this afternoon, when you were getting into the cab, that you were sorry you'd been mad at me yesterday.' 'Well, yes, I am,' he said. 'I am sorry.' 'Yes, well, that's good. I'm glad. But what were you mad at?' 'Oh,' he said. 'Oh. Well, yesterday I had to tell Eric he was fired. And it was pretty terrible. His parents and his friends were all coming to the first night. You know – none of them's even been to a Broadway show before, and so – he cried, and said, "What am I going to tell my mum?"' I thought about this. 'But do you think he shouldn't have been fired?' 'Oh, he had to be fired. No question of it. And I should have done it before you came. And then I kind of hoped he'd be all right. I kept telling myself he was getting better, and believing it, until you spoke up. And I knew it was true. Everybody knew it, really.' 'Well,' I said, 'if I'd been here from the beginning of rehearsals and got to know him I probably wouldn't have spoken up.' I really don't know if this is true or not. Certainly it had helped that I'd only had one conversation with Eric, although that had been one conversation too many, as I'd found him touching and likeable. As I suppose one would find any young man who was in a sense already posthumous. Like Chidiock Tichborne, really, when you think about it. Anyway, Chidiock Tichborne was long dead, Eric had left the building, Nicholas Martin had had a rotten day which he'd been unable not to share with me – and so the conversation moved on, to other things, and eventually he went back to the Booth, and a few minutes later I followed, smoking a cigarette along the way, and got in and sidled to a spot along the back, and watched the new Gardner come on stage, where he looked eerily like the old Gardner, the way he stood, his expressions, the same blond hair, and almost the same voice – the difference was he was in every respect stronger, more present – even his blond hair was blonder, more assertive, and Nathan was seeing him and playing to him, and therefore I felt much better about the end of the play. He got a good hand, the new Gardner, and even one or two low-key bravos and the yip in yippee! But that might have been family, of course, or a partner. Fleshily and Lissom gave him a good clap – no, unfortunately put – applauded him vigorously, as they did all the actors, then went wild when Nathan took his curtain – not bravos or yippees, but both of them clapping their hands above their heads and thrusting out their chests, and I don't think they were family, Fleshily and Lissom, wrong physical types, but there was no doubt they'd enjoyed their evening. I found myself looking on them with doting eyes as I slipped out behind them. They had a limousine waiting on the kerb on 45th, with a man in a peaked cap holding the door open for them. As they clambered in Lissom put the cell to his ear, then passed it to Fleshily as the car slid into the traffic.

SKIDDING ON VOMIT

Most of the recent nights I've come back to the hotel, and sat with a pad in front of me, thinking about how to describe the day, or whether I want to. I put down a few words, then stop, look out of the window, down at the little dots of the car lights going up and down the street – our street – and the sight stirs a memory that doesn't stay, as if it's nudging me to a memory beyond it, and so I flounder, look down at the traffic, then put on the Mozart and wait for Victoria if she's out, or for Stephen Hollis, an old friend who put on several of my plays when he was artistic director at the Palace Theatre, Watford, in the 1970s, then directed three, I think it was, in London, and three or four in New York, where he now lives, still directing and teaching drama at a university in a town nearby. Stephen sometimes joins us for dinner, sometimes afterwards, at the large, outside café on the corner of 50th Street which takes its style from Parisian pavement cafés. You can get wine, beers, Cognacs, *pâtisseries* and coffees, then sit over them for as long as you want. In the section we go to, which is the one in which you are almost sure to find a table straight away, you are allowed to smoke. There are always clean ashtrays on the tables, and the people who come to use them are mostly regulars, who don't bother to hang about until the *maître d'* comes to escort them, they stroll straight on through, their cigars and cigarettes unlit but ready between their lips. They never come in smoking, they relish sitting down first, then lighting up with a degree of ceremony, but there are a few who have become so furtive and cowed that they don't really believe, in spite of the evidence provided by a dozen or so tables of smokers, that it's allowed. They stand at the entrance apprehensively, waiting for the *maître d'*, who after midnight tends to be a robotic but quite pretty Russian girl, and they ask her, 'Hey, is it all right to smoke?' and she smiles in a friendly, slightly unseeing fashion, and says, 'Yes, yes, you can smoke, yes, it's OK, yes', and leads them to a table, and when she's sat them down she moves the ashtray a few inches, then turns it around a few times, not complete revolutions but partial revolutions almost as if it were a combination lock and the top of the table the door of a safe. It sometimes makes me think of chastity belts, though I doubt if chastity belts have combination locks, they'd have neat little padlocks, I'd guess, made of gold with pearls inlaid – well, the female ones, I can't imagine the male ones – anyway, she creates the sense, with these needy and ill-at-ease smokers, that whatever had to be opened has been opened, they may now smoke, but they check several times before taking out their cigarettes and lighters. Perhaps they'd relax and light up with more of a flourish if they weren't conscious of being closely watched by an ill-kempt, elderly man, I suspect that I'm a clumsy and ostentatious observer, I know that I stare directly at people. When Victoria catches me at it she says that it's more like a glare than a stare, an accusing glare that must be alarming to those it's fixed on – the fact that I'm smoking clearly doesn't reassure them, perhaps they see me as an *agent provocateur*, I don't know what they see me as, probably just an ill-natured old man, a sort of Evelyn Waugh but with small, malevolent eyes instead of protuberant, indignant ones.

I wrote too soon about Liz McCann being on the way to recovery. I suppose it was having written about her that made me think of her when I went to the matinée – I was hanging about in my usual spot, smoking, when a young lady from the McCann office came over with an envelope containing my tickets – I always have trouble finding something to say to her, she's small and pleasantly brisk in her manner, but she always, on giving me the envelope with the tickets in, stands rooted, as if waiting for me to say something to follow the thank you that I've just said. We sometimes stand there for up to a minute, she staring up at me, I bending over her. Then she says, 'Well, I'd better get back,' and goes through the stage door or towards the lobby. This afternoon, though, I said thank you, and then I said, 'Oh, and how's Liz getting on?' and she said, 'Oh, didn't you know, she's broken her leg.' 'Yes,' I said, 'but it's getting better, isn't it?' 'No,' she said, 'she's had another accident,' and she told me that a few evenings ago, at her home, Liz had skidded on some cat vomit and taken a tumble down the stairs. I think she said down the stairs, or have I just added that because that's how I imagined it – Liz McCann heaving herself along on her crutches, coming to the top of the stairs, putting her foot down on an unnoticed puddle of mess, then whoops! and crash. But it may have happened quite differently, of course. I don't think the ticket lady told me how it happened. I could scarcely pursue the matter once I'd got the essential fact of her skidding on cat vomit.

Apart from that, I enjoyed the play very much.

THREE SCORE AND TEN

It's nearly four in the afternoon and I'm sitting at a low table in our hotel suite, Suite 1410, writing this down into a pad on my lap while a youngish man, short and dark, with a ragged goatee and holes in his socks and a broad Boston accent, is taking photographs of me – posed photographs – he keeps putting me into completely phoney and unnatural positions, and when I break free to do something that is actually natural, e.g. lighting a cigarette, he stabs a word out – a word like 'Freeze!' or 'Hold!' – while I'm in the middle of the action – he's a very courteous, slightly anxious-mannered man of Greek origin, and you wouldn't think he had such sharp peremptoriness in him, but he has managed to keep me frozen in positions that become phoney immediately I've taken them up, and he keeps me in them until every part of me begins to ache, and reminding me of the various punishments to which I was subjected by my powdered and pouchy-eyed prep-school teacher

Mr Burn, who most particularly liked to keep me in positions that were no doubt eloquent for him. He would walk, slightly crouched, around and around me, watching me, much like this photographer, but of course my reactions now are totally different – instead of shy and furtive and tortured pleasure, a kind of self-mangling self-love, I feel a terrible weariness, the ache is the ache of age protesting, aged muscles, creaking limbs, stiffening back – the difference between being eleven and knowingly desired and seventy and being photographed – vanity the only connecting element –

Actually I wasn't actually quite seventy when I wrote the above, but I am now, and have been since midnight four hours ago. We celebrated my becoming it at a restaurant called La Miseria, something like that anyway, on 48th Street, between Broadway and Eighth. It was recommended by Nathan, who'd had one of his forties birthdays there a few years back, and it seemed OK when we explored it. The staff, or cast really, were entirely Italian – I mean, not simply every one of them, but every bit of every one of them, no one spoke English fluently, some of them seemed not to speak it at all, and the portly, no, roly-poly laughing Italian who was in charge of parties spoke lots of half phrases and clichés that he managed to make adequate to his needs and ours – so his reply to our anxious enquiries as to whether there was really enough room in the back half of the restaurant which was where he proposed we should hold our party was 'OK. Sure. Yeah. Be all right on the night, trust yes?' and there was so much merriness in him, he shook and rolled about with it, that we took him at his word, the one that mattered, and we did indeed trust – well, Victoria did indeed, I only did in patches – 'I'm sure it'll be all right, as he says, just don't see how we're going to fit nearly fifty people in that small space', to which, from Victoria, 'He's very experienced, and he wants to do it, and he won't want to let Nathan down.' 'People who let people down don't usually want to' was my usual answer to this – in fact I can't think of anyone out of all the many I personally have let down that I actually wanted to, or set out to, let down. So this *maître d'* etc. certainly seemed determined to let us down on the night of the party. Victoria and Stephen Hollis and I arrived at just after 10 p.m. Most of our guests were at the theatre, either watching *Butley* or acting in it, and as the curtain comes down at 10.15 and it's a five-minute walk from the theatre they could be expected from around 10.30 on. So what did we see in the back part of the restaurant, the set-apart-for-the-party part, at 10.15 but two long tables at which were sitting, at each table, about a dozen diners. Italians. Of the sort that roll spaghetti around their forks while raising glasses and shouting loving messages across the room, some of them sounded like loving birthday messages – yes, two long tables of birthday revellers in the space reserved for my forty or so birthday guests.

My brother Nigel and his wife, Barbara, had flown in from Toronto, and had come along early, with Stephen, to help seat the guests and settle my nerves. So there were five of us waiting to receive forty-eight – I"ve just checked with Victoria – it was forty-eight guests. Well, minus the five of us, come to think of it. So forty-three guests in a room currently occupied by about twenty noisy Italian diners, celebrating, from the sound of them, a birthday per head.

I went out on the pavement and smoked, not being allowed, of course, to do it anywhere else, even on my birthday. *Signor il padrone* came out on the pavement and smoked with me, not anxiously, as I did, but patiently and benevolently, a man who enjoyed his cigarette wherever he might be, and in whatever company – in this case a suppuratingly angry man of exactly seventy years of age – now here is an odd thing about age, this proprietor, let me call him Giuseppe, no, that's too long, can't be bothered to write that out each time, what about Gino? Yes, Gino, Gino was about, I should say, fifty years old, no more, perhaps a month or so less, yet I had the distinct sense that he was older than me by more than a few months, by about thirty years, in fact – I don't mean that I felt him to be a hundred, but that I felt that he was my senior, in responsibility, in authority, in the kind of maturity that counts, in life as opposed to years, as it were, and therefore, though I was livid with him –

No, let me go back to that thought, about my being in physical terms about twenty years older, but feeling in real terms, in life terms, that I was thirty years his junior – I realize, now I've put it down, that this has become quite a common experience with me, and it's not a recent one, to do with my being seventy. I've had it most of my adult life, as if at a certain stage I just stopped adding years to my sense of my self, and have gone on seeing people, people I don't know, from a constantly juvenile perspective. But what do they see? What did Gius – no, Gino see, but a seventy-year-old – he knew my age to the day, as he was organizing the party that celebrated it – a seventy-year-old Englishman being petulant and ill-tempered on the pavement. Or did he see a noble wreck of an English gentleman, irritated and impatient but only in a manner that became his years? 'Eet weel be OK. They are frands,' he kept saying to me. 'They weel be gone in tree four meenits.' The most infuriating thing about him was his smiling certainty, which turned out to be completely justified – I went for a very short walk, about three, four minutes, and when I got back Gino was holding open his restaurant door and ushering his frands on to the street, and beyond him, in the back part of the restaurant, his waiters were converting the two long tables into four smaller tables, moving all the other small tables out of the wings and into place, putting down the tablecloths, the knives and forks etc., and at the upstairs table, in the alcove, I could see Victoria laughing and relaxed with Nigel, Barbara, Stephen –

So it should have been all right. How now to explain that it wasn't – not in my soul it wasn't. It wasn't really the problem with Gino or the unwanted diners, it wasn't simply that I didn't want to be seventy – it was as if I wasn't there, or as if I was at an oblique angle to what was going on, an oblique angle to my birthday, to the event itself and the people who'd come, a number of them from far away. The food was very good, everybody said, and there was certainly enough to drink, perhaps more than enough if the strange suggestions and propositions put to me by an actress I was once very close to were anything to go by. And it passed, it all passed, this too has passed –

Perhaps the problem for parties with me is mundane – that I no longer drink, I'm not allowed to smoke, therefore etc. But what is unarguably true about this particular party is that now that it's over and retrospective I find that not only can I enjoy it at last, but that I'm moved by the memory of it, and grateful that people came, that friends came, and that I have a wife like Victoria to organize it. What do I mean, a wife like Victoria? She is not like Victoria she is Victoria. Is my wife.

ALAN, NATHAN AND ALAN

Something else from the party that has stuck like a burr in my mind, and that I wish I could dislodge – several people who had seen Alan's Butley on stage in London or New York or who have seen the film, and who have now seen Nathan's Butley, came up to me and asked, in rather too low and intimate a manner, as if they were prying into family matters, which Butley I preferred, Nathan's or Alan's. And in fact I felt that they were prying into family matters – being asked to choose between two blood relatives or – or – absurd, of course, because it's a reasonable question to ask, even though it's one I can't answer reasonably, at least not in terms of preferences, although I could, perhaps, in terms of comparisons, elementary comparisons, starting with Nathan. His performance is extraordinary, not because it's immensely funny and full of bravura comic moments with impeccable timing – the things that one would expect from Nathan, the great comedian – but because there's a darkness and a loneliness to it as of a man living out the last hours of his life. One feels that for this Butley the loss of Joey is a death of the spirit, from which there can be no resurrection. For Alan, not only an attractive man but a beautiful one, in whose eyes the light never quite went out, one felt that tomorrow – no, not tomorrow, he'd be too hung-over, and the next day too and perhaps the day after that – but anyway before the week was out he'd be on the rampage once more, back at his desk despoiling students' essays, at his office door blocking their entrance, on the telephone buggering up the college's administration, above all in and out of Joey's new office – back in his life, turning it into a chaos. Alan's Butley was an exhilarating experience, really, his triumphant curtain calls an extension of his last moments on the stage – on Broadway women came armed with flowers, which they flung at him as he bowed and beamed, and whatever you thought the character would be doing the next evening, you knew the actor would be back for his flowers. It seemed to me a miracle that Nathan was back for the next performance, I would have looked for him where I would have looked for his Butley, exhausted and drained, adrift in the night. Well, these are extravagant and generalized statements, I know, and subject to mundane qualifications – some nights, when the mischief is on him, Nathan is more Alan, just as some nights Alan prefigured Nathan in his final moments of desolation, clutching at the curtain-call bouquets as if he'd been thrown lifesavers, wrapping his arms around them, and hugging them to his stomach. It would be meaningless to say which of the performances was better. If one had been able to see them on alternate nights over a couple of weeks one couldn't have kept a scorecard, they were different experiences that emanated from different cores, and when they were bad, they were bad as I would expect them to be bad, with Nathan demanding more pity from the audience than the audience had at its disposal, Alan coasting along with too many flourishes and sometimes the hint of a smirk –

Well, of course I didn't go into any of this at the party, muttering vaguely to the effect that really the only performance I could see at the moment was Nathan's, it blocked out all other performances, even Alan's, especially while we were in preview, and indicated that perhaps there were other topics of conversation, indeed other plays. And it was a bit odd, really, to have people asking whether I preferred Alan's or Nathan's Butley with Nathan sitting only just out of earshot and highly visible, having just a short while ago given his performance. There was an elderly actor with a withering tendency when discussing other actors, and who has become slightly deaf, and you would think from his behaviour slightly blind too, as he seemed to be looking straight towards Nathan when he said – 'But Alan's performance is on film. I've got the DVD. I'll send it over to your hotel, if you want.' I said, rather tersely, that I couldn't imagine why I would want it. 'So you can compare the two performances. You can come back from Nathan's in the theatre and put on Alan's on film, see them consecutively.' I said yes, and there was probably some way I could get the film up on my mobile, so I could actually watch Alan's film performance and Nathan's stage performance simultaneously. I think he thought this a pretty stupid idea.

Alan though –

Of course I have the DVD at home, somewhere in the basement, along with a lot of other memorabilia. The film was meant to be – in accordance with the avowed intention of Ely Landau, the somewhat messianic producer – a filmed record of the stage performance, but given cinematic authenticity by being filmed in a studio, where the camera could travel to all the secret nooks and crannies of the specially built office, as well as the nooks and crannies of the actors' faces. It wasn't, in other words, a mere static filming of one of Alan's theatre performances, but a scrupulous rendering of the performance in cinematic terms. I saw it on its first public showing and remember having only one clear critical thought – that the playwright should have turned himself into a screenwriter at least to the extent of cutting twenty minutes or so out of the script, but I don't believe I knew then, and certainly don't know now, which twenty minutes. I've never been tempted down to the basement to forage around for the DVD because the thought of having it in my hand, putting it in the DVD player, then sitting calmly watching Alan alive, breathing, laughing, subsiding exhausted, remembering the days I sat in the studio observing the various takes, then sat with him during the interminable settings-up between scenes – it was odd enough at the time, just to be in what was an exact reconstruction of my daily office, but when I sat beside Alan he would be wearing a version of the suit I wore to my office, and when he entered my office he was wearing a copy of my mackintosh and carrying in his hand my actual briefcase, as he'd done every night on stage at the Criterion Theatre, it had become for him a sort of talisman, my briefcase. He'd also borrowed my walk, some of my gestures and my manner of talking, so I was told – who knows how they appear to walk, what habitual gestures they make, how their voice sounds when they speak, but I had an odd sensation about which I can't be precise – I didn't feel I was being stolen from or imitated or in some sense doubled, nor that there was some conspiracy between the actor and the director which involved me from which I was also excluded – actually what I felt was an extremely heightened sense of the shame that I always feel when a piece of my writing is being acted out, the only approximate image for which is a variation on the familiar nightmare of discovering oneself naked in a public place, the variation being the element of deliberate intent – that one of me has positively and arrogantly strutted naked on to a public stage, while another of me is an aghast spectator, unable to speak out confessionally and penitentially. The result is a jumbled self, yes, that's me, look at him, isn't he something! Please, please forgive me, I know not what he does – that sort of jumble of self, of selves really – well now, that's a heightened version of the heightened version of shame that I experienced when I watched Alan giving his version of me in the filming of *Butley*. It wasn't happening in a dream or a nightmare, it was happening in a recognizable world of everyday consciousness, and when someone, usually Harold, asked me what thoughts I had about what I was seeing, I answered in a composed enough fashion, and probably tried to demonstrate my eye for detail – 'Just wondering whether those essays look right on Butley's desk, a bit too neatly piled, mmm?' and Harold would run an alert eye over the essays, shuffle them about a little. Sometimes Alan and I would go to the canteen, where he would have me buy for him three or four large chocolate biscuits rather gaudily packaged in the shape of wagon-wheels that he was too embarrassed to buy for himself. So we both had our embarrassments, but Alan being Alan passed them on in uncomplicated fashion.

In some obvious respects I could never be confused with Alan, especially by myself. He was the most beautiful and attractive

man, of course, but there was also the sexual mystery of him. Such
a solid, purposeful-seeming, peasant-like body, so male, but the
suggestion of something soft and feminine in his smile, the subtle
and pleasing physical expression of the cruder psychological truth,
that Alan was all over the place emotionally. He had long, painful
affairs with men and longer, more painful affairs with women, and
sometimes with both simultaneously. It was as if he never knew,
from one minute to the next, what his sexual direction was, or as
if the sexual nature of his next, intended partner was incidental to
a greater need, the precise nature of which left him baffled but not
particularly tormented. The painfulness of his affairs with both
men and women came from trying, almost immediately after
starting them, to find a way of ending them. He would emerge
from the protracted and ghastly struggle of separating himself
from her or him with exhausted triumph, like a football player
whose team has just won the cup, while the other party – well, it
would depend on which sex they were. As a matter of fact I can't
really speak of the men, I only met them long after the
tumultuous part of the relationship was over, sometimes years and
years after, when they would pop up again in Alan's life and be
introduced with impersonal warmth, as if they were distant
cousins rather than the ex-lovers that he'd imitated, analysed and
caricatured with comic and bitter brio that would give way to
irritable confusion – 'What did they want? Why did they start it?'
From time to time he would attribute base motives – they were
after material goods (a car, perhaps?) or a connection with his
glamorous reputation. These dark speculations would usually
conclude in a comic gesture of resignation, and the admission of
a suspicion that perhaps he himself wasn't really very interested in
sex, except as the giving and receiving of short bursts of affection
and pleasure. I think that was the truth of it, that he liked men's

and women's bodies mostly for the comfort they could give him, physical intimacy bringing a more intense form of the companionship he loved – and of course for some years after his wife Victoria's death his only companions at night were his two spaniels, who slept on his bed I think, and to whom he was devoted. One, a marvellously fluid runner, perished under the wheels of a car when chasing a cat across the road. The other survived to a considerable age, becoming incontinent and senile. He would say when he went home at night to first the pair of them, and then to just the one of them, something along the lines of – well, what more did a man want after all, but creatures who were unchanging in their needs and affections. The thought of his preference for dogs over lovers made him laugh sardonically but cheerfully – and always there was his work on stage and screen, where he was such a complicated and romantic presence –

But really, what do I know? The above is merely gossip, or more accurately merely a report of Alan's gossip about himself, and it leaves out entirely the main story of his life, the death of his wife Victoria, his devotion to his twin sons, Tristan and Benedick, the death of Tristan – there was an afternoon one Easter in Lyme Regis. My first wife, Beryl, and I in my father's house in the town, Alan and Victoria in small hotel just up from the Cobb. It was a gorgeously soft and warm afternoon, Beryl and I were walking on the beach when they suddenly appeared, running hand in hand down the slope towards us, they had come looking for us, had something to tell us. 'We're very happy,' Victoria said. 'Aren't we, Alan?' Alan said that they were, and his beam confirmed it. 'You see,' Victoria said, 'we've just made love.' They spoke of it as of a rare and mysterious event. And in truth it was, as it had scarcely ever happened before – they'd been married about a year – and was, according to Alan, never to happen again – and it was right that their manner should have been both ecstatic and ceremonial, because what they were announcing turned out to be not only an almost unique act of love but a conception. They were for those few hours on the beach unambiguously happy and proud, they looked almost as if they belonged to each other.

THE PRODUCER CALLS

I had a brief encounter with Liz McCann this afternoon, at the matinée. She was in a wheelchair, in Shubert Alley, outside the box office. There were several people clustered about her, among them Nicholas Martin, whose head when standing was on a level with Liz's when sitting, which at least made conversation between them physically easy. Nicholas Martin was talking a lot and laughing a lot, he has a way of throwing his head back when he laughs, have I described this before? His spectacle lenses seem to glitter with mirth and his teeth, which he bares, sparkle with it – he is, when he laughs, a completely laughing creature. I couldn't tell whether Liz McCann was laughing with him, as she had her back to me, and I couldn't tell who was pushing her wheelchair when the little party moved towards the theatre lobby, it was almost as if she were being propelled collectively, by a small mob. I finished my cigarette and went in. She had been rolled to the head of an aisle at the back of the stalls. Her partner, a stout and very pleasant English woman of about Liz's age, I should imagine, who coincidentally walks with a stick, was standing beside the wheelchair. She called me over and bent to Liz McCann's ear, to tell her that here I was, standing behind her – given her position it was difficult to get into her line of vision, she had to twist her head at an awkward angle to see me. I asked her how she was, and she said, 'Coming along, coming along,' slightly irritably, clearly tired of the question. I said I hoped she would enjoy the show, she said she hoped she would too. It was a bit strained, this exchange, I had the feeling that she was angry about something – well, who could blame her, to skid on cat vomit and break your leg just as you were recovering from a broken leg – anyway, I didn't try to stretch the conversation, and moved away in search of Nicholas Martin. I spotted him an instant before the lights went down. He was sitting at the end of an aisle, whispering anxiously to his tall young assistant, who was taking notes – but about what? The show hadn't begun – perhaps on the conversation he'd had with Liz McCann?

It was the usual full house, with people standing beside me at the back. I thought the show was distinctly sluggish in places – some pauses that had been cut reintroduced themselves, in the way that pauses do, they're often as hard to exterminate as a virus, if you get them out of one scene, they turn up in another, where they've never been before, which sometimes makes one feel that they actually breed. Nevertheless it was OK really, it seemed to me, and is certainly much better, much more fully expressed than it was, say, four nights ago – previews don't get better from performance to performance, in my experience, but in fits and starts, with occasional little steps backwards before forwards again. The audience was fine at the curtain, with yips, bravos etc. for Nathan, but as for Liz McCann and her reaction –

I kept half an eye on the back of her head during both acts, but it didn't tell me much – it didn't seem to bob about when the audience laughed, though, and once or twice I saw it shake, slowly and possibly negatively, but body language is difficult to read when you don't have the front of the body to work with – Liz McCann might have been smiling and even chortling all through the show until we got to Nathan alone and forlorn, when she might have wept a little – still, it seemed to me wise to keep out of sight at the interval and speed off at the end – Nicholas Martin can deal with Liz McCann, it's his job, after all –

Hah! I've just put down the phone on Liz McCann. I don't mean I hung up on her, it's my policy never to hang up on people, however offensive you think they're trying to be, because it's almost a physical act, like a blow. I don't believe she hung up on me, either, it's just that her goodbye and the clicking-off noise were almost simultaneous – well, the 'good' and the click off were simultaneous, I'm taking the 'bye' as understood – she's probably in a considerable amount of pain from her leg, and also there'll be the painkillers – so hurting and a bit muzzy would explain why she was so curt, she couldn't cope with a long conversation – what there was of it went like this: 'Simon, it's Liz McCann.' 'Hello, Liz, how –' 'Simon, I think you better get out your scissors and make some judicious cuts.' 'Oh, really? Well, where exactly should I –' 'Don't know. Just make some judicious cuts. Better do it straight away, Simon. Good –' click. 'Bye' understood. Although perhaps it was boy, as in 'good boy' as in 'There's a good boy!' In a moment I'll phone Nicholas Martin, and tell him what she said, although I expect he knows already, they probably discussed it after the show yesterday. I'll also tell him that I've no intention of making any cuts, as far as I'm concerned any cuts would be completely injudicious. Now. Do it now.

Done it. He agrees with me. We discussed the need to close down further on pauses and to speed up various passages and speeches, in other words to go on as we're going on – and to hell with Liz

McCann really, when it comes down to it, though we didn't actually say that out loud, at least not to each other.

QUESTIONS. PERTINENT AND IMPERTINENT, FROM MY WIFE

The other night, after she'd come to a preview, Victoria said that she thought *Butley* was probably the most misogynist play that she'd ever seen. Also she thought it was strongly homosexual in its feelings and sensibility. I asked her if she thought it had therefore been written by a misogynistic homosexual, and would that therefore strike her as an accurate description of her husband. I didn't say this in a particularly abusive or threatening manner or in a misogynistic or homosexual manner, at least I don't think I did, because I was quite anxious to pursue the subject a little, having – I admit it – been coming to something like the same thoughts myself. I can't say that in myself I detect any impulses that I could categorize as homosexual or misogynistic – on the other hand, by his fruits shall ye know him, and there is my fruit, early fruit, in the form of a play that has as its central story the desperate attempt of a male university lecturer to maintain emotional possession of a younger and homosexual male colleague, furthermore the play teems with – that can't be the right phrase, 'teems with', 'is rife with' doesn't seem appropriate either, but get to what it teems with, or is rife with, and let's face it, if it's not misogyny it's the next best thing – So let's leave it at that, after all the early fruit is not the only fruit, there are lots of later fruits, mature, which are full of love for women, compassion for them too, and as for the works of my dotage, the fruit that follows the mature fruit – yes, better leave it at that.

A LETTER TO NATHAN

It's all over, really, this New York experience, apart from the reviews, which are already out, but which we haven't yet read. Victoria's in bed, asleep, I've turned off my mobile and told the hotel operator not to put any calls through, as I don't want news of the reviews until tomorrow, I want first of all to write a letter to Nathan, and then, when I've done that, to get on with this – an account of the first night. But I may skip that, write the letter to Nathan, and go to bed. Or sit smoking, and listening to Mozart.

I've written the letter to Nathan. I've smoked three cigarettes. I've listened to half a CD of Mozart. I've also taken a sleeping pill and two co-proxamol. I feel tired and am a little dizzy, but here I am, nevertheless, with my pen in my hand, and a befuddled sense of a duty yet to be completed. Begin at the end is perhaps the best route, going backwards from here, rather than forwards from there, partly because I can't really work out which is the appropriate there to start from, every backwards point from which I might go forwards immediately suggests another backwards point, so that ultimately I'd start from my birth, or go backwards from there to my parents' birth, it would therefore take me more than a few lifetimes to get forward to the moment when I sat down to write to Nathan at the round table in the kitchen area of this preposterous apartment with its views over New York, which is obscurely magnificent at four in the morning, a triangle of deep caverns at the bottom of which specks of light move up and down, and across – oh Nathan, Nathan!
  It was actually a bit like that – oh Nathan, Nathan! – the impulse to write to him – it was something to do with the way he looked at the party, not at all like an accomplished and experienced performer

of some fifty years – his suit looked so smart, and his face so clean
and his hair so shiny – really he looked like a spruced-up, anxious
child at an adult's very important birthday party – and actually it was
difficult to say who was giving the party – there seemed to be a lot
of elegant young women and men who greeted us once we'd got into
a dining room the size of a banqueting hall – they greeted me as if
they knew me, though I'm sure I've never seen any of them before,
and ushered us to one of the large round tables which had my name
on it, then pointed to long tables to the side where there was food
and drink in abundance, and so perfectly arranged that though a lot
of people were busying themselves with plates and glasses, there
wasn't the hint of a queue – I have simply no idea how many guests'
tables there were, sixty, seventy, a hundred? – the eye couldn't take
it all in, the sweep and glitter of it, table after table with winking
cutlery and sparkling glasses and there was enough space between the
tables so that people could move easily about, dropping in on friends
here and there – it was, the whole thing, I was going to say
magnificent, and it was, and it was also grotesque, and it kept
reminding me of a scene that I knew well but couldn't quite place,
from a book, I think, and not a film, not simply because of the
opulence on display, and the opulence of the people, most of them
sumptuously dressed in dinner jackets and gowns and so forth – I
mean one's seen scenes like that in lots of films, and generally
something momentous happens to disturb the vibrant, worldly and
organized glamour – a gun is fired, a man collapses with a red spot
on his otherwise spotless shirt front, women scream, men yell and
dash about, some of them with guns they've had concealed in
holsters under their armpits, and then a little gang of men run with
their arms around a shrouded bundle who is in fact the president of
the United States being hurried away from an attempted
assassination – of course *In the Line of Fire*, Clint Eastwood as the

president's bodyguard and John Malkovich the leisurely psychopath with a grudge against the government and a self-damaging fondness for the Clint Eastwood character – and of course *Towering Inferno*, when another, equally magnificent banquet with famous character actors scattered around the tables, thrillingly unready for the fire that the audiences know will presently sweep on to the screen and burn everything up, including a large handful of the famous character actors – much of the fun of the film comes from 'a spot the survivor game' – which of these famous actors will go first, which will be there, drenched and sooty, at the end – really one wishes they'd made many versions of the film, each one with a different schedule, and possibly a very limited edition, a collector's item, in which Steve McQueen and William Holden are crisped in the fire's first moments, and that actor with the atrocious wig is left standing on the pavement, surveying the hosed-down rubble of what was once – well, two hours ago – the proudest and tallest building in San Francisco. I'm not saying that at the *Butley* first-night party one found oneself yearning for a blazing gun, or a purging blaze, but there was something one yearned for, something there was that wasn't there – I think this is why it reminded me more of a book than a film – I mean although I've only managed to remember *In the Line of Fire* and *Towering Inferno*, I could think without stirring my brain of at least five more films with imperilled banquets – Buñel's *Exterminating Angel*, any film made about the Battle of Waterloo or Napoleon's invasion of Moscow, *Giant* (the peril there being James Dean's performance) – but none of these quite caught the atmosphere of uncompleted luxury, of almost irrelevant opulence and display, the sense that the real story hadn't arrived, or perhaps that the real purpose hadn't arrived and never would, whatever narrative there was, was the narrative of separate tables – all the producers' tables, one imagines ten or so, the lighting designer's table, the set designer's table, the various actors' tables – all kinds of things could be happening at those tables, marriages breaking up, new adulteries developing, children planning their parents' anniversary parties or deaths, so forth and so forth, they might have been terrifically interesting stories in all sorts of ways, far beyond the reach of my imagination, but they weren't subplots to a strong, coherent narrative because, as I've already said, there wasn't one – it's almost as if there would have been no clear answer to the question, 'Why are we here?' although the ostensible answer would, of course, have been, 'To celebrate the first night of *Butley*.' So perhaps what was predominantly missing that one yearned for was the spirit of celebration – there was a lot of noise, people shouted and clapped their hands at each other and embraced and laughed but these didn't seem like celebratory acts, more like tribal routines. We'd come into this remarkable restaurant, if it was a restaurant, by way of an enormous lobby, walking down a passage formed by two ropes, on either side of which were showbiz journalists and photographers, most of them quaint and middle-aged, with academic stoops or hunched-up shoulders – not at all like the occasions I've seen on television, which were all hustling intimacy and a 'Hey, Si, whaddya think of Nay-tan?' sort of approach, instead these journalists had a formal, rather stilted way of addressing you: 'Please, Mr Gray, could I just have a word?' – and I would be escorted over the rope, a matter of raising first one foot and then the other higher than comes naturally to me, and then standing still and smiling with a few cameras aimed at my face while replying to a number of carefully thought-out but dowdy questions. In fact, I had the feeling that I was attending a rather austere postgraduate ceremony rather than a high-octane first-night fanfare – I had to do about six of these almost identical interviews, the middle-aged, bespectacled man being replaced by a middle-aged bespectacled woman, and then a drooping sort of woman followed by a drooping sort of man. I found it quite easy to relax into the role of playwright emeritus, and wouldn't have minded a gown and a mortarboard, a scroll in my hand – it did cross my mind that this might be an elaborate trap to catch another preening, clapped-out, opportunistic Brit but it clearly wasn't, because for two of the interviews Nathan was brought to my side – he'd done a dozen or so on his own before we arrived, and there was no change of tone when we were interviewed jointly, Mr Gray and Mr Lane was how it went, with discreet enquiries into our relationship, when and where had it started? How it had come to this blossoming? – so a quick trudge back to New Haven where we'd first met, on to Los Angeles, where we'd suffered together at the Matrix Theatre, ninety-nine seats and nobody gets paid, on to our triumph in New York, at the Promenade Theatre, 499 seats and a steady income for months and months – we'd both told the tale in separate interviews before the opening, and now we were telling it together before going off to our separate tables – he to sit with his two brothers and various friends, I to sit with my brother Nigel, his wife Barbara, my nephew Chris, my wife Victoria, and one of her nieces, Alice – I was very dull company, I expect, I wasn't at all hungry and all that glamorous-looking food made me feel queasy, and as I couldn't smoke, I had only my Diet Coke to occupy my hands, which were twitching, as if they wanted to do violence to somebody, perhaps just to myself – occasionally I looked over to Nathan's table, I could see his face, red, shiny, laughing too much – once I got up and went over, we met in a no man's land between tables occupied by elderly people, producers from the look of them – have I noted down how many producers there are on *Butley*, I mean I can't actually note down how many, I mean it rhetorically, how many producers! On the trip from the lobby to our table I was accosted by half a dozen who rose from their tables to thank me and congratulate

me on their being where they were, at the first-night party of *Butley* –
and then you think of all the tables you didn't pass at many of which
producers almost certainly sat and you can say with confidence that
there were probably two herds of them –

What Nathan and I talked about in this interlude was the
reviewers – it wasn't really a conversation, but a series of
interrogatives – 'Have you heard anything?' from him, 'No, have
you?' from me, and then from him, 'Who do we know who might
have heard?' and from me, 'Well, there's that friend of yours who
does publicity – do you think she's heard?' and from him, 'Who,
Jackie, no, I just asked her, and she hasn't heard a thing, isn't there
somebody –?' and so it went, repetitiously, until Jackie happened up
to us, smiling underneath her controlled and dead-pan eyes, giving
Nathan the opportunity, which he took, to ask her if she knew
anything. 'No,' she said, 'no more than I knew five minutes ago.' A
flash of doubt befuddled Nathan's innocently enquiring expression.
'Surely somebody must know something, for God's sake!' Jackie took
off her glasses, so to speak, though I don't think she wears glasses. 'I
would never,' she said intensely, 'ever hold back on anything with
you, Nathan, for the sake of our friendship.' Probably not precisely
those words, but absolutely that meaning. Off she went, leaving us
to hang around for a few minutes longer, to eye the great scene, all
those guests sitting at all those tables eating all that food and drinking
all that drink and wearing all that money, all because of us – yes, it
is the case that if Nathan hadn't been born some fifty years ago and
become a Broadway star who wanted to do *Butley*, and if I hadn't
been born seventy years ago and written *Butley* before I'd lived for
half of them, then neither he nor I nor the hundreds upon dozens
of producers would have been wherever it was we were this evening
(must find out its name and address) waiting, some of us, for news
of the *New York Times* review. Neither of us expressed this thought,

nor indeed any particular thought, as we stood together for a bit longer, then we smacked each other on the shoulder and laughed both at and with each other, as if diverted by our feebleness and fear, and went back to our tables – producers rising to both of us as we passed – now here's the thing I'm getting to –

I knew for a fact that the main review, the *New York Times* review, was out, in the sense that its content was known to quite a few people in the room, doubtless to at least a few of the producers and I was going to write 'almost certainly' as 'almost certainly' is a kind of writing tic of mine that I am aware of and can't control – well, that's the nature of a tic, after all – but in this case 'almost certainly' won't do, the words you have to write down are 'most certainly' as in – Jackie, the publicity girl, 'most certainly' knew the content of the *New York Times* review, and furthermore knew that it was bad, when she stood among the tables and told Nathan that she knew nothing, and would never jeopardize their friendship by withholding information from him.

Now how is it I knew what seemingly other people, far more experienced in the ways of Broadway and New York reviews, didn't know – or at least didn't know that they knew? I think Nathan knew. He'd been on stage in New York very regularly over the last decade, had been through the whole business again and again, and would surely have understood, at a higher level of certainty than mere guesswork, that information about the review would have been in circulation before he arrived at the first-night party, but probably he persuaded himself that there would be an unusual explanation for the unusual delay – for instance that the review was so intensely favourable that it had to be vetted by specialist policemen for signs of a conspiracy – bribery, corruption etc., or that the reviewer had delayed publication because he wanted to insert some extra compliments that had occurred to him just as the paper was going to press, or that the reviewer had shot the editor or the editor the reviewer in a crime of passion and revenge – anyway he persuaded himself, against all previous experience, to hope for the best, or at least postpone facing up to the worst until it was plonked directly in front of him and there was no escaping it. That's the thing about a certain sort of hope, it's merely despair delayed by an act of will. But as I say, I think he knew all right, he just hadn't got around to acknowledging it yet.

My own case is slightly different. I am always eager to acknowledge the worst, and well in advance of the evidence. My temperament is to assume it, in fact, which is not to say that I welcome it, although there's possibly a bit of that perversity in it – I blame the usual suspect, my mother's womb, which is where I first learnt of disappointment – though whether in the being in it or in the getting out of it I can't really say, probably a case of out of the frying pan –

So we begin with my predisposition to suppose that there was a bad review in the *New York Times*. We add to that my sense of the improbability of the contents of this review not being known by someone or other by 10 p.m. on the night before its publication. We heap on top of that my conviction that a publicity person who begins a sentence with 'I'd never ever' is already more than halfway through the beginning of a lie. Underneath all that was my feeling that there was something awry – 'awf' or 'orf', as some of my older and classier English friends would put it – in the festive atmosphere, something uneasy circulating around the hall, possibly in the form of a muttered piece of gossip or even hard news. Then perch on the very top of that this fact:

That at the interval I'd sloped away from the theatre to the small bar where they allow you to smoke in the passageway leading to the front door, where they have four tables and two stand-up ashtrays.

I sat at one of these tables with a Diet Coke and gaped vaguely towards the pavement, thinking of nothing in particular but admiring Nathan's performance in a grateful and hazy sort of way, when a young lady came around the corner from the pavement and into the passageway. She had her cellphone to her ear and a stricken look on her face, as if hearing something she didn't want to hear, and when she saw me at the table she looked aghast, as if seeing something she didn't want to see. She did a little skid and spin and went back around the corner – just that glimpse I had, that glimpse of Jackie the publicity lady on her cellphone, looking first stricken and then aghast – there was a pause and then she reappeared, the cellphone no longer visible. 'Hi, Simon,' she said, as she squeezed past me, 'having a Diet Coke?' I said I was, yes. Had she been in for the first act? 'No,' she said, she'd had some business to see to. Was she going in for the second act? No, not until the last moments, for the curtain call, she had to see some people – she gestured towards the door to the bar, and let the gesture carry her towards it, and then through it, a bit like a ballet dancer leaving the stage, really, except not on her toes, and not particularly gracefully, so not like a ballet dancer at all, although that was the image that came to mind, it must have been the gesture with the arm and the way her body followed on –

I sat for a few minutes, trying to imagine how Victoria would have dealt with my suspicions: 'Oh, really! She could have been talking to anyone, her mother, her boyfriend, her girlfriend, her dogsitter – some domestic worry.' Yes, I would have said, but then why was she so upset to see me? 'Actually,' she might have replied, 'people are often upset to see you, especially when they're not expecting to. And she was probably embarrassed at missing the performance, the first night –' No, I would have said, it was the review. The *New York Times* review. 'Oh, really!' and on like that, for a bit, but her protests would have got feebler because she would have known I was right. I usually am, on such matters. I got up to go back to the theatre, then thought I'd better have a pee, and went into the bar. It was quite empty except for a table by the lavatory. There were half a dozen people, men and women, I didn't really take them in because I was firstly conscious that there was one of those silences that happen when people suddenly stop talking because somebody who is connected to what they're talking about has suddenly appeared, and secondly that Jackie the publicity lady was sitting at the head of the table, rather formally, as if she were chairing an urgent meeting. I raised my hand in salute as I went into the lavatory, she raised hers, smiling radiantly, and she was still smiling radiantly, the table still in complete silence, when I came out. Of course it's possible that this group of people were always silent, they may simply have liked sitting with each other, not saying anything because wise to the many disasters, violent death etc., that are among the consequences of speech. On the other hand they could have been people who had clustered together to discuss the *New York Times* review and its implications, and naturally fell silent when one of the subjects of the review passed and repassed their table, on the way to and from a pee.

I hung about outside the Booth for about twenty minutes, smoking in the wind – it was really very windy, and I spent most of the time hunched, to protect the cigarette. Then I went in, with my head down so that I wouldn't see anyone coming out, and they wouldn't see me – there was a bit of activity around the door to the auditorium as I approached it, it opened and closed several times, quite violently, as if a rather feeble person were trying to leave, and a stronger person preventing him or her – perhaps a child and a parent? But would any sensible parent bring a child to the first night of *Butley*, and then forcibly stop him or her from leaving? When I opened the door myself, to sidle in, there were no signs of disruption, and no discernible explanation for the door's behaviour. In fact, there was an attentive row of people standing at the back of the stalls, and an attentively packed house, no one had failed to come back from the interval, not even Victoria, who was settled comfortably in her aisle seat, brave and concentrating, in fact as far as I could see, there were no empty seats, unless some of the audience were doing what we call in the trade 'double-shuffling' – i.e. and e.g. a chap uses his ticket for the first act, hands it to his wife at the interval who uses it for the second act – a variation on what we call 'single-shuffling' – i.e. and e.g. when a chap uses the same ticket for both acts, which happens more often than you would think, and is profitable to the management, although not as profitable as the 'single shuffle twice over' – i.e. and e.g. a husband and a wife with a ticket each sitting through both acts, which is nothing like as profitable as the 'double booking times X', X being the number of tickets the management can sell twice – apart from the possible financial gain, the confusion and rows that break out in the auditorium can lead to excellent publicity, with i.e. and e.g. 'They're fighting for seats at the Booth Theatre, where Simon Gray's *Butley*, starring etc. etc. –'

Well, the fact is that the play was mightily well received, with bravos and yippees and assorted screeches, screams and howlings at the curtain – I tried to join in but my husky rattlings went unheard except by the plump young man next to me, who turned away with what might have been revulsion. Nevertheless he yippeed and clapped his way to the exit – he might have been one of the producers, of course, eager to get on to the party.

We went in a small van hired by the management – Victoria and I and Michael Musso, a small, pleasant man who is the chief administrator of the Huntington Theatre in Boston, where the production had originated three years before. He considered the evening to be a total triumph, and smiled and chatted calmly and confidently of what it would mean for the Huntington, which had a share in the royalties, and for his close colleague Nicholas Martin. Then we arrived at the place I've described above, I still can't remember its name or its precise location but it seemed to be right downtown, around 20th Street, anyway in an area I'd never visited before, at least to my knowledge – but in New York who knows where I've been at other times in my life? Then we did all the stuff in the lobby, then we sat at the table and then I got up and had that conversation with Nathan and Jackie the publicity lady and then we left and came back here – oh, one thing I've forgotten to put down, that shortly after the conversation with Nathan I went out to the pavement with Victoria's niece, Alice, for a cigarette. Alice is tall and blonde and very pretty, has just finished at Oxford and gets into the English papers now and then because she has an active social life in London of a sort that is incomprehensible to me, because in my day, etc. and so forth, modern youth so forth and etc. Anyway, though, she is vastly more sophisticated at twenty than I am at seventy. But perhaps not when I was forty. I have a sense that I've become less sophisticated in the last ten years or so, less at ease in company, I find conversation more difficult and am sometimes awed and even frightened by the prospect of meeting people I don't know – but then it's ten years since I stopped drinking, so perhaps that explains it. Anyway it would have been pleasant on the pavement, smoking and chatting with Alice, and looking for resemblances to her father, a very intelligent and charming man who died young and unfulfilled in life – pleasant to note his expressions in hers, his gestures in hers, if I hadn't been conscious of people exiting from the party. They walked quickly, in couples and threes, their heads together, their voices low, like conspirators – not quite like the exits from my first Broadway first-night party, which had taken place on the top floor of Sardis, the

famous – more famous then than now – show-business restaurant, in
1969 – the room had been crowded and abuzz when I slipped out for
a pee and virtually empty when I returned a few moments later, guests
scampering past me in the hallway and down the stairs. 'Why, what's
happened, what's going on?' I asked the producer, who sat slumped
at the head of the table. 'The *New York Times*,' his wife said in a dead
voice, as she left the room. Well, as I say, it wasn't quite like that
tonight, people weren't leaving in an unseemly rush, it was more like
a dignified and measured withdrawal from a slightly unseemly event,
but still there was something in their manner that reminded me of my
first night thirty-nine years ago.

We stayed on at the table, I longing to go because I felt tired and
couldn't eat, Victoria keeping an alert eye on me as she continued
in a lively and unworried vein. Nathan came over and we had the
same conversation again, almost word for word – 'Have you heard?'
'No. Have you heard?' and then I said I was thinking of leaving,
what did Nathan think? Yes, he said, he'd give it a few more minutes
and then he'd leave. We agreed not to wait for each other, as we were
going in opposite directions.

So we went back to our respective tables and stayed a few more
minutes, and then a few more, and a few more after that, and then
Victoria and I left, after a quick embrace with Nathan. We'll talk in
the morning, we said.

Victoria and I had some coffee sent up, lolled about going over the
evening. I kept my suspicions to myself for once, although I
suspected she suspected them. She went to bed, and I turned off my
mobile, phoned down to the operator, had a 'do not disturb' on our
lines, and then wrote my letter to Nathan. I started from the
premise, which I didn't state, that the *New York Times* review was
going to be, at the least, a disappointment. I could have gone on to

say how much I admired his performance, but I'd already said it, in Boston and in New York, and in the end he knew what his performance was, and nothing that the *New York Times* printed would alter that – at least I hoped it wouldn't. What I really wanted to write to him about was something quite different, and for me, as I've been feeling these last few days, far more important than the first night, or the immediate future of the revival of an old play. I hope I've written all that I wanted to write, but the thing is – the thing is – I can't at this moment remember a single sentence. It's as if I'd written in a trance, not easily and flowingly, but very meticulously – knowing how difficult my handwriting is to read, I'd made each letter as distinct as I could – that's actually my memory of the letter, finished only an hour or so ago, the careful grip on my pen as I laboured for legibility. But what exactly did I say? Now I have the letter in front of me, in an envelope, sealed and with Nathan's name on it. It would be perfectly easy to open the envelope, read the letter – but I don't think I have another envelope, I'd have to go down to the lobby and ask at the front desk – down 110 floors, at what is it? 4.13 in the morning – go to the front desk and ask for an envelope. Or I could try and reseal this one – but it wouldn't look right, it would look slightly grubby around the flap, as if I'd opened it and resealed it. Besides it would be wrong to change anything, whatever I wrote was full of feeling and intention, the fact that I no longer remember what it was apart from its being an expression of friendship, and of gratitude to the play for bringing me three close, true and good friends, the other two being Alan, of course, and Harold – without *Butley* I'd never have met them, and my life would have been completely different, in almost every respect.

Oh yes, well that's what it was, that's all it was, a simple and natural thing, no wonder I've had trouble remembering it.

NO MORE HEYDAYS

It's the end of the next day, not quite one in the morning, which actually, I suppose, makes it the beginning of the day after, in other words tomorrow. But can you ever be in tomorrow? Can you ever be out of today? But then what the hell is one in the morning, neither today nor tomorrow in any way that makes sense. I'm back from dinner with Nathan, Victoria is still not back from dinner with friends in Brooklyn, so it's just me, here in Suite 1410, determined to write about a day I'm unwilling to think about. Do it quickly. See if you can get it done before Victoria gets back.

When we got up at about eleven, we ordered breakfast and the *New York Times* – we've made it a rule over the last few years never to read reviews of my plays, but this morning had to be an exception, the concern being Nathan and his feelings rather than me and mine. We noticed that the messages light was winking on the telephone, but we decided not to listen to them until we'd found out what they'd be saying.

We ate breakfast with the *New York Times* lying unopened on the table between us, then I lit a cigarette, Victoria poured us each a cup of coffee, we went into the loungey half of the room, I sat in a corner of the sofa, she sat in an armchair beside me, I opened the arts section, and there was the review, a lot of it in the sense that there were quite a few paragraphs and a photograph of Nathan, but somehow laid out so as not to be eye-catching, in fact sort of squeezed in and lumpish-looking, and finishing over the page where you can't find it without searching. It's mostly bad for Nathan, and while it's good for the play it mainly mentions it parenthetically, or compliments it as a way of insulting Nathan – Nathan not being up to the part of Butley being the main theme, with side dashes at the other actors for not being up to their parts either, and for working so hard at their English accents that they're all accent and no character – this is odd, really odd, as Julian Ovenden, who plays Joey and virtually shares the stage with Nathan for most of the evening, is English born and bred, is in fact an Old Etonian, and all the other actors were assumed by all our English friends who saw the play on my birthday to have been imported from England specially, so natural and easy and unlearnt did their English accents sound – but the *New York Times* chap clearly has an ear of his own, and knows his English accents as other men know their French wines –

Well, what's to be said? what's to be said? I said to Victoria, who said, that what was to be said, all that could be said, really, was that this chap Ben Brantley wasn't really reviewing Nathan at the Booth Theatre, really he was reviewing the review of his colleague Bruce Webber, who'd been sent by the *New York Times* to review *Butley* at the Huntington Theatre in Boston three years earlier, arguing with him and contradicting him, sometimes almost by the sentence – Webber, for example, had said that Nathan and Butley were a perfect match, that Nathan was, in a sense, Alan's heir apparent, it was worth the thirty-five-year wait – while for Brantley, but I've already written down what Brantley said about Nathan, wrong for the part, not up to Alan etc. – Webber admired Nicholas Martin's production, Brantley therefore despised it.

I picked up the messages from the telephone. They were from Nathan and Nicholas Martin and were grave in tone and disappointed, though both, being the men they were, also laughed quite a lot. I phoned them both up and we talked at length and purposelessly, so much the usual conversation when there's a bad review – happily Brantley has an unhappy prose style, aiming to be simultaneously colloquial and elegant it comes out in a bit of a muddle, here snobbish and there vulgar, and sometimes both in the same sentence, so again we laughed quite a lot – but really it was a bit like finding comedy in the deformities of a man who has harmed you, a bit schoolboyish, really, but I suppose the point is that though Brantley can't help the way he writes, any more than he could help it if he speaks with a lisp or a slur, for instance, he's still responsible for the opinions he expresses, and there's no getting away from it, Brantley's opinions are the official opinions of the *New York Times*, and might do us harm at the box office.

According to my American agent, Charles Kopelman, who has just phoned, the Brantley review won't do us much harm, if any. The box office is ticking away, the advance is huge. He also said that there were lots of very good reviews for Nathan, including one from Clive Barnes, in the *Post*, who had reviewed Alan in both the original London production and the subsequent Broadway production for the *New York Times* – there was also going to be a rave in the forthcoming *Newsweek*. The producers were already preparing a monster ad, full of marvellous quotes, to appear in the *New York Times* on Saturday, I think he said.

I phoned Nathan again to report my conversation with Kopelman, but I don't think it cheered him up particularly, he knows the box office is OK, what is depressing him is the thought that the *New York Times* review will be most audiences' only preparation for the show, they will bring the memory of it in with them, and they will actually look for him to disappoint them, because Brantley has promised them he will.

We arranged to have dinner after the show, which means I shall have to see it, half of it at least, actually I think I might enjoy it – of course I shall have the advantage of not expecting to be disappointed. I must remember to take the letter – it hasn't moved from the table where I left it last night, but already has a slightly shop-soiled look, as if somebody has opened it and resealed it. I've just examined the back of the envelope – it has a smudge at the apex of the flap, as of a thumb pressing into a spot of moisture, now dry – a teardrop, perhaps, but if so, whose?

I thought Nathan was terrific. The first few moments, appearing as a silhouette at the door and then coming on in the dark, the intricate stage business with the lights, were pretty awful, he said afterwards, when I went up to his dressing room, he felt that the audience for the first time in his experience of the play was tentative and ill at ease, probably cursing themselves for having bought tickets before the *New York Times* review came out, now having to sit through the evening out of respect for the money they'd paid and a grudging politeness to the star – that's how it felt to him, anyway, with the review stinking away in his consciousness, but gradually, by concentrating on the performance moment by moment, keeping his eyes and ears fixed on the other actors, he forgot the audience and the review and began to enjoy himself – and as so often happens the enjoyment became contagious, the audience relaxed, Nathan became free, the evening took off – perhaps not into full flight, as in the best of the previews, but sufficiently for Nathan to feel that the worst was over, that it hadn't been too bad, nothing like as bad as he'd expected, in fact it had been OK, tomorrow he'd be OK too, and one evening soon he'd be better than OK.

Just before we left his dressing room to set out for dinner I handed him my letter. He took it from me with an odd, set smile, as if he knew what it contained, and then ripped it across, rolled it between his hands until it fitted into his fist, and then threw it across the room, into the wastepaper basket behind the sofa, a

perfect shot. 'Olé,' he said, 'and to hell with your crappy letter.'
Well, no he didn't. He took the letter, with a serious little smile, put
it in his pocket and said he'd read it when he got home. But one has
these fantasies of rejection, one should express them sometimes, as
a way of knowing oneself better.

We had dinner in the restaurant in which we'd had my birthday
party. The waiters were subdued and the portly owner, with whom
I'd smoked cigarettes on the pavement while he assured me that all
would be well, came over bowing gravely and shook us by the
hand – he was in undertaker mode, quite unsuited to his
personality, but perhaps he'd read something in Nathan's
expression, or something in this morning's *New York Times*, anyway
the service was compassionately attentive and the food was good.
Nathan's account of the evening came out in spontaneous fits and
starts, interspersed with digressions of an inevitably vituperative
nature on the subject of Brantley, and the old absurdity of it – that
really Brantley was merely Brantley, no doubt the sort of chap whose
opinions you'd greet with a concealed scowl if he tried to press them
on you over a dinner table, especially if he speaks as he writes, but
by virtue of his job he ceases to be the socially unwelcome B.
Brantley and becomes the fearsome Ben Brantley of the *New York
Times*, or consider it another way around, if Bruce Webber, who'd
reviewed us in Boston, and writes readable and literate as well as
glowing prose, had instead reviewed us in New York, Nathan would
now be the toast of Broadway, instead of merely the apple of the
playwright's eye –
    Here's the sound of the door opening, Victoria back – and has
now gone to bed. She says she had a good time over there in
Brooklyn, it's really lovely, gardens, trees, flowers, you must try and
see it, you'd love it – yes, I said, I must, it sounded really lovely, I'd

heard that trees grew there, in Brooklyn, but flowers too, eh? This was formulaic, we both knew that there was as little chance of my getting to Brooklyn as the sisters had in getting to Moscow. I told her about Nathan's performance, the dinner etc., and then she went to bed, and here I am again, thinking that what I'd really like is to go into the bedroom, wake her up, and say, 'Hey, why don't we go home? Go home immediately? Go home tomorrow?'

We're all packed, the limo to take us to the airport is due in half an hour, Victoria is having a shower, and I'm sitting at the table in the kitchen writing this. In front of me is the *New York Times*, open at the page in which there is the promised advertisement for *Butley*, and I have to say that it's mightily impressive – the compliments for Nathan snake on and on, down the length of the page, a full page in the *New York Times* concluding with the name of the play in bold black type – BUTLEY – there it is! what playwright could wish for more, apart perhaps for a quote for himself, or if not that, for the play, and if not that, then at least to have the play ascribed to him. In justice it has to be added that, as in the lights above the theatre, it hasn't been ascribed to anyone else instead, it has no authorship whatsoever, as if self-generated. Of course there's a theory in modern literary criticism that the author is merely the accidental point at which historical trends and influences meet, and that he should therefore be treated as if he were anonymous. It's entirely possible that the producer of *Butley* subscribes to this theory, and is putting it into practice both on Broadway in lights and in the *New York Times*, though like the authors of the theory she herself likes to be named. There it is, her name, for all the world to see. And there is the bellhop to take down our bags. And there is my wife, wearing a towel and a top hat, ready for flight, and here are the last words I shall write in New York. It was a vile month. There. I've got it down.

It was a completely vile month. I don't think there was a day in it that I enjoyed. The New York of my splendid heyday, of my thirties, forties and early fifties, has vanished, no doubt about that.

No, no, let's face it, the truth is more likely that the I of my splendid heyday has vanished – the bellhop has gone with the bags, and my wife, fully dressed, is standing by my chair, waiting to assist me to my feet, and the returning home has begun.

We're home. Got in this morning, very early. It would have been earlier, if the specially cheap airline – let's call it Soar – the producers had put us in hadn't lost one of our bags, the one with my nail clippers in it. A woman who started off by being very calm – 'Don't worry, we'll have it in a minute or two, it's somewhere about' – ended with panic in her eyes – 'It's never happened before, we've never lost a bag before.' I said it might be the computer, Soar had installed a new one at Kennedy airport, which is why we'd had such trouble boarding – She said she hadn't heard about the computers, that had never happened before either – Hints of accusation emerging in her tone, as if she were putting two and two together and coming up with us – the couple that caused things to happen to Soar, the specially cheap airline, that had never happened before. We left Stansted without the bag, which somehow we know we'll never get back, but we're home now, George and Toto, Errol and Tom all well, so who cares about the bag with my nail clippers in it?

PART SEVEN

ANCESTORS

We've been back a week now, I've spent most of it in bed with a version of flu, I suppose it's flu, my head aches and my nose is running and my eyes are red and smarting – these might not be the symptoms of physical flu, but of moral flu, anyway of a contagion picked up in the course of the month in New York, I cut an altogether disgusting figure to myself and to others – although very few others, as I've scarcely been out, except once or twice, up to the Renaissance for coffee, sitting outside at one of the tables because they've banned smoking inside – so in a sense I'm repeating an aspect of my life in New York, sitting outside in the cold in order to enjoy a cigarette – it must be merely a coincidence that I could smoke inside the Renaissance until I went away to New York, that I've spent a month dreaming of being back in my favourite and personal coffee shop in Holland Park Avenue, that I've actually trudged with weary, flu-drained limbs through the cold, up Holland Park Avenue, to my personal and favourite coffee shop, to find that I'm returned so to speak to New York, where I used to sit at a table on a cold pavement dreaming of being back in the Renaissance, while now I sit at a cold table on the pavement outside the Renaissance dreaming of being back inside it – but the old Renaissance is a month ago, never to return. Actually this is flu-generated self-pity, I never sat inside the Renaissance if I could help it, even on the coldest days I chose the outside, just as I did at the New York café, which I believe was called Café Maison. I suspect it was at the Café Maison that I picked up the cold in my chest that turned to flu when I got home.

*

I'm sitting in front of a new computer, these are my first words on it, and I worry that they may be my last – it really is so neat and compact, compact – yes, that's the word – no, the word the man who sold it to us used was 'sexy' and indeed it's a ladylike thing that reminds me of face powder in small containers, silk stockings, a pistol half the size of the slim and dainty hand that holds it, a knife in an especially fitted thigh-clasp, a poisonous lipstick, and a two-way mirror, not to mention a two-way bra and a pussy-whip – perhaps that's what he meant when he called it sexy, a sexy little computer, the sexiest on the market, because all these images from the flowering of my adolescence swarm into my consciousness – but then they swarm out once the lid is lifted and I see a keyboard and a screen and a pad and I wonder again at my folly – for years I've had a perfectly good system of working, I type out my first drafts on my typewriter if they're plays, and scribble them down on yellow pads if they're random musings that come to me where no technological help is available i.e. when I'm an unadorned writer in need only of the simplest of implements, I like to believe I could make out with a sliver of flint and the bare wall of a cave, as my ancestors did, although I'm not sure if at that stage of my evolution I would have had a vocabulary, I might have had to make do with pictures, which would be difficult, as I have no gift for drawing, no sense of perspective – but then nor did they, from examples I've seen of their work, which has mainly been in newspapers or in cartoons in the *New Yorker* – odd thought, that, that the cartoons on a cave wall from many, many thousands of years ago become the subject of cartoons in a shiny metropolitan magazine of today – what was he doing? What did he think he was doing as he scratched the outline of three bison, for instance, on his wall, was he keeping accounts, but if so, of what? Three live bison herded, three dead ones stored, three eaten, three dreamt of, hoped for, regretted – the fact is that we don't have a clue what he was doing in his cave, if it was a he – but why not she, alone with the babies, anxious, bored, scratching a dream on the wall of the cave, figuratively a stomach's dream, but perhaps not figuratively, the bison embodiments of an impulse, a prayer, a message to the *New Yorker* –

I would have needed sounds, however brutish and short, to record the narrative of my life, and more complicated sounds than grunts, groans and yodellings – what was the first word spoken, what can it have sounded like? There must have been a first word, chronologically, a sound uttered for the very first time that wasn't simply an angry or satisfied or terrified expulsion of air, a sound that had a content and was directed towards a fellow creature, perhaps it was a sound that meant 'help!' and that could be understood to mean 'help!' – When did we first laugh, what made us first laugh? In films and novels and so forth people are constantly laughing in happiness, but I have never heard or seen anyone laugh in happiness, though in joy – physical joy, yes, when the body is suddenly liberated from itself, in sex, say, or tobogganing downhill in a Montreal park when I was six or seven, or in the water, the first time in a warm sea after months of overcoated land-life, I have sometimes let out a yelp of joy, but not a laugh, really –

And when he heard himself laughing for the first time, what did he make of it, this ancestor of mine, of yours, of everybody's, who has given rise to so much laughter in the pages of the *New Yorker*, when presented as a cartoon? And why do I resent the *New Yorker* for it, it's not reasonable, really –

Nathan phoned to say that business is very good and that the houses are full, if sometimes of eccentric composition – at one of the matinées, halfway through the first act, a gang of middle-aged women, evidently from out of town, began to dispute among themselves in the stalls, at the tops of their voices, the ushers had to come in and calm them down. Apparently they kept away from each other during the interval, coming back in separate little groups, but ten minutes or so into the second act they started again, standing up and bawling at each other, even aiming slaps and punches until the ushers descended once more – Nathan couldn't give a completely clear account as each time he'd gone on playing the play, not daring to look out front – the good news though was that their rage was with each other, and not with the actors or the playwright – or so the ushers told the stage management. Or so the stage management told the actors.

He said he'd had one extraordinary performance, when the role had taken him over so completely that he seemed not to be acting but just happening – he'd never experienced anything like it, nor expected to again.

HITS AND MISSES

I was sitting where I am now, doing the sort of thing I'm doing now, when I heard Victoria scream – well, it wasn't exactly a scream, rather a shocked calling out of something I couldn't hear properly, but my name came into it somewhere, I could hear it distinctly, but I went on doing what I am now doing, on the rather lunatic, I now see, assumption that if she could call out my name, in however much alarm, it couldn't be for too serious a reason, it would only be serious if she couldn't call out my name, besides I had a sentence to finish – when I finished it I noticed that she was still calling my name, so I went to see what it was she wanted –

She was standing at the top of the stairs, outside the bedroom, with the almost serene look people sometimes assume when they have a calamity to announce. 'The ceiling's just fallen in,' she said, in a tone that made it clear that she wasn't speaking metaphorically. Rose, our elegant young cleaning lady, was standing just behind her, also looking calm, but with a graze on one of her arms, which she was dabbing at with a handkerchief. Apparently she'd been putting a garment into the chest of drawers, and from some instinct, had done a little skip-skip sideways just as the ceiling dropped, yes, it just dropped, dropped from whatever ceilings are attached to, in a cascade of heavy plaster, a small lump of which had caught, only very lightly, her arm – She was lucky, she said, with one of her brilliant smiles, she wears quite a lot of lipstick and has fine white teeth so her smiles are often radiant – She said it had happened to her in a café she'd worked in, a few years ago, when for the same 'some reason' as in our bedroom she'd found herself taking a little skip into the only spot in the café the ceiling didn't fall on, it had fallen all around her but on that occasion she hadn't even been grazed – I thought this was interesting, was there any possibility that we were getting it the wrong way around, that the skipping had caused the ceiling to fall by first arousing it with what it might have interpreted as an invitation, or a challenge, or an act of hubris? – was it something peculiar to Rose, that she possessed unknowingly, a kinetic power that contained within it another power that guaranteed her safety? – after all twice, twice in a few years, while surely for most people who live in an earthquake-free area once in a lifetime would still be well above the average – but there's nothing about Rose that suggests that she has an intense inward relationship with inanimate matter – inanimate matter? Is that a tautology, or can matter be animate? – Well, poets, novelists, playwrights, musicians, mystics, all those types, talk of the spirit of place, so why not be particular and talk of the spirit of a place's ceiling, and if of its spirit, then why not of its will? And then of a will that exhausts itself and collapses from the sheer strain of *being*, to put it in existential terms, and especially from the sheer strain of being a ceiling, and a bedroom one, at that? – But what am I doing? Why am I writing about matter and spirit and ceilings collapsing from boredom etc.? I'm completely missing the thing I should surely be thinking about – that the ceiling could have collapsed during the night while Victoria and I were underneath it, in bed – if you take eight hours as the average time in bed – actually it doesn't work like that in our case, as our sleeping overlaps, Victoria is generally in bed from 1 a.m. to 9 a.m., I am generally in bed from 5 a.m. to 1 p.m., so there are four hours in which we could have been buried in rubble together, and eight hours in which one of us could have been buried in rubble, so that makes a total of twelve hours in which one or both of us could have been buried in rubble, therefore there was a 50 per cent chance – Christ, 50 per cent! One in two! Doesn't bear thinking about, which was probably why I wasn't thinking about it – but now that I am thinking about it, I notice that I wrote that to have a ceiling fall on you once in your lifetime would be well above the average, but I've just remembered that when I was a child of about six in Montreal, residing at 4047 Vendome Avenue, I was sitting on the lavatory one day when the ceiling did in fact fall down, filling the little room with lumps of plaster and a cloud of dust, but leaving me unscathed, like a little prince enthroned on a battlefield is how I like to think I looked –

I wonder how many other near misses I've had, not just from ceilings but from all conceivable sources, that I can't remember, or possibly never knew about, or was too drunk to notice – the ones I can recall are probably routine, appropriate anyway to an Englishman who has lived most of his three score years and ten in peacetime, but an eighteen-year-old Englishman born in 1897 and dispatched to Mons, Marne, Ypres might have been able to list five times as many near misses by the end of a morning and not lived through the afternoon – although many of even the youngest soldiers apparently believed there was no such thing as a near miss, every bullet reached its correct destination, and it was either you or it wasn't.

I could say that I'm lucky to have been born in 1936, and not forty-five years earlier, in good time for World War One, or not fifteen years earlier, in good time for World War Two – I hit what might turn out to be a parenthesis, because I also sense that I'm lucky not to have been born fifteen or forty-five years later either – I have a sense, from what I've glimpsed of it, that the future's not going to be my kind of period, well, it will be a different century and a different country after all, they'll do things differently there –

DO I BELONG ON THE SEX OFFENDERS' REGISTER? AND OTHER WORRIES

And they're already doing them differently here, so perhaps the present's no longer my kind of period either – why today, this very day, in fact here, underneath my desk where I've thrown it, there's a copy of today's *Evening Standard* with a headline and a front-page story about a new law that is being proposed to the effect that women who give consent to sex when they're drunk can withdraw the consent after the event, when they've sobered up, and have the man involved – assuming it's a man they consented to have sex with – charged with rape. There's no mention of what happens if it's with a woman – presumably, if both women are drunk, then they could both withdraw their consent, and charge each other with rape. The story is followed up by an editorial of almost stupefying stupidity celebrating the probability of vastly increasing the number of successful prosecutions for rape – or that form of rape which could I suppose best be described as non-consensual consensual sex – actually I see it as yet another major step in the infantilizing of women, one of the bizarre consequences of the woman's liberation movement – but in the name of equality, which I've ever championed, I'd like to enter a plea for a quid pro quo infantilizing of men – let me reach into my own rubbish bin of experience and draw out a memory of something appropriate – well, there are several along these lines: when I was a research student at Cambridge I went one evening to a reception for a professor newly appointed from a provincial university, where I met a young woman, a Cambridge graduate and an assistant lecturer in the professor's old department, who was known to be his mistress – he was married, with a child or two. She was lively and attractive, with an easy laugh and a soft, shapely manner, about twenty years younger than the professor, and about eight older than me. There was something about me that appealed to her, mostly I think that I listened to her with close attention and apparent sympathy when she spoke of how Cambridge's gain was her loss, she there in the provinces, he here – and here he certainly was, in the centre of the room, his large, shaggy head inclined towards attentive young faces, his cheeks popping to the commands of his celebrated pipe, which he had once, in the middle of a seminar, crammed still alight into his jacket pocket along with his half-open box of Swan Vestas – the ensuing explosion, his attempts to scuffle off his smouldering jacket while still pursuing his thoughts on *Antony and Cleopatra* were the stuff of his legend – endearingly and comically absent-minded, yes, but with all-obliterating powers of concentration – a short, stooping man with visible dandruff and bad teeth, yes, but he held full lecture halls entranced, students mesmerized, he had genius and animal magnetism – this was the nature of her conversation, though I have to admit that the dandruff and bad teeth are my contributions, inserted here, out of spite. She was slightly drunk when we began our conversation and three times drunker by the time she suggested we take our leave and have coffee somewhere, what about my flat? It wasn't altogether my flat, I said, I shared it with two other chaps, and didn't mention that they were both away. She said that was all right, she'd like to meet them, let's go, why not, or did I have an objection to introducing her – ? She wasn't exactly aggressive and I wasn't exactly sober, but though I was no longer completely new to sex – see various *histoires* above – I was completely new to the prospect of having sex with someone I didn't know. So we set off through the soft Cambridge night – something of a phenomenon in nature, most nights in Cambridge were hard, very hard, even in warm weather – she clinging to my arm and talking now of her departing professor, now of other men in her life, perhaps to reassure me that I was not to take this, whatever it was going to be, too seriously, I was to see myself as a trifle, a toy in the blood etc. – My tactic was to lead her around and about, this way and that, until she was worn out and wanted to get back to where she was staying the night, but I'd only managed a few diversions when she did that thing that drunks sometimes astonish us by doing, she achieved a complete concentration on what she wanted – 'I thought you said you lived in Green Street,' she said, pulling me by my arm in a circle, 'We're going the wrong way.' 'It's a nicer way,' I said, 'we're going around by the Backs, for a peek at the river.' 'No,' she said, 'we're going to Green Street, to see your friends.' We got to Green Street in no time, it seemed to me, and then we were up the stairs and into the flat, which consisted of a small sitting room, three bedrooms, a kitchen and no bathroom, not even a lavatory, which was off the stairs on the way up to the flat, and contained as a washing facility only a small sink – we took our baths, when we had them, in our respective colleges. At this moment I can remember the disposition of the flat very well, because she led me from room to room, on a tour of inspection, rather as if she sensed there'd be nobody there but us. 'Back any moment,' I said, 'they're always around when you least want them.' Or never around when you most want them, would have been at that moment a more accurate way of putting it. She lay on the sofa, which was a squat ragamuffin of a thing, and spilled voluptuously over it. I went to make some coffee, and when I brought it back she had adopted a new position, in the centre of the room, and her clothes were everywhere but on her. I handed her a mug, and sat down. I'd ruined the previous occasion when a woman had undressed on my behalf by explaining that I was a virginal sort of man – i.e. inexperienced and probably inept, but very, very willing – I believe I've gone into the incident somewhere else, but the point is that here, with this girl, let me call her Mo, for Maureen, say, also out of spite, I was not a virginal sort of man, I was a quarter drunk, was a little more than half willing, out of primeval excitement, but then again almost half not, because she really was a little too excitable, a little too determined, a little too drunk and there was the professor and all the other chaps she'd told me about somehow somewhere in the room, and I wasn't sure she wasn't mistaking me for one of those – well, not the pipe-puffing, dandruff-headed genius of a professor, of course, but one of the subsidiaries, many of them known to me as serious men who read literature with moral intent, but now also known to me as men who'd been laid by Mo – as I might soon become known to them. Would being laid by Mo elevate me into a morally serious reader? was not a thought that was occupying me when Mo launched herself at me in a flurry of fists and kisses – I won't claim that I was passive, or that I remained fully dressed for long, but I still retained the top part of my clothing when we hit the floor. There was a slip-shod chaos between our legs, terrible farmyard sounds (poultry section) as we rolled on top of each other, and then away from each other. She came unsteadily over to me on her hands and knees, her face hovered over me, cheeks white and eyes staring as if she had an urgent message most of which she then delivered over my exposed chest, and the rest of it over my genitals, which were already in a fairly depressed state. Ever the gentleman, I went to the sink in the lavatory off the stairs, while she made do with the sink in the kitchen. I can't remember much in the way of conversation as we got dressed. I like to think I walked her to wherever her bed for the night might have been, but I have a strong suspicion, based on what I have come to learn of my character, that I probably merely offered to – in mitigation I should say that the streets of Cambridge weren't particularly dangerous in those days, except for men like me when women like Mo were about in them.

A few days later a letter arrived, in which she apologized in a deft and witty manner for the 'rather shameful incident the other evening', she'd had 'rather more than far too much to drink', for one thing she'd been 'grieving', for her the reception had been a little like a funeral as it marked the loss of her professor from her daily life. She went on to make a few penetrating remarks about the state of English studies in the provinces, with particular reference to her own province, and hoped we'd meet again some day. There was an indecipherable squiggle at the end, to serve as 'sincerely', 'ever', 'best wishes', whatever I chose to make of it, followed by her first name – Mo, if we're still sticking to Mo, and then, oddly, her surname in brackets.

We never met again, although I heard of her now and then, her steady rise up through English departments in this university and that, until she became in due course a professor herself, in the States, somewhere in the Midwest, I believe, and then I have the impression that a few years ago I heard that she was dead, but I'm not altogether sure about that. One's always thinking one's heard that someone's dead, and then they turn out to be alive, and vice versa, of course.

But to return to the reason I found myself recalling my night with Mo: the headline in the *Standard*, announcing that a parliamentary committee had proposed new legislation to the effect that a woman who has sex with a man when she's drunk can change her mind when she's sobered up, call the police, and have him charged with rape – this followed up in an imbecilically pious editorial insisting that such legislation was necessary to increase the number of rape convictions, and so reverse the current tendency of juries to hold women responsible for their own actions when drunk. Under this new law, should it come to pass, Mo could have pressed charges, I might have found myself in court, then quite plausibly convicted of rape, and the Crown Prosecution Service – Service! Can that be right? Crown Prosecution Service, the accused now seen as a customer, as passengers on the railway services are now seen as customers? Will convicts become customers of the prison services? Well, whether as customer or convict the Crown Prosecution Service would have added me as one more statistic in their successful drive to increase the number of convicted rapists in the nation, and one more name on the sex offenders' list to congratulate themselves on. Thus would a life have been destroyed – well, no, you can't say that, not for sure, my life as a convicted rapist and listed sex offender would certainly have been different from my life as, say, an unconvicted rapist and unlisted sex offender, which is what I am, really, when you think about it, thanks to the historical accident of having come to my sexual prime decades before the proposed new law was even a malevolent glint in the eye of the future – and anyway who can argue with authority that my life would have been destroyed by being convicted and listed? My writing, if I'd chosen to continue as a writer, might have been richer for its being darker, profounder for its being more pessimistic, and more commercial, far more commercial for its being brewed out of suffering and injustice. At least I could put my middle-class public school and university education behind me. I would have had a best-seller story to tell. Or perhaps I wouldn't – if the parliamentary committee has its way there would be too many like me with pretty well the same story to tell.

But what about Mo's life? Let us fast-forward Mo into a quite other creature, a young woman of today as hoped for by the Crown Prosecution Service – a young woman who is a fearless drinker and an equally fearless fucker, for what has she to fear on either count? On either count, drinking and fucking, the only consequence will be the pain, or will it be the pleasure?, of ruining the life of her drinking and fucking partner. They did the same thing, but she's a woman, so it doesn't count for her, it's not her fault, she's a woman. They did the same thing but he's a man, it does count for him, it's his fault, he's a man. In fact the woman doesn't really exist, at least in name – she's a nameless, anonymous victim and remains so until the end of her life. The man is named the moment he's charged, and remains so until the end of his life, whether convicted or acquitted. He can be listed, named, shamed, acquitted, with possibly many months in jail after he's listed, named, shamed, and before he's acquitted.

Come back to my own case. I would submit that if there was a victim it was myself. I tried, within the gentlemanly and therefore limited means at my disposal, to prevent Mo from coming back to my flat. I was reluctant to have sex until it became positively discourteous to refuse, by which time my penis, head-strong in the way that penises tend to be (in this respect they resemble C. S. Lewis's dog, who never obeyed him, but sometimes agreed with him. If only men could train their penises as they frequently manage to train dogs – Down boy! Stand! Sit! Beg! Down, I said!). Anyway, my view would be that I could certainly claim, in an imaginary world where men were as equal before the law as women, that Mo pretty well raped me. An adequate lawyer could make the case, furthermore, that her vomiting over my chest and genitals was a serious abuse of my human rights, and what's more, what's more you are seventy, and you sound it, so stop it, stop it! The fact is that you don't drink any more so you won't even get yourself to the first stage, the Mo stage, therefore you're most unlikely to appear in court or on the sex offenders' list – besides there are far more serious and complex issues around, which might touch on you personally and affect the course of your life in your remaining years, why don't you worry about them – ?

Because I don't think you can be a selective worrier, or – in another of those phrases I hate so much – 'cherry-pick' your worries, this business of non-consensual consensual sex has grown and grown in wherever it is in my consciousness that is the seat of worry – seat of worry? Well, what is worry, anyway? – I mean, what is its relation to memory and imagination, is it a separate faculty, how do we come by it? What would we be like if we didn't worry? It seems to me that my stream of consciousness is really a stream of worry, from the moment I awake, when I contemplate getting out of bed – is somebody other than Victoria in the house? Can I potter down to my lavatory naked, which is what I really want to do – no, perhaps slip downstairs to the kitchen, pick up a newspaper, slip back up – slip? Slip? Hah! Plod, plod down naked, plod back up the stairs, potbelly swinging – they will say, how his arms and legs are grown thin – no, they won't, if the girl who walks the dogs is in the hall and looks up the stairs and sees you coming down, she won't think how his legs are growing thin, she'll think, how disgusting ees thees man – she's Spanish, South American, anyway she speaks English with a Spanishy accent – thees man, with his beeg belly swinning thees wye and thees wye – but no, she won't think in English with a Spanish accent, she'll think in Spanish with a Spanish accent, or will she? Do we actually think in words, come to think of it, well, however she thinks she'll probably be thinking of not walking our dogs again, or if she's an advanced and practised child of our time she'll think of calling the police – sexual harassment, *si, si* – or a lawyer, she'll sue me, *si, si, si por favor* – very shameful, embarrassing for Victoria – back on the sex offenders' list – what do you mean back, you haven't been on it yet, this continual, in fact almost continuous fretting about being on the sex offenders' list is perverse, to say the least, you haven't done anything for years and years that would qualify you – and do you think of committing a sex crime as a qualification for a distinction? like getting an honour, Simon Gray, *quondam* playwright, was honoured in the New Year sex offenders' list, his autograph and photograph are available from a police station near you – or is it the sad dry form that an old man's sexual fantasy now takes, is this what I've come to? fretting or dreaming about getting on the sex offenders' list while still in bed at – oh Christ, it's half past one, Victoria's out, where's she out, the dogs are out, you're alone, I'm alone, he's alone – we're all alone – and I have to write, I'm a writer, writers write – but what about? – get up, get up, need a pee – incontinence, yes, when does that begin? Or will death snatch me first? I really and truly don't want to be incontinent, Alzheimer's, incontinence, look at him shuffling naked down the stairs for his first pee of the day – but it's amazing that you can get through six, seven, sometimes even eight hours of sleep without needing a pee, especially when you consider all that Diet Coke you drink, all those cigarettes you smoke, and yet here you are at seventy, continent – but for how long?

That's pretty well how it goes, something like that, in that vein anyway, when I have nothing specific to worry about.

PART EIGHT

SOME BEWILDERMENTS

We've got through Christmas without anything bad happening. We had the usual Boxing Day dinner with Harold and Antonia. Harold looked wonderfully well above the table, but he said that beneath it his legs were creaky and painful. He said it cheerfully, though, and got angry once or twice.

Here comes the New Year. 2007. What an unlikely number. The question, though, is whether you're going to make yet another promise to yourself to give up smoking. Let's start by putting down yet again all the reasons for giving up. No, let's not. Let's sit by the window, light a cigarette, and see if we can see the fox in the garden. It's a bright night, the sort of night that foxes like. The one I'm looking for sometimes strolls along the back wall, laughing. At least it sounds like laughter. It may be a mating cry, or desperation.

Last night was the last night of *Butley*. Nathan phoned to say it had gone very well, the company relaxed and at its best, the house packed, terrific reception. Afterwards there had been a party to celebrate the success of the run – we'd actually made a profit, very rare for a straight play on Broadway these days – it had been a pleasant and slightly melancholy party, only slightly marred by the late arrival of the producer, Liz McCann, who'd spent the evening at *A Chorus Line* rather than at *Butley*, which she hadn't looked in on since its opening night. I asked whether by any chance she was still in her wheelchair. He said he hadn't noticed, he thought not.

We agreed that whether she was or not she might be again very soon, unless she'd got rid of the cat, of course.

We hung about on the line for a while, mixing inconclusive sentences with laughter, then finally said goodbye, we'd keep in touch, and of course we will – we might even celebrate another birthday together, one that falls somewhere between Nathan's sixtieth and my ninetieth, why not?

When Nigel first saw me he was sixteen months old, and I was three days old. According to our mother he looked at me for a while, then slapped her face. Nevertheless, he was as kind an older brother as a man could have. He died last night in Oakville, Ontario, of heart failure, and I am suddenly all at sea, a brotherless man – there are many of us, of course, but I have never been one before.

I have a tumour in my lung, discovered by accident during the annual scan of my aneurysm, which itself has apparently grown or swollen apace and will have to be dealt with in due course – if there is a due course, which will depend, I suppose, on the tumour and whether it's confined to the lung or has come from somewhere else. If from somewhere else, would it explain why a lymph gland on my neck is swollen and has to be investigated? Or has that come from the lung? So. So ahead of me – biopsies, scans, tests, consultations, more scans, an operation if I'm strong enough and lucky, otherwise radiotherapy or chemotherapy, or both, so forth and so forth, but absolutely certainly, one way or another, I'm coming up to the last cigarette.

Well –

I went there this afternoon. Piers's little section was *en fête*, quite extraordinary, not simply the abundance of flowers on every grave, including Piers's, but flags, bunting, balloons, dolls, as if transformed into the setting for a party, a victory party, where was the music, one wondered, and where the voices? – because it was as quiet as it usually is, with just the sound of a car or a mower in the distance, and it was as sunny as it usually is – there's always bright sunshine when I visit Piers, not at all a coincidence or a mystical harmony between me and the weather, it's simply that I never go there unless the sun is out, partly to make sure that I associate his grave with cheerfulness and brightness, though not entirely with warmth, as my favourite time is on a cold, bright winter midday, and partly because I never want to go unless the sun is out, in fact the impulse only comes with the sun, and I can see myself now, as I write this – yes, there I am, an elderly man, sitting on the bench in the sunshine. I am smoking a cigarette, coughing slightly and perhaps, if you catch me at the right moment, slightly squinting so that I have the verses on the next-door tombstone in the corners of my eyes. I have half a newspaper on my lap. The other half – the business, travel and property sections – is under my buttocks, to cushion them against the wood of the bench. I imagine that the few people who pass by, usually in clusters of three or so, would take me for what I am, a brother visiting a younger brother, rather than a husband grieving for a wife, or a father for a lost child. I don't know what precisely would make this evident, it wouldn't really be anything in the detail, more a general effect, but one can always distinguish the brothers from the husbands and the fathers, at least I can, I think, and I therefore assume others can as well, but we might all of us be wrong, I might be identified, for instance, as one of those creatures who likes to visit graveyards, I was going to say 'strange creatures', but when I think about it I see nothing strange in it, there are few more interesting places in London than Kensal Green Cemetery, and few more enchanted and eloquent spots than Rowan Gardens, or more vivacious, at least on an afternoon when the bunting and the flags are out, and balloons floating, and there is the sense of victory in the air, not grim and forceful victory, as in 'Death, be not proud –', but a jolly victory, a celebration as of a – what? I can't think what sort of event would be collectively celebrated in Rowan Gardens Cemetery in a manner that made it look like a village fair from a different age – how come the balloons and flags? and who put the flowers on Piers's grave? there were two bunches, a bunch of fresh daffodils and a bunch, a clutch, really, of artificial poppies, they must have been laid by different hands – now, as I sit here writing this, I realize that none of it makes sense – if it was in memory of a momentous event, a great battle won or a country liberated, they would leave a sign, surely – it begins now to feel like a hallucination, the question being whether I had the hallucination when I visited Piers this afternoon or am having it now, in memory, in memory decorating with flags, bunting and balloons that sedate and pleasant place I know so well.